100 CLASSIC HIKES

NEW ENGLAND

100 CLASSIC HIKES

NEW ENGLAND

2nd Edition

JEFFREY ROMANO

Maine, New Hampshire, Vermont,
Massachusetts, Connecticut, Rhode Island

**MOUNTAINEERS
BOOKS**

To Richie for inspiring me to do what I have to do and
Jude for providing so many opportunities to do so.

———————————————

MOUNTAINEERS BOOKS is dedicated to
the exploration, preservation, and enjoyment
of outdoor and wilderness areas.

1001 SW Klickitat Way, Suite 201, Seattle, WA 98134
800-553-4453, www.mountaineersbooks.org

Printed in China

Distributed in the United Kingdom by Cordee, www.cordee.co.uk

First edition, 2010. Second edition, 2023.

Copyeditor: Erin Cusick
Series design: Kate Basart
Layout: Melissa McFeeters
Cartographer: Bart Wright, Lohnes+Wright
All photographs by the author unless credited otherwise
Cover photograph: *Looking south across Franconia Ridge from the summit of Mount Lafayette (Hike 61).*
Frontispiece: *Mount Passaconaway rises high above Mount Hedgehog's east ledge (Hike 63).*

The background maps for this book were produced using the online map
viewer CalTopo. For more information, visit caltopo.com.

Library of Congress Cataloging-in-Publication Data is available at https://lccn.loc.gov/2022052188.
The ebook record is available at https://lccn.loc.gov/2022052189.

Mountaineers Books titles may be purchased for corporate, educational, or other promotional sales,
and our authors are available for a wide range of events. For information on special discounts or
booking an author, contact our customer service at 800-553-4453 or mbooks@mountaineersbooks.org.

Printed on FSC-certified materials

ISBN (paperback): 978-1-68051-609-8
ISBN (ebook): 978-1-68051-610-4

An independent nonprofit publisher since 1960

Contents

Rhode Island: The Ocean State

Connecticut: The Nutmeg State

Massachusetts: The Bay State

Vermont: The Green Mountain State

New Hampshire:
The Granite State

Maine: *The Pine Tree State*

Hikes at a Glance

Notes: Difficulty is estimated based on length of hike, elevation change, and terrain. Seasons to hike are based primarily on road access; hike descriptions include other seasonal considerations. Also note that Vermont asks hikers to avoid high elevations—noted with an asterisk (*)—during mud season (mid-April to Memorial Day).

NO.	NAME	DISTANCE (ROUNDTRIP)	DIFFICULTY	SEASON	HIGHLIGHTS	STATE
SHORT HIKES (LESS THAN 3 HOURS)						
1	Sachuest Point	2.6 miles	Easy	Year-round	Coastal, birds	RI
2	Block Island Greenway	6 miles	Easy–Moderate	Year-round	Coastal, birds	RI
3	Napatree Point	3 miles	Easy	Year-round	Coastal, birds	RI
6	Bluff Point State Park	4.5 miles	Easy–Moderate	Year-round	Coastal, history	CT
7	Devils Hopyard State Park	2.8 miles	Easy–Moderate	Year-round	Waterfall, views, geology	CT
8	Mashamoquet Brook State Park	4 miles	Moderate	Year-round	Geology, history	CT
10	Talcott Mountain	4 miles	Moderate	Year-round	Cliffs, views, history	CT
13	Hidden Valley Preserve	3.8 miles	Easy–Moderate	Year-round	River, history, views	CT
18	Great Blue Hill	2.8 miles	Moderate	Year-round	Views, geology	MA
24	Sugarloaf Mountain	4.7 miles	Moderate	Year-round	Views, geology	MA
28	Monument Mountain	2.8 miles	Moderate	Year-round	Views, geology, cliffs	MA
31	Lye Brook Falls	4.6 miles	Moderate	Year-round	Waterfall, wilderness	VT
36	Little Rock Pond	4.8 miles	Easy–Moderate	May–Nov	Pond, wildlife	VT
38	Deer Leap	3.2 miles	Moderate	Year-round	Views, ledge	VT
45	Niquette Bay State Park	3.7 miles	Moderate	Year-round	Views, lake	VT
52	Harris Center	4.6 miles	Moderate	Year-round	Views, wildlife, wetlands	NH
69	Pondicherry Wildlife Refuge	5.1 miles	Easy	Year-round	Views, birds, wetlands	NH
84	Black Mountain	2.6 miles	Moderate	Apr–Nov	Views, ledges	ME
HALF-DAY HIKES (3–5 HOURS)						
4	George Parker Woodland	6.5 miles	Moderate	Year-round	Wildlife, geology, wetlands	RI
9	Breakneck Pond	7.4 miles	Moderate–Challenging	Year-round	Ponds, geology, wildlife	CT

NO.	NAME	DISTANCE (ROUNDTRIP)	DIFFICULTY	SEASON	HIGHLIGHTS	STATE
11	Sleeping Giant State Park	5.8 miles	Challenging	Year-round	Views, cliffs, geology	CT
12	Peoples State Forest	5.1 miles	Moderate	Year-round	Views, ledges, wetlands	CT
14	Macedonia Brook State Park	6.4 miles	Moderate–Challenging	Year-round	Views, ledges, wetlands	CT
16	Great Island	6.8 miles	Challenging	Year-round	Coastal, beaches, wildlife	MA
17	Borderland State Park	7.8 miles	Moderate	Year-round	Wetlands, history, birds	MA
19	Battle Road	10.3 miles	Easy–Moderate	Year-round	History, birds	MA
20	Mount Watatic	3.7 miles	Moderate	Year-round	Views, ledges	MA
21	Wachusett Mountain	4.3 miles	Moderate–Challenging	Year-round	Views, geology	MA
23	Holyoke Range	7.6 miles	Moderate–Challenging	Year-round	Views, ledges, history	MA
25	Mount Tom Reservation	7.6 miles	Challenging	Year-round	Views, cliffs, birds	MA
29	Hoosac Range	5.6 miles	Moderate	Year-round	Views, geology, ledge	MA
32	Haystack Mountain	4 miles	Moderate–Challenging	Year-round	Views, ledge	VT
34	Mount Ascutney	5.6 miles	Moderate–Challenging	Year-round	Views, cascades, geology	VT
39	Moosalamoo National Recreation Area	6.7 miles	Moderate	Year-round	Waterfall, wetlands, birds	VT
42	Spruce Mountain	4.4 miles	Moderate–Challenging	Year-round	Views, birds	VT
47	Laraway Mountain	4.8 miles	Moderate	Year-round	Views, cliffs, geology	VT
48	Belvidere Mountain	5.2 miles	Challenging	Year-round	Views, geology	VT
49	Mount Pisgah	4.6 miles	Moderate–Challenging	Year-round	Views, cliffs	VT
50	Jay Peak	3.4 miles	Challenging	Year-round	Views, ledge	VT
53	North Pack Monadnock	5.6 miles	Moderate–Challenging	Year-round	Views, cascades, cliff	NH
54	Mount Monadnock	5.8 miles	Challenging	Year-round	Views, ledges, geology	NH
57	Mount Cardigan	5.4 miles	Challenging	Year-round	Views, ledges, geology	NH

NO.	NAME	DISTANCE (ROUNDTRIP)	DIFFICULTY	SEASON	HIGHLIGHTS	STATE
59	Welch and Dickey	4.4 miles	Moderate–Challenging	Year-round	Views, ledges	NH
63	Hedgehog Mountain	4.8 miles	Moderate–Challenging	Year-round	Views, ledges	NH
67	Arethusa Falls and Frankenstein Cliff	5 miles	Moderate–Challenging	Year-round	Views, cliff, waterfalls	NH
74	Dixville Notch	5.2 miles	Challenging	Year-round	Views, cliff, waterfalls	NH
76	Monhegan Island	5.1 miles	Moderate–Challenging	May–Oct	Coastal, cliffs, birds	ME
77	Ragged Mountain	7.2 miles	Moderate–Challenging	Year-round	Views, ledges	ME
79	Great Pond Mountain Wildlands	5.5 miles	Moderate	Year-round	Views, birds, ledges	ME
81	Cadillac Mountain Traverse	6.5 miles	Moderate–Challenging	Jun–Oct	Views, ledges	ME
82	Jordan Pond and the Bubbles	4.2 miles	Moderate	Apr–Nov	Views, wetlands, geology	ME
83	Sargent Mountain Multi-Peak Loop	6.1 miles	Challenging	May–Nov	Views, ledges, pond, cascade	ME
86	Quoddy Head	4 miles	Moderate	Year-round	Coastal, views, birds	ME
90	Tumbledown Mountain	6.4 miles	Challenging	May–Nov	Views, geology, pond	ME
93	Borestone Mountain Sanctuary	5.6 miles	Moderate–Challenging	May–Nov	Views, ledges, wetlands	ME
94	Eagle Rock	6.8 miles	Moderate–Challenging	May–Oct	Views, ledges, cliff	ME
95	Mount Kineo	3.4 miles	Moderate–Challenging	May–Oct	Lake, views, cliffs	ME

DAY HIKES (5–8 HOURS)

NO.	NAME	DISTANCE (ROUNDTRIP)	DIFFICULTY	SEASON	HIGHLIGHTS	STATE
5	Arcadia Loop	11.9 miles	Challenging	Year-round	Geology, wetlands, birds	RI
15	Bear Mountain and Sages Ravine	7.9 miles	Challenging	Year-round	Views, cascades, geology	CT
22	Tully Lake and Jacobs Hill	10.5 miles	Moderate–Challenging	Year-round	Wetlands, birds, waterfalls	MA
26	Race and Everett	10.6 miles	Challenging	Year-round	Views, waterfalls, pond, ledges	MA
27	Alander Mountain	12.6 miles	Challenging	Year-round	Views, birds, wetlands, ledges	MA

NO.	NAME	DISTANCE (ROUNDTRIP)	DIFFICULTY	SEASON	HIGHLIGHTS	STATE
30	Mount Greylock	11.4 miles	Challenging–Strenuous	Year-round	Views, cascades, birds	MA
35	Baker Peak and Griffith Lake	8.8 miles	Challenging	Year-round	Views, wilderness, lake, ledges	VT
37	Killington Peak	7.6 miles	Challenging	Year-round*	Views, ledges	VT
43	Camels Hump	7.6 miles	Challenging–Strenuous	Year-round*	Views, ledges, alpine	VT
44	Worcester Range	7.8 miles	Challenging–Strenuous	Year-round*	Views, ledges, waterfall	VT
46	Mount Mansfield	6 miles	Challenging–Strenuous	Year-round*	Views, ledges, alpine, geology	VT
51	Pawtuckaway State Park	9 miles	Moderate–Challenging	Year-round	Wetlands, geology, birds, views	NH
56	Mount Roberts	9.4 miles	Moderate–Challenging	Year-round	Views, ledges, birds	NH
58	Smarts Mountain	7.2 miles	Challenging	Year-round	Views, ledges, cliff	NH
60	Cannon Mountain and Lonesome Lake	8.2 miles	Challenging–Strenuous	Year-round	Views, lake, ledges	NH
61	Franconia Ridge	8.8 miles	Strenuous	Year-round	Alpine, waterfalls, views	NH
64	Mount Chocorua	8.5 miles	Challenging	Year-round	Views, ledges, geology	NH
65	South and Middle Moat	6.6 miles	Moderate–Challenging	Year-round	Views, ledges	NH
66	Davis Path	9.8 miles	Challenging	Year-round	Views, ledges, cliff	NH
68	Mounts Webster and Jackson	6.5 miles	Challenging	Year-round	Views, ledges, waterfall	NH
75	Mount Agamenticus	8.2 miles	Moderate–Challenging	Year-round	Views, geology, birds	ME
78	Camden Hills	7.3 miles	Moderate–Challenging	Year-round	Views, cliff, ledges	ME
80	Great Head, Beehive, Gorham Mountain, and Ocean Path	7.8 miles	Challenging	May–Nov	Coastal, views, geology	ME
85	Cutler Coast	9.7 miles	Challenging	Year-round	Ocean, views, birds	ME
87	Goose Eye and Carlo	7.7 miles	Challenging–Strenuous	May–Nov	Views, alpine, geology	ME
88	Puzzle Mountain	7.5 miles	Challenging	Year-round	Views, ledges	ME
89	Baldpates and Table Rock	8.2 miles	Challenging–Strenuous	Year-round	Views, cliff, alpine	ME

NO.	NAME	DISTANCE (ROUNDTRIP)	DIFFICULTY	SEASON	HIGHLIGHTS	STATE
96	Gulf Hagas	9.7 miles	Challenging	May–Oct	Waterfalls, geology, birds	ME
97	Debsconeag Lakes Wilderness	8.6 miles	Moderate–Challenging	Jun–Oct	Wetlands, wildlife, views, birds	ME
98	Mount O-J-I	8.7 miles	Challenging–Strenuous	Jun–Oct	Views, ledges, geology	ME
99	Doubletop Mountain	7.2 miles	Challenging	Jun–Oct	Views, ledges	ME

LONG DAY HIKES / BACKPACKS (MORE THAN 8 HOURS)

NO.	NAME	DISTANCE (ROUNDTRIP)	DIFFICULTY	SEASON	HIGHLIGHTS	STATE
33	Stratton Pond and Mountain	12.7 miles	Challenging	Year-round*	Views, pond, wildlife	VT
40	Vermont's Presidential Range	13.6 miles	Challenging–Strenuous	May–Oct	Views, wilderness, ledges	VT
41	Mounts Abraham and Ellen	12.3 miles	Challenging–Strenuous	Year-round	Alpine, views, ledges	VT
55	Belknap Range Trail	12.9 miles	Challenging–Strenuous	Year-round	Views, ledges, wetlands	NH
62	Pemigewasset Wilderness	26.4 miles	Strenuous	Year-round	Alpine, views, cliffs, wilderness	NH
70	Presidential Traverse	19.5 miles	Strenuous	May–Oct	Alpine, views, ledges	NH
71	Mount Madison	10.6 miles	Strenuous	May–Oct	Alpine, views, wilderness	NH
72	Carter Dome and Mount Hight	10.2 miles	Challenging–Strenuous	Year-round	Views, geology, ponds	NH
73	Baldfaces	9.8 miles	Challenging–Strenuous	Year-round	Views, ledges, cascades	NH
91	Saddleback Mountain	10.2 miles	Strenuous	May–Nov	Alpine, ponds, views, ledges	ME
92	Bigelow Range	12.8 miles	Strenuous	May–Nov	Alpine, ponds, views, ledges	ME
100	Katahdin	11.1 miles	Strenuous	Jun–Oct	Alpine, views, wetlands, ledges	ME

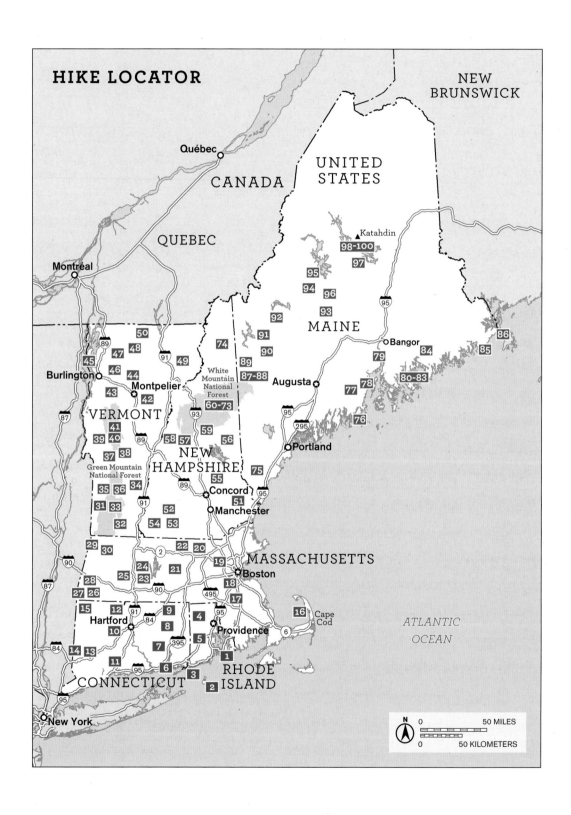

Introduction

The hundred classic hikes described in this guidebook showcase the breadth and diversity of New England's landscapes: from the sandy beaches of Long Island Sound to the lofty summits of the White Mountains, from the rolling ridges of the Berkshires to Maine's rocky coastline, from the traprock cliffs of the Connecticut River valley to the lush hardwood forests of Vermont. Hikers can take advantage of a patchwork of conserved lands protected over the past century with this book in hand, as it highlights the region's premier hiking destinations, including national parks, forests, and wildlife refuges; state parks, public lands, and wildlife management areas; and land trust properties.

Selecting the hundred classic hikes in New England is a challenge with so many trails and destinations from which to choose. In addition to capturing the region's varied landscapes, the final list includes hikes with different degrees of difficulty, multiple interesting features (natural and/or historical), and, when possible, trailheads that offer the option to adjust the described route for either a longer or shorter adventure.

New England is noteworthy for many reasons, not the least of which is the cycle of the seasons. Exploring these hikes covered in snow, sprouting with wildflowers, warbling with songbirds, and afire with colorful foliage will undoubtedly lead you to discover what I did long ago: New England is a hiker's paradise that invites outdoor discovery throughout the year. I look forward to crossing paths as you discover these 100 classic hikes of New England!

CLIMATE

New England's climate is as diverse as the months of the year. While all four seasons offer unique attractions, the conditions of each require special consideration prior to hitting the trails.

Spring Hiking

Spring hiking can be deceptively winter-like. Warm weather at lower elevations and in southern regions of New England does not mean spring has arrived everywhere. In fact, it is not unusual for snow and ice to be abundant throughout April and May (sometimes into June) in northern New England, especially at elevations over 3000 feet. Proper equipment like snowshoes, ice grips, and warm clothing may be necessary additions to your backpack. When considering a spring hike, keep in mind that slopes melt more quickly, especially south-facing ones, and that flat areas and high-elevation ridges, particularly when shaded by evergreens, stay snowy for longer.

While winter-like in some respects, spring can also mimic summer. The sun's rays, for example, can cause sunburn as quickly in April as in August. Adding to the sunburn threat is the reflection of light off snow and the lack of leaves to provide shade. Be sure to add sunscreen to your pack by March. Insects are also a concern on spring hikes. The swarming, biting, and eye-, mouth-, and ear-filling black-flies usually arrive in late April in the southern areas described in this book. By Memorial Day most places in New England have ushered in their arrival. Although short-lived, the blackfly season can be frustrating. Spring also marks the start of prime tick season, and the bloodsucking parasites seem to be spreading farther north each year (see the Ticks and Insects section for additional information).

Finally, spring can also be very spring-like, and nothing says spring more than water. A constant issue on many hikes in this season is the number of and size of water crossings. It is hard to hike in New England without encountering running water. To ensure that the worst-case scenario is only wet boots, use caution at all stream crossings and be prepared to turn around if necessary. The increased water also creates muddy trails that lead to wet feet and increased erosion. Avoid mud and help protect trails by picking hikes in the southern and coastal areas earlier in the spring and slowly work your way north as the season progresses.

Summer Hiking

Few things put a damper on a summer hike more than swarming insects. Clouds of mosquitoes lurking in shady, moist areas and circling deerflies on the hottest, most humid days of July can be annoying and painful. To ease the situation, use an effective bug repellent; avoid low, wet areas; and remind yourself that without the insects we would not be blessed with so many species of colorful songbirds.

Summer heat and humidity are other factors to consider. This combination, most common in July, quickly saps your energy. Try to start hikes early in the day and make sure to drink plenty of fluids. Heat and humidity may also trigger thunderstorms. Many of the hikes in this book describe trails with a lot of exposure. These are excellent hikes when the weather cooperates, but they are potentially very dangerous when lightning is in the air. Storms most frequently hit later in the day but often come on suddenly. Be alert and seek cover quickly at the sound of thunder. Lastly, heat and humidity tend to mix with smog from the Midwest, diminishing views that can be far more impressive at other times of the year.

If you are looking for the optimum summer day, wait for the day after a strong thunderstorm, which is often followed by cooler, cleaner air from Canada. When ideal summer weather arrives, take advantage of the plentiful daylight, and enjoy long days high above tree line or in the forests, where wildlife and wildflowers abound.

Autumn Hiking

While autumn is often a wonderful time to hit the trails, remember that the days shorten quickly. Conditions may tempt you to take long adventures, but be prepared to finish before the sun sets. Unlike in summer, once the sun goes down in autumn, the temperatures quickly follow. In addition, it is not uncommon to experience winter-like conditions during the day, especially in northern New England. Be sure to bring plenty of warm clothing, including a hat and gloves. The cool temperatures often make water crossings more difficult too. When crossing rocks that look icy, step on sections slightly submerged in water rather than wet spots exposed to the open air.

A final consideration for the autumn is that it is also prime hunting season throughout the region—for deer and a variety of other wildlife. Many of the trails described in this book are located in areas open for hunting. Although it is quite uncommon to encounter hunters near hiking trails, it is good practice to wear bright colors such as blaze orange (required in some places). To avoid hunters altogether, head for Massachusetts or Maine on a Sunday, when hunting is prohibited. (Note: Not all hunting takes place in autumn; consult each state's fish and wildlife agency for specific information on hunting laws, schedules, and regulations.)

Winter Hiking

When choosing a winter hike, keep in mind that many trailheads are inaccessible from November to May. And even those roads that are regularly plowed might not be cleared immediately after a snowstorm. Before heading to a particular trail, check on the accessibility of the access road and/or be prepared to change plans.

The margin for error when hiking in winter is slim. Carry more than you think you will need: clothes, water, and food. It is especially helpful to have dry clothes in case you get wet. In January, the sun sets between 4:00 and 4:30 p.m. and slowly shifts later and later. On cloudy days or on northern slopes, it can grow dark even earlier.

Finally, always bring and expect to use snowshoes. Surprisingly, many hikers shy away from

The Beehive stands over Sand Beach in Acadia National Park (Hike 80).

using snowshoes and use spikes or smaller ice grips instead. While crampons are essential in certain circumstances, they are needed infrequently, even while climbing 4000-footers. Smaller ice grips can be useful when trails are reduced to very hard-packed snow, but be prepared to wear snowshoes on most winter hikes. Using snowshoes makes for an easier journey and prevents the creation of ruts in the snow-filled trail for future hikers. When choosing snowshoes, opt for narrow ones with metal grips below. This design will allow maximum control and maneuverability, particularly in mountainous terrain.

OUTDOOR ETIQUETTE

With more folks enjoying hiking and backpacking each year, the need for outdoor ethics has never been greater. Few things on a hike are more frustrating than, for example, encountering inconsiderate trail users or campers who ignore Leave No Trace principles. Tents might be perched improperly on the banks of a stream, threatening water quality. Hikers may take shortcuts, causing erosion. A peaceful day in the woods can be interrupted by a loud group oblivious to the enjoyment of others. These experiences can sour an otherwise glorious day in the outdoors. In some cases, these types of activities violate the rules that govern a particular area; but more importantly, these activities diminish the experiences of other hikers.

Leave No Trace

To ensure that we all can enjoy the same opportunity to renew our spirits in the wilds of New

Waves pound the shoreline along Maine's Bold Coast (Hike 86).

England, it is essential for each of us to commit to basic outdoor ethical principles. The Leave No Trace Center for Outdoor Ethics, a national nonprofit organization dedicated to promoting and inspiring responsible outdoor recreation through education, research, and partnerships, has developed eight simple principles all hikers should follow.

Plan Ahead and Prepare. Know applicable regulations and special concerns for each area visited; be prepared for extreme weather, hazards, and emergencies; schedule trips to avoid times of high use; and understand how to use a map, guidebook, and compass.

Travel and Camp on Durable Surfaces. Use established trails, routes, and campsites. Remember that good campsites already exist and should never be located closer than 200 feet from wetlands. Also, minimize erosion by walking single file in the middle of the trail, even when wet or muddy. Remaining on the trail is especially important for the high-elevation hikes described in this book that use trails surrounded by fragile vegetation.

Dispose of Waste Properly. For garbage and toilet paper, follow the basic rule of waste disposal: pack it in and pack it out. When depositing solid human waste, dig a small hole 6 to 8 inches deep at least 200 feet from water, camp, and trails. Cover and disguise the hole when finished. Avoid washing yourself or your dishes within 200 feet of streams or lakes and use small amounts of biodegradable soap.

Leave What You Find. You are not the first to visit any of these places and likely will not be the last. Preserve the experience for others who follow: examine, but do not touch, cultural or historical structures and artifacts; leave rocks, plants, and other natural objects as you find them; avoid introducing or transporting nonnative species; and do not build structures or furniture or dig trenches.

Minimize Campfire Impacts. Lightweight stoves and candle lanterns leave less impact than campfires. Where fires are permitted, use established fire rings, fire pans, or mound fires, and keep fires small. Only use sticks from the ground that can be broken by hand. When done, burn all wood to ash, and then scatter cool ashes. Put campfires out completely.

Respect Wildlife. Wildlife is best observed from a distance and should never be fed. Feeding wildlife damages their health, alters natural behaviors, and exposes them to predators and other dangers. Protect wildlife and your food by storing rations and trash securely. Control pets at all times or leave them at home.

Think Before You Post. When you post on social media about a place you visited, consider your potential communications through a leave-no-trace lens by modeling responsible outdoor recreation in your posts.

Be Considerate of Others. Respect other visitors and protect the quality of their experience. Be courteous and yield to other users on the trail. Let nature's sounds prevail—avoid loud voices and noises.

SAFETY

Before beginning your next New England hiking adventure, prepare adequately for potential hazards. Taking the necessary precautions to avoid or minimize exposure to the following safety concerns will help to ensure a more pleasurable outdoor excursion and allow you to experience countless future hikes in the region.

Weather above Tree Line

Weather concerns increase on hikes that climb above tree line, like Katahdin, Saddleback, and the Bigelows in Maine; Mansfield, Abraham, and Camels Hump in Vermont; or Franconia, the Pemigewasset Wilderness, and the Presidential Range in New Hampshire. The weather in these areas can be dangerous and, in most cases, there is no safe shelter once you are above tree line.

Pay attention not only to the existing conditions but also to the forecast that day and any incoming systems noted in the weather report. Remember that weather conditions above tree line are not reflective of conditions in the lowlands. Expect a minimum drop in air temperature of 3 degrees Fahrenheit for each 1000 feet in elevation gain, combined with the windchill from increased velocity as you climb. Plan for the best possibilities, but also be prepared to change plans to accommodate weather conditions. Do not try to outsmart the weather or push hesitant members of your party if conditions are not ideal. The mountain will be there another day, and hopefully you will get a chance to try again; this decision will be made all the sweeter by the fact that you have exercised discipline and shown respect for the elements.

Lightning

Lightning storms are common throughout New England. Most electrical storms occur from June to August, but thunderstorms are possible any time of year. Since many of the hikes described in this book traverse exposed ridges and other high locations, the threat of being struck by lightning should not be underestimated.

Take precautions to minimize your risk of being injured or killed by lightning. First, be aware of the day's weather forecast and avoid hikes with a lot of exposure when the threat of thunderstorms is great. Second, pay attention to the sky and avoid being caught on exposed ridges, open areas, or above tree line if a storm is brewing. Third, if a storm hits, spread out so that if one person is struck, others can help. Lastly, if you do not have time to get to a lower elevation or out of an open area: squat down to reduce your height, minimize your contact with the earth (only your feet should touch the ground), and avoid metal objects.

Hypothermia

Though it is most often a threat during colder months, hypothermia—the lowering of your body's core temperature—can strike at any time of year. To protect yourself or a fellow hiker from succumbing to hypothermia, it is important to understand the early warning signs, which include poor judgment, a slight sensation of chilliness, and trouble using your hands for simple tasks. Should these early signs go unnoticed or unaddressed, hypothermia can lead to more-serious conditions such as uncontrolled shivering, unconsciousness, and even death.

The best way to prevent hypothermia is to dress in layers and to wear clothes that keep you warm even when they are wet. Be sure to wear good wind and rain gear because your body loses heat three times as fast when it is wet. Finally, it is important to eat and drink properly. Even when the temperature is cold, drinking plenty of water is critical to your health. Avoid alcohol and caffeine since both can contribute to hypothermia. When eating, opt for many small meals.

Water

Carry plenty of water as well as a water-treatment system. Unless faced with extreme dehydration, you should not drink any water before treating it. In fact, the cleanest mountain streams could be home to microscopic viruses, bacteria, and parasites such as giardia, that can wreak havoc on your digestive system. Treating water can be as simple as boiling it, chemically purifying it with iodine tablets, or pumping it through one of the many commercially available systems for filtering and purifying water. Drinking untreated water is a mistake you will remember for a long time, and one that will provide you ample time to "sit down" to think about the poor decision you made.

Wildlife

New England is not known as a hiking destination fraught with dangerous wildlife encounters. However, there are a few animal species that can potentially be problematic. Male moose during the fall rutting season and female moose with young can be aggressive if their space is violated, but they typically do not go looking for trouble. To minimize your risk, maintain a distance of at least 75 feet. Your safety is more important than getting a photo! Similarly, black bear sows with their young are another possible concern; however, they usually sense your presence first and are long gone before you arrive. When camping overnight, properly storing food will also help to avoid interactions with bears. This could mean hanging the food from a tree, using a portable bear-proof canister, or taking advantage of bear-proof containers when provided

Bull moose roam throughout northern New England.

by the land management agency. Lastly, some of the southern hikes in this book are in rattle-snake country. Pay attention to where you step and place your hands. If bitten, seek immediate medical attention.

In the end, do not let your fear of wildlife deter you from a hiking adventure. Use common sense with all animals (view from a distance, do not feed them, and respect their space), and you will likely avoid threatening encounters. In fact, the animal you are most apt to be threatened by on a hike will be an unleashed dog, and that can just as easily occur on a walk around your neighborhood.

Ticks and Insects
The smallest creatures you encounter on a hike in New England are the ones most likely to injure you. The most common antagonists are black-flies, mosquitoes, deerflies, greenheads, ticks, and yellow jackets. Since their presence varies depending on the region, the time of year, and the current conditions, you will not encounter each of these on every New England hike during the year's warmer months. Still, it is possible you will encounter at least one of them if you go for a hike between March and November.

Encounters with these critters are typically manageable with little effort. However, if you suffer allergic reactions to any of them, their numbers are high, and/or your tolerance is low, consider using insect repellents, hats, long pants, or commercially available gear to help ease the annoyance, threat, and pain inflicted by them. To avoid picking up ticks, which carry Lyme and other diseases, tuck clothes in and wear light col-ors. In addition, after every hike, do a thorough scan of your body to ensure no ticks are present and use fine-tipped tweezers to quickly remove any ticks you find.

Getting Lost and Found
While the hikes described in this book are located on well-developed trails in areas fre-quently used by hikers, the possibility of becoming lost, injured, or stranded after dark is something to consider. Most importantly, do not rely on technology to save you. For example, cell phones cannot receive signals in many regions covered in this book, and even if they could, their batteries may run out of juice. If you find yourself lost or injured, it is much safer to rely on basic outdoor skills, preparedness, common sense, and a few simple rules: It is always safer to hike with companions; if you choose to hike alone, be sure to let someone else know of your plans; study the area you are visiting beforehand to have a better understanding of the topography; keep all hiking groups together; and always carry and know how to use the Ten Essentials (see the following section).

BEFORE YOU GO
Before hitting the trails, it is prudent to be prepared with proper gear. While it may be tempting to head up the trail with minimal gear, you never know what may occur: injury, change of weather, illness, or other circumstances. The bottom line for any hike is to bring more than you think you will need; the worst that could happen may be that you build stronger back and shoulder muscles. The point of the Ten Essentials, originated by The Mountaineers, has always been to answer two basic questions: Can you prevent emergencies and respond positively should one occur (items 1–5)? And can you safely

spend a night—or more—outside (items 6–10)? Use this list as a guide and tailor it to the needs of your outing.

1. **Navigation:** Carrying a map of the area, and knowing how to read it, provides options in case of emergency. For example, often there are multiple trails in an area that provide shorter or easier alternatives to a given destination. Know where you are and how to quickly get to safety in an emergency. Also, while the trails in this book are generally well marked and easy to follow, harsh weather, leaves, and snow can sometimes obscure the way, so carrying and knowing how to use a compass can help ensure you'll return home safely. Other navigation tools to consider are an altimeter, GPS device, and a personal locator beacon or other device to contact emergency first responders.

2. **Flashlight or headlamp:** If you are forced to spend the night outdoors or when still on the trail after sunset, artificial light can be a big help in returning to the trailhead safely. Don't forget spare batteries.

3. **Sun protection:** Sun protection, including sun-protective clothing, is a must throughout the year. In fact, the low angle of the sun and the reflection off snow and ice can make sunglasses very important during colder months. A broad-spectrum sunscreen rated at least SPF 30 is also beneficial, especially from April to October. Late winter through mid-spring can be your most vulnerable time of the year when the sun is strong and bare trees provide little protection.

4. **First-aid kit:** Cuts, stings, twisted ankles, and other ailments are distinct possibilities, even for the most prepared hiker. Standard supplies include bandages, skin closures, gauze pads and dressings; roller bandages or wraps; blister prevention, nitrile gloves, tweezers; nonprescription painkillers or important personal painkillers, including an EpiPen if you are allergic to bee or hornet venom and an inhaler if you are susceptive to sports-induced asthma; anti-inflammatory, anti-diarrheal, and antihistamine tablets; topical antibiotic;

Mushrooms of various sizes and colors brighten many New England trails throughout the summer.

A hiker enjoys the quiet view of Tully Lake (Hike 22).

and antiseptics. Knowledge of first-aid procedures can also help instruct how to react in certain emergency situations to ensure an injured party receives the necessary help.

5. **Knife:** A knife or multitool with pliers is a handy device to carry. While neither may be necessary 99 percent of the time, that one time you need it, you will be happy to have brought it along.

6. **Fire:** Having something that will catch fire, even when sticks and brush are wet, can be a huge help in an emergency, such as having to spend the night in the woods. Carry at least one butane lighter (or waterproof matches) and firestarter, such as chemical heat tabs, cotton balls soaked in petroleum jelly, or commercially prepared firestarter.

7. **Shelter:** In addition to a rain shell, carry a single-use bivy sack, plastic tube tent, or jumbo plastic trash bag.

8. **Extra food:** Hiking is a strenuous activity that burns calories quickly. Fill your pack with high-energy food and more than you expect to eat. For shorter trips a one-day supply is reasonable.

9. **Extra water:** Begin each hike with at least two quarts of water per person, even during colder months. An otherwise enjoyable hike can be spoiled by a headache resulting from dehydration. It's also a good idea to have the skills and tools required to obtain and purify additional water.

10. **Extra clothing:** Even on the hottest days of summer, carry a rain jacket and a water-resistant layer of clothing at a minimum. During colder times of the year or while venturing above tree line, additional layers are a must, including warm hats and gloves. The highest locations described in this book can experience winter-like conditions throughout the year. Pack additional layers needed to survive the night in the worst conditions that your party may realistically encounter.

In addition to these ten items, there are other gear considerations to make. Many of the hikes in this book and throughout the region take place on rocky terrain. To provide optimum comfort and effectiveness, choose sturdy boots with good ankle protection and seal the boots with a waterproofing material. There are commercially available products that will cause water to bead up and run off your boots, leaving your feet dry. Gaiters that wrap around your lower leg are also handy for keeping water and debris out of your boots. When choosing clothing, avoid cotton; it is not the best material to wear when wet, as it does not dry easily.

Last but not least, a camera and binoculars can add a lot of enjoyment to a hiking adventure. Similarly, books that help in the identification of birds, wildlife, trees, mushrooms, and wildflowers offer many new dimensions to your adventure.

How to Use This Guide

This book is designed to introduce you to one hundred of New England's best hiking destinations. Extra care was used to choose locations that not only exemplify the region's most iconic features but also offer you the greatest variety of trip choices. While each recommended hike includes a description of one specific itinerary, many of the hikes also provide information on other optional excursions (of various lengths and difficulties) from the same trailhead or a nearby starting point.

Each hike begins with a list of information that provides helpful facts about the destination. Use this information to decide whether the hike is a good fit for you.

The **distance** category provides the full length of the described hike in miles and indicates whether the journey is roundtrip (using the same route both ways), a loop, or a one-way hike (beginning and ending at different trailheads). In other words, a hike that leads 2.3 miles to its destination and then returns along the same 2.3 miles of trail will be listed as 4.6 miles roundtrip. If, on the other hand, the hike returns on a different trail or trails, it will be listed as a 4.6-mile loop.

When referring to the **hiking time**, please bear in mind that this is an estimate for the average hiker, based on experience. You may find the estimates to be high or low based on your pace. Use the estimate as a tool rather than a way to judge success or failure.

Map Legend

Symbol	Description	Symbol	Description	Symbol	Description
- - - - - -	Featured trail	❶	Trailhead	🗼	Tower
· · · · · · ·	Other trail	ⓣ	Alternate trailhead	～	River or creek
· · · · · · · · ·	Unmaintained trail	℗	Parking	⫣	Falls
→	Direction-of-travel arrow	Ⓟ	Alternate parking	⬭	Water
11	Hike number	Ⓡ	Restroom	⩘	Wetland
⬆	Appalachian Trail	▪	Point of interest	●——	Ski lift
═══	Highway	⚠	Campground	⸭⸭⸭	Park or forest boundary
═══	Paved road	⚠▶	Backcountry campsite	⸭⸭⸭	Park or forest boundary (selected maps)
═ ═ ═ ═ ═	Gravel road	Ⓥ	Viewpoint	⸭⸭⸭	Wilderness boundary
⑨⓪	Interstate highway	🎋	Picnic area	— — —	State boundary
① ⑪	US highway	)(	Pass	— · —	National boundary
⑧ ⑧⑨	State route (SR)	][	Bridge	◆—·—◆	Powerline
56 556	Forest road (FR)	▲	Peak	🧭	True north (magnetic north varies)

Block Island's Black Rock Beach (Hike 2)

Each hike is also evaluated based on degree of **difficulty** (easy, moderate, challenging, or strenuous). This subjective tool seeks to categorize the hikes based on their length, elevation gain, exposure, steepness, and terrain.

To gain a better sense of the terrain, refer to the **elevation gain** and **high point**. The elevation gain is an estimate that adds up all the individual ups and downs along the hike.

The **season** listing is another subjective tool meant to be a guide—not an absolute. Anyone who has lived in New England knows that the weather can be quite unpredictable. The amount of snow and ice on a given trail or access road varies from year to year. In most cases, hikes that have trailheads accessible twelve months a year are listed as year-round destinations. However, some hikes with year-round-accessible trailheads are recommended only for times of the year when snow and/or ice are typically not a factor. This does not mean that these hikes are not possible other times of the year with proper equipment and experience.

The list for each hike also includes a **management** category that provides the name of the respective landowner or agency responsible for the management of the trail or trails along the described route (some hikes take place on lands owned and managed by more than one organization, individual, or governmental entity). While most land in New England is held privately, the hikes in this book are mainly on publicly owned and managed lands. However, the book also includes hikes accessible over private roads, hikes crossing sections of private land, and hikes on conservation land owned by nonprofit conservation organizations. Each landowner and manager associated with hikes in this book has unique missions and regulations. For your enjoyment, and to ensure that others that follow can enjoy these same special places, it is important to know and obey all regulations and to be especially considerate of private landowners. For the most up-to-date information on fees, trail conditions, camping requirements, and regulations, contact the respective landowner or visit their website (see Resources for contact information).

While every hike includes a map outlining the trails and various other important features, each hike summary lists a website where the landowner features an official **map** of the property, when available. Most of the hikes in this book include this information, but some landowners do not offer online maps.

At the end of the list of information for each hike, there are **GPS coordinates** in decimal degree format. These are based on a **getting there** section that provides driving directions to the parking areas connected with the trailhead or trailheads outlined for the hike. In a few cases this section also includes ferry and shuttle directions that are helpful for accessing the trailhead.

Each hike also includes a **notes** section with other background information, such as whether admission fees are required, specific regulations about dogs, and the availability of backcountry campsites.

A Note about Safety

Safety is an important concern in all outdoor activities. No guidebook can alert you to every hazard or anticipate the limitations of every reader. Therefore, the descriptions of roads, trails, routes, and natural features in this book are not representations that a particular place or excursion will be safe for your party. When you follow any of the routes described in this book, you assume responsibility for your own safety. Under normal conditions, such excursions require the usual attention to traffic, road and trail conditions, weather, terrain, the capabilities of your party, and other factors. Because many of the lands in this book are subject to development and/or change of ownership, conditions may have changed since this book was written that make your use of some of these routes unwise. Always check for current conditions, obey posted private property signs, and avoid confrontations with property owners or managers. Keeping informed on current conditions and exercising common sense are the keys to a safe, enjoyable outing.

—Mountaineers Books

Opposite, top: The great blue heron is one of the largest wading birds in New England.

Opposite, bottom: Napatree Point attracts birdwatchers and beachcombers.

Rhode Island: The Ocean State

Although it is New England's smallest state, Rhode Island invites hikers to explore its network of land trust preserves, state public lands, and national wildlife refuges—most within a short drive from Providence. The Ocean State is also home to the North–South Trail, a long-distance route that traverses rural conservation areas along the Connecticut border and connects the Blackstone River valley in the north with Block Island Sound in the south.

The state's most picturesque spots are found along its 400 miles of coastline, especially the dramatic cliffs surrounding Block Island. Moving away from the shore, find family-friendly treks across a rolling landscape interspersed with wetlands that are home to a wide diversity of plants and wildlife. Rhode Island is a four-season hiking destination, especially late fall through early spring, when other corners of New England are experiencing more winter-like conditions.

1 Sachuest Point

Distance: 2.6-mile loop	*Management:* Sachuest Point NWR
Difficulty: easy	*Season:* year-round
Hiking time: 2 hours	*Map:* NWR website
Elevation gain: 50 feet	*GPS coordinates:* 41.47976°, −71.24351°
High point: 30 feet	

Sachuest Point's rocky shoreline

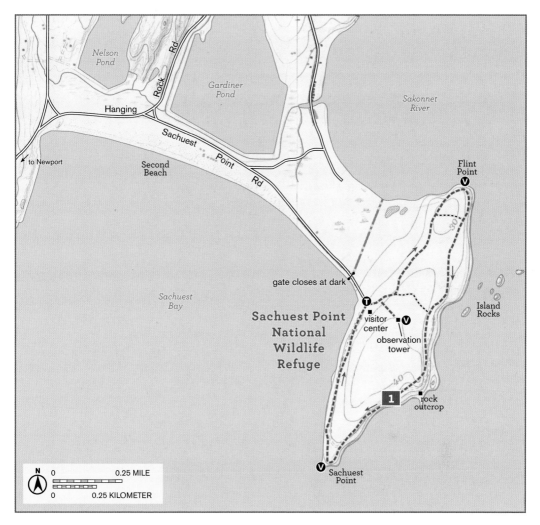

Nelson Pond

Gardiner Pond

Rock Rd

Hanging

Sachuest Point Rd

to Newport

Second Beach

Sakonnet River

Flint Point

gate closes at dark

Sachuest Bay

Sachuest Point National Wildlife Refuge

visitor center

observation tower

Island Rocks

1

rock outcrop

Sachuest Point

N

0   0.25 MILE

0   0.25 KILOMETER

Getting there: From Easton Beach on the Newport/Middletown line, follow Route 138A east. In 0.1 mile stay straight on Purgatory Road and drive 0.8 mile. Bear right on Hanging Rock Road and continue 0.4 mile to the intersection with Sachuest Point Road and turn right. Drive 1.1 miles to the visitor center. *Notes:* Ticks and poison ivy are common here, though the refuge's wide trails minimize potential encounters with both. Dogs are prohibited.

Lying east of Newport's famed Cliff Walk and popular sand beaches, this prominent peninsula served as a strategic US Navy rifle range and communications center during the Second World War. Today, Sachuest Point features a 242-acre National Wildlife Refuge where visitors can enjoy more-peaceful pursuits, such as exploring gentle hiking trails across a coastal oasis that welcomes more than two hundred bird species throughout the year.

From the parking area, follow a short path east to an observation tower. Here, gaze out to the distant waters and, perhaps, spot a northern harrier or other raptor gliding over the low-lying terrain.

Return to the main path, turn right, and hike 0.1 mile to a junction. While the nearby shoreline is straight ahead, stay left to complete a longer journey. Winding along the edge of a field, the path slowly swings northeast and in 0.5 mile arrives at Flint Point. Check out the viewing platform and survey the mouth of the Sakonnet River for wintering waterfowl, the adjacent marshlands for summer wading birds, and the rocky shoreline for migratory shorebirds.

Begin the 1.4-mile walk to the refuge's namesake point by following the trail south. Quickly pass the first of eight ocean-access points. Only use these well-marked locations to approach the water. Near Island Rocks, a collection of small near-shore ledges, a viewing platform serves as an excellent location to spot harlequin ducks—blue, white, and chestnut-colored birds that nest in Canadian streams but winter along the North Atlantic's turbulent coast. Sachuest is home to one of New England's higher concentrations from late fall to early spring.

Continue along the shore and wrap around a cobble beach to shore access number 6, where you can cautiously meander to a scenic rock outcrop on the water's edge. To the south, the trail slices through a mostly open landscape, where an interpretive sign describes resident songbirds. After entering thickets, arrive at a three-way intersection. Follow the short spur left to the point for dramatic ocean views.

The 0.6-mile journey back parallels the eastern shore of Sachuest Bay. As you take in the scenes of the expansive cove, you may spot a white-tailed deer or two in the adjacent thickets before reaching the trail's end. If you have time, check out the visitor center; open daily.

Nearby Options: Second Beach, popular for swimming, is an excellent place to explore during colder months too. Also, check out the popular Cliff Walk in Newport. Partially paved, this route provides excellent views of the water and the community's famous seaside mansions.

2 Block Island Greenway

Distance: 6-mile loop
Difficulty: easy–moderate
Hiking time: 3 hours
Elevation gain: 625 feet
High point: 170 feet

Management: Block Island Conservancy, The Nature Conservancy (TNC)
Season: year-round
Map: TNC website
GPS coordinates: 41.16878°, −71.58334°

Getting there: There are many ferry services to Block Island. Visit blockislandinfo.com for the latest information. In the summer, bringing a car can be challenging, but during the off-season, it is easier. From the Old Harbor ferry terminal, follow Water Street right and immediately turn left onto Chapel Street. In 0.2 mile, turn left on Old Town Road. Drive 0.9 mile and turn left onto Center Road. Head south 0.4 mile to Nathan Mott Park on the right. Options without a car include walking to the trailhead or taking advantage of the island's many bicycle-rental companies (bike rack at trailhead). Use caution along the narrow roadways.

In 1972, the Block Island Conservancy was formed to "maintain habitat for birds and animals, to protect the views of hills rolling to the sea, [and] to provide walking trails and quiet recreation to islanders and visitors." In subsequent decades, they have joined forces with many public and private partners to conserve nearly 50 percent of the island and develop

View of Black Rock Beach

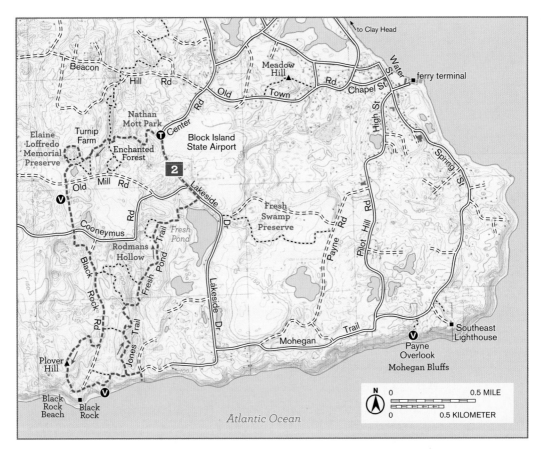

Atlantic Ocean

more than 28 miles of inviting trails, known as the Block Island Greenway. Nowhere are these land protection successes more evident than along the paths that are in and around the Nature Conservancy's Rodmans Hollow Preserve, a glacial outwash that was one of the island's earliest conservation victories.

The loop begins at Nathan Mott Park, which was donated in 1949 as the island's first park. Heading west from a kiosk, the route leads through a tree-lined corridor before crossing a grassy meadow. Hike over a small knoll and descend into the heart of the Enchanted Forest, a small basin covered in shade trees. The trail winds up the steep hillside to the first of many junctions, 0.5 mile from the start.

Stay right and then immediately veer left, following the signs 0.2 mile to Turnip Farm, a wide expanse of open fields. Head south along

its edge and then swing right where a path continues straight to Old Mill Road.

Parallel a stone wall a couple hundred feet to enter the Elaine Loffredo Memorial Preserve. Named for a victim of the TWA flight 800 crash, the trail soon forms a 0.4-mile loop. Complete three-quarters of the circuit and then head south. The main trail bends left, right, and then left again en route to Old Mill Road. Once across the dirt road, wind 0.1 mile through an open field to a bench showcasing views of Long Island. Head over a stone wall and turn sharply right, remaining near the edge of the field. The footway reenters the forest and leads 0.2 mile straight to Cooneymus Road.

Carefully cross the pavement and rejoin the greenway on the far side as it proceeds 0.2 mile east to a junction. Turn right onto Black Rock Road (no vehicle traffic, but bikes are allowed) and follow the wide corridor south past two entrances to TNC's Rodmans Hollow Preserve. In 0.5 mile, bear right on an inviting trail that rises 0.4 mile through meadows. Near the top of Plover Hill, the grassy route descends gently while affording sweeping ocean views and aerial shots of the impressive cliffs that rise above Black Rock Beach.

In 0.2 mile, hike past the southern end of Black Rock Road to another vista. Here, the route heads inland to an intersection. Follow the dirt road leading right. Just beyond the start of the Jones Trail, reach a small parking area at the end of a private road. To the right, an unmarked route drops steeply through a small chasm to the rocky beach below. Enjoy dramatic scenes of the rugged bluffs and opportunities to explore the shoreline, especially during lower tides.

Carefully make your way back to the Jones Trail and follow this route north toward Rodmans Hollow. At a junction, stay right and climb up a small hill to a second intersection. This area is especially vibrant in May, when the shadbush is flowering. Take the trail east and descend into the heart of the hollow. Bear right onto the Fresh Pond Trail to aggressively rise out of the depression. The well-marked route levels off before passing through a small neighborhood. Back in the forest, stay right at the next two intersections. Through a field, the path meanders 0.3 mile to a bench on the pond's picturesque northern shore. A final climb ends on Lakeside Drive. Turn left and follow the pavement 0.4 mile to return to Nathan Mott Park.

Nearby Options: If you are looking for additional areas to explore on the island, consider visiting nearby Mohegan Bluffs and Southeast Lighthouse. Both offer exceptional views of dramatic cliffs. Another great hiking destination, the Clay Head Preserve, is located on Block Island's northern half. Here, a network of trails meanders through a TNC preserve that showcases scenes atop breathtaking coastal bluffs.

Rhode Island Land Trust Council

Rhode Island has an active coalition of community-based land trusts that collectively protect scenic open spaces, farms, forests, historical sites, wildlife habitat, and beautiful places for recreation. Coalition members make available to the public many preserves that are traversed by hundreds of miles of walking trails.

3 Napatree Point

Distance: 3-mile loop	**Management:** Watch Hill Conservancy (WHC)
Difficulty: easy	
Hiking time: 2 hours	**Season:** year-round
Elevation gain: 50 feet	**Map:** WHC website
High point: 15 feet	**GPS coordinates:** 41.31053°, −71.86110°

Getting there: From the junction of Route 1A and Route 1 in Westerly, follow Route 1A south toward Watch Hill. In 3.9 miles, stay right on Watch Hill Road. Continue 2 miles to the village of Watch Hill. Public parking is limited, especially in the summer. Look for spots along the road and non-reserved spots in the adjacent parking lot. **Note:** Dogs must be leashed and are prohibited during the day from early May to early September.

A delightful peninsula to explore near the village of Watch Hill, 1.5-mile-long Napatree Point is Rhode Island's westernmost piece of land. The sandy spit features intact dunes, an inviting beach, and a rocky point. Napatree is also an oasis for avian life throughout the year. Choose lower tides for better footing, and visit during the colder months to avoid summer crowds. Throughout the year, watch your step and remember that wildlife—such as piping plovers, least terns, horseshoe crabs, and American oystercatchers—always have the right-of-way!

Across from the small stores and restaurants in Watch Hill, walk through the parking area to the edge of the protected bay. The pavement leads to a large sign welcoming you to the Napatree Point Conservation Area and outlining various policies, including the need to stay off the dunes. There are a handful of designated paths marked with yellow stakes that are available for crossing from one side of the spit to the other. The most obvious of these are located closest to town.

Hiking the point in a counterclockwise direction, remain on the bay side of the narrow peninsula. Follow the shoreline and take advantage of the inviting terrain to scan the surrounding waters for ducks, geese, and wading birds. At the same time, check the ground below for signs of horseshoe crabs and other sea creatures. About a mile from the start, you will encounter a small obstacle. Here, a stream exits a small cove. It is possible to follow the circuitous route around the inside of the cove, but the footing is not ideal. The best option is to wade across the stream. If neither option is desirable, backtrack and take an official path across the dunes to explore the beach.

Beyond the stream, the sandy spit grows increasingly rugged. To the right lies the Connecticut coastline. Fishers Island, an unconnected extension of New York's Long Island, is visible straight ahead. Take your time navigating 0.2 mile over the uneven rocks and large boulders near the tip of Napatree Point. Your reward is the gorgeous sand beach that awaits on the other side.

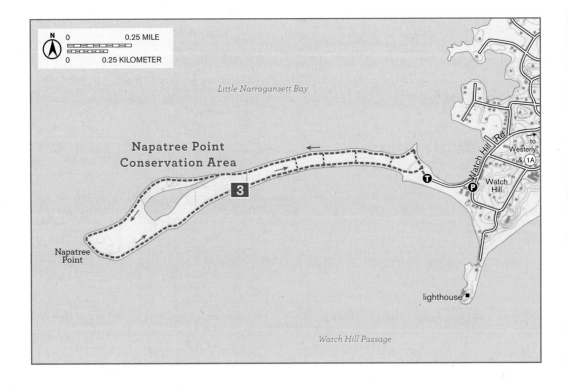

Driftwood near the tip of Napatree Point

Enjoy the crescent-shaped expanse, often pummeled by crashing waves. Look for plovers, sandpipers, and sanderlings feeding on the edge of the surf as you hike 1.2 miles along the picturesque shoreline. With a little luck, discover sand dollars, interesting shells, and polished beach glass at your feet. The beach ends near a rock barrier. Follow the wide path to the left. It leads up and over the dunes, completing the circuit.

If visiting during the colder months, come prepared. While the spit is a great place to soak in the sun, there is little protection from the winds that frequent this exposed landscape.

4 *George Parker Woodland*

Distance: 6.5-mile loop
Difficulty: moderate
Hiking time: 4 hours
Elevation gain: 800 feet
High point: 595 feet

Management: Audubon Society of RI
Season: year-round
Map: ASRI website
GPS coordinates: 41.71685°, −71.69795°

Getting there: From the junction of Routes 102 and 6 in Scituate, drive 9.3 miles south on Route 102 and then turn left onto Maple Valley Road. The parking area is 0.1 mile on the left. **Note:** Dogs prohibited.

The George Parker Woodland property features delightful trails that form three loops along the remains of Revolutionary-era carriage roads once home to pastures lined with stone walls. Today, this wildlife-rich forested landscape is dotted with exposed ledge, immense boulders, and serene bubbling brooks. When your exploration is complete, check out the Audubon Society of Rhode Island's other wildlife refuges scattered across more than 9500 acres in every corner of the state.

Beyond the kiosk, the orange-blazed Meadow Trail immediately forms a loop. Stay right and descend gradually, reaching a junction in 0.2 mile. The route continues right, dropping quickly before leveling off. Boardwalks and bridges wind across the Flat River and accompanying wetlands. The path soon rises to a well-marked intersection.

Turn right onto the blue-blazed Paul Cook Memorial Trail, which forms a 2.3-mile loop. Head up the rocky landscape, the first of the circuit's many short ascents. Swing right and meander through a collection of cairns before reaching the banks of the Flat River. The route continues straight through a junction and parallels the running water for 0.4 mile. Swing north and ascend easily to a four-way intersection at the base of an impressive boulder.

Before completing the Cook Memorial Trail, take the yellow-blazed path exiting right. Winding past large rocks, it eventually hugs the rugged sides of Pine Swamp Brook. Near a small cascade, cross a wooden bridge to the other side. After climbing away from the water, proceed to a three-way junction.

Table Rock on the Gowdy Memorial Trail

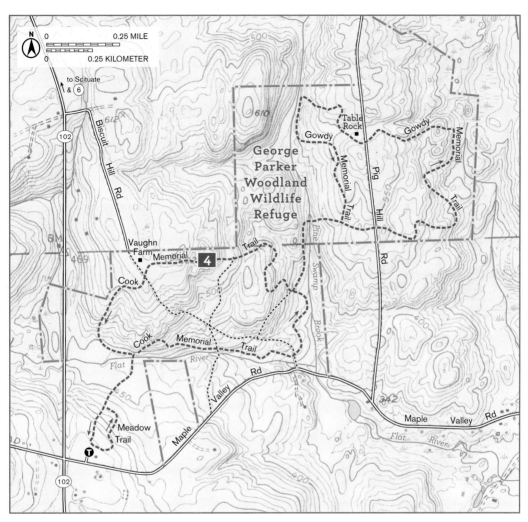

Follow the blue-blazed Milton A. Gowdy Memorial Trail to the right. It forms an attractive 2.4-mile loop through the refuge's northeastern corner. It crosses and recrosses Pig Hill Road, winds over undulating terrain covered with stones and ledges, passes forested wetlands, and visits Pine Swamp Brook before concluding. Beyond the loop's halfway point, a short spur leads to the aptly named Table Rock, a small but intriguing natural feature.

Retrace your steps 0.4 mile along the yellow-blazed connector to rejoin the trek around the Cook Memorial Trail. The northern 1.3-mile stretch of this circuit begins with two short but steep inclines. Hike up lichen-covered ledges to reach the loop's highest point. Just beyond, pass what is left of the Vaughn Farmhouse foundation, further indication of a history when open meadows dominated the now thickly forested landscape. The footing becomes more inviting over the final 0.5 mile.

Turn right to rejoin the Meadow Trail. After crossing the Flat River, head up the hillside. This time, explore the loop's western half, which quickly emerges onto the edge of a field covered in bluebird houses. Look for these bright-colored songbirds as you complete the hike.

5 *Arcadia Loop*

Distance: 11.9-mile loop
Difficulty: challenging
Hiking time: 8 hours
Elevation gain: 1150 feet
High point: 430 feet

Management: Rhode Island DPR
Season: year-round
Map: no official online map
GPS coordinates: 41.57299°, −71.72158°

Getting there: Take exit 14A from Interstate 95 and head south on Route 102. Turn right onto Route 3 in 0.7 mile. Drive 1.3 miles and bear right onto Route 165. Follow Route 165 west 3.5 miles. Cross the Wood River and turn left on the short driveway that leads to a parking area and picnic pavilion. *Note:* Blaze orange required during hunting season.

At more than 14,000 acres, Arcadia Management Area is Rhode Island's largest public land unit. Popular year-round, it is managed for multiple uses, including hiking, fishing, hunting, mountain biking, and horseback riding. Explore this 11.9-mile circuit for a comprehensive tour of the state's wildest landscape, or break it up into multiple shorter hikes. Along the way, enjoy flowering mountain laurel, wildlife-rich forests, secluded wetlands, and an optional extension to Rhode Island's highest waterfall.

Pick up the white-blazed Mount Tom Trail as it departs southwest through a pine stand. The route turns sharply left and briefly follows a dirt road. Bear right before reaching a bridge and proceed along the banks of Parris Brook, a peaceful flowing stream. Once across Mount Tom Road, the day's most difficult section ensues. Rising rapidly up ledge-covered slopes, the path reaches the first of several pleasant viewpoints. Continue up and around the uneven terrain past many geologic formations protruding from the

Reflection on Breakheart Pond

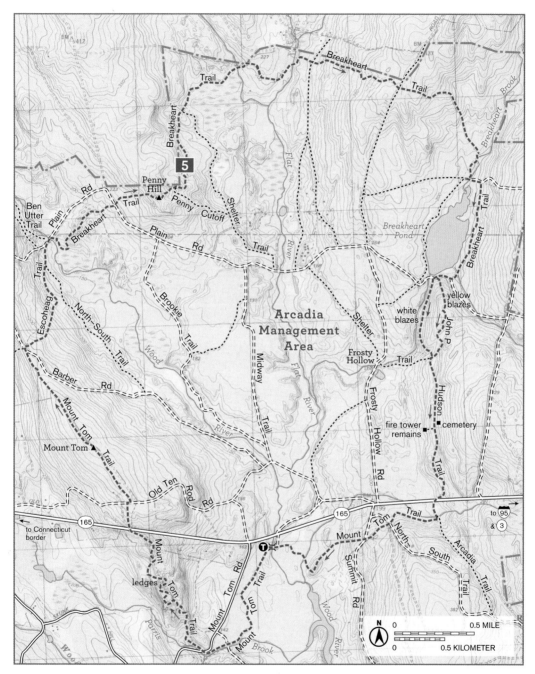

landscape. A sudden descent leads to busy Route 165, 2 miles from the start.

Cross with care—it is hard to see oncoming traffic from the west—and rejoin the path as it climbs quickly to a three-way intersection. Over the next stretch, the once thickly forested landscape is slowly regenerating after a timber harvest in 2019 removed numerous oaks decimated by years of caterpillar infestations. Turn right and then immediately veer left, remaining on the Mount Tom Trail. Continue straight 0.8 mile across Mount Tom's indiscernible 430-foot high point before dropping easily to Barber Road.

Hike over the dirt road and pick up the Escoheag Trail as it gradually descends 0.6 mile northeast to an intersection with the North–South Trail, a 75-mile path that begins in Charlestown and ends at the Massachusetts border. Follow this long-distance trail north 0.2 mile to Plain Road. Turn right to quickly reach a bridge. Before crossing, consider an optional, 3.5-mile roundtrip extension along the mostly flat Ben Utter Trail to scenic Stepstone Falls.

The main loop crosses the Wood River and then immediately joins the yellow-blazed Breakheart Trail as it enters the forest on the right. Briefly following the running water, the path then swings left and ascends a long esker. Continue straight over Plain Road in 0.5 mile and begin a short but steady 0.3-mile climb to a small ledge atop Penny Hill. While the views are limited, the topography is interesting.

Descend steeply, only to climb more easily to a second knoll. Here the Penny Cutoff exits right. Remain on the Breakheart Trail as it swings north and drops moderately past a junction with the Shelter Trail in 0.5 mile. A relatively level section follows over the next mile, which includes crossing two tributaries of the Flat River. Once over the second bridge, traverse the undulating terrain 1.5 miles before briefly heading south

along Breakheart Brook. Upon reaching a dirt road, bear sharply left and cross a wooden bridge at the northern tip of Breakheart Pond. Up a small rise, turn right and parallel Breakheart Pond's eastern shore from a distance. In 0.7 mile, at another intersection of woods roads, hike west to reach the pond's southern shore. As you approach the outlet and small dam, enjoy excellent views of the expansive wetland.

Pick up the John P. Hudson Trail, just south of the dam. This route offers two options to start. A yellow-blazed route leads up an evergreen-draped ridge, while a more rustic, white-blazed path exits right and follows the brook more closely. The two options reconnect in 0.6 mile, near a junction with the Shelter Trail. Continue south through an area thick with mountain laurel. Past a small cemetery and a short spur to the site of a former fire tower, the yellow blazes lead to a parking area in 0.8 mile.

Proceed along the driveway, carefully cross Route 165, and follow the pavement west to a parking area. Together, the Arcadia and Mount Tom Trails lead south for 0.1 mile. At a junction, remain on the Mount Tom Trail as it swings sharply right. The final 1.2-mile stretch rises gradually past stone walls near a sprawling forested wetland. Hike straight through an intersection of woods roads that includes the North–South Trail. After crossing Summit Road, the trail rises up and over a low hill, passes marshy wetlands, and soon arrives at the banks of the Wood River. Cross the bridge to complete the loop.

Shorter Options: If you are looking for shorter excursions, consider combining the Mount Tom Trail with Barber Road (roughly 6 miles); or park at Breakheart Pond and combine the Breakheart and Shelter Trails with Plain Road (roughly 5.5 miles); or start at the John P. Hudson trailhead and hike out and back to Breakheart Pond (roughly 3 miles). There are countless other possibilities with the many trails and roads in the area. (Note: Many of the roads have gates that are open at certain times of the year, allowing vehicular access.)

Opposite, top: Heublein Tower in Talcott Mountain State Park

Opposite, bottom: Cliffs surround Devils Oven in Devils Hopyard State Park.

Connecticut: The Nutmeg State

The Nutmeg State is blessed with an extensive network of well-maintained hiking trails that traverse state parks and forests, many with infrastructure built by the Civilian Conservation Corps nearly a century ago. In recent decades, land trusts and the Connecticut Forest and Park Association have led efforts to greatly expand hiking opportunities throughout the state.

While not home to high summits, Connecticut is blanketed with a rolling landscape of hills, low mountains, and traprock mountain ridges on both sides of its namesake river. The mostly forested landscape invites exploration through the year, but early summer is a great time to hit the trails, when mountain laurel, the state's official flower, is bursting in whites and pinks.

6 *Bluff Point State Park*

Distance: 4.5-mile loop
Difficulty: easy–moderate
Hiking time: 3 hours
Elevation gain: 200 feet
High point: 115 feet

Management: Connecticut DEEP
Season: year-round
Map: DEEP website
GPS coordinates: 41.33605°, −72.03345°

Getting there: From Interstate 95 in Groton, take exit 88 and head south 1.1 miles on Route 117. Turn right onto Route 1, drive 0.2 mile to a traffic light, and then turn left onto Depot Road. Continue 0.3 mile and stay straight. Go under the railroad tracks and drive 0.3 mile to a large parking area. **Notes:** Non-resident fee required. Dogs prohibited on the beach from April to September.

Look for piping plovers while exploring Bushy Point Beach.

Bluff Point State Park, at 800 acres, is the largest piece of conservation land on Connecticut's coastline. The property was first acquired in 1644 by John Winthrop Jr., one of Connecticut Colony's first governors, and the state purchased the point in 1963. This 4.5-mile loop visits Winthrop's former homestead, heads to the top of scenic bluffs, and explores Bushy Point Beach before completing a relaxing stroll alongside the marshy banks of the Poquonnock River.

The wide trail begins near a picnic area at a gate. Walk 0.1 mile to a junction and stay left to start the loop. After rising steadily up the slope, the old road soon levels off under a canopy of towering trees, where paralleling stone walls offer a glimpse to an agrarian past. Here and throughout the hike, expect to encounter narrower, unmarked paths exiting in both directions. These are popular with mountain bikers.

One mile from the start, arrive at the former Winthrop homestead. A side trail descends east to Mumford Cove and another drops west toward the Poquonnock River; remain on the ridge by swinging right and then left around the foundation's remains. Follow the pleasant trail and scan the surrounding forest for resident songbirds taking advantage of the thick understory. In 0.5 mile, reach a short spur right to Sunset Rock, a granite protrusion surrounded by trees that no longer offers distant views. Beyond the geologic feature, arrive at the first of many unmarked paths that lead left to the water's edge. Follow the main trail as it winds west to the top of scenic bluffs more reminiscent of the Maine coast than Connecticut.

Dropping north, the trail quickly leads to the eastern end of 1-mile-long Bushy Point Beach. Occasionally, soft footing may slow you down; however, journeying at least 0.5 mile along the picturesque extension of the point provides an excellent perspective of the bluffs and offers ideal locations for picnicking. Be alert for piping plovers, diminutive shorebirds with plumage that matches the beach's sand and crushed shells.

Upon completing the exploration of the beach, make your way back to the main loop. The 1.2-mile return trek to the parking area exclusively follows the lower trail on terrain that is generally flat. In this area, you are likely to notice the nearby airport. Fortunately, the occasional noise does little to undermine the abundant natural beauty. With some patience, you might spot an egret or heron feeding among the tall reeds in the adjoining marshland.

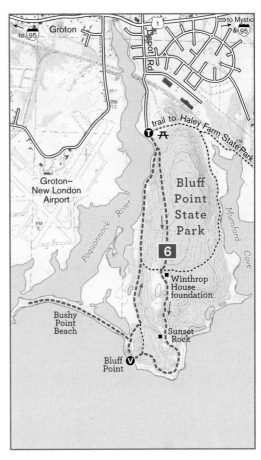

7 *Devils Hopyard State Park*

Distance: 2.8-mile loop
Difficulty: easy–moderate
Hiking time: 2 hours
Elevation gain: 500 feet
High point: 450 feet

Management: Connecticut DEEP
Season: year-round
Map: DEEP website
GPS coordinates: 41.48434°, −72.34202°

Getting there: Take exit 70 off Interstate 95 in Old Lyme. Follow Route 156 north 8.5 miles. Turn right onto Route 82 and in 0.2 mile turn left onto Route 434 (Hopyard Road). Drive 3.4 miles and turn right on Foxtown Road. The parking area is immediately on the left. **Note:** Camping is available in the state park.

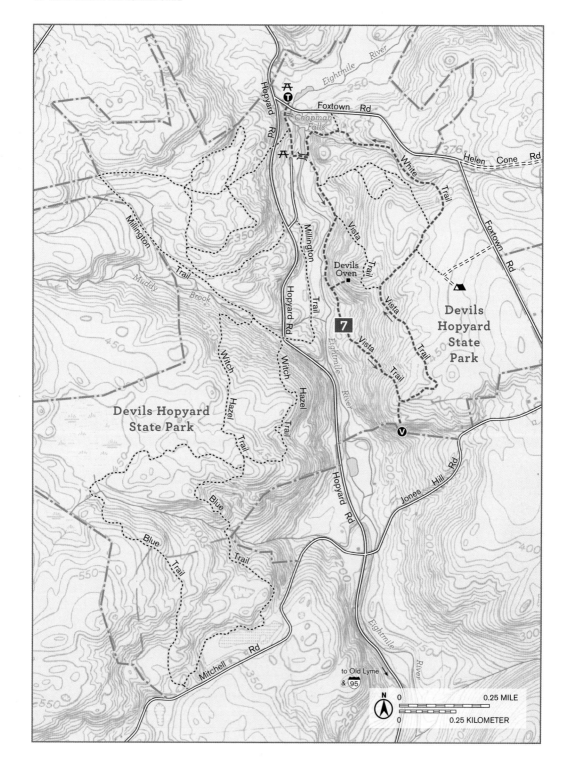

Featuring 12.5 miles of trails, 1000-acre Devils Hopyard State Park is a perfect destination for discovering gnarly geologic formations, maturing forests shading groves of mountain laurel, and bubbling mountain streams. While exploring the well-marked trail network, contemplate which of many explanations is the true origin of the park's name: perhaps the mispronunciation of a local farmer named Dibble who grew hops for beer, or a folktale describing how an angry, pitchfork-packing deity stamped the deep potholes in the river upon dampening his long, pointy tail.

The hike begins near the banks of the Wild and Scenic Eightmile River. Cross Foxtown Road, join a wide path, and quickly reach a view of Chapman Falls. Cascading 60 feet down a steep rock ledge, the falls are a popular attraction. A few hundred feet ahead, a spur leads left to its base. Beyond the spur, make your way down to a picnic area.

Cross the charming covered bridge and stay straight on the orange-blazed Vista Trail. Proceed 0.2 mile to a junction where the path forms a loop. Continue right under the shady canopy of towering evergreens. The trail weaves up, over, and around numerous boulders and rock outcrops while paralleling the peaceful river. Occasionally, unmarked paths diverge to the water's edge. Follow the many orange blazes to a signpost. Here, an extremely steep but very short climb ends at the Devils Oven, a dark crevice in an impressive rock face. Carefully return to the main route.

The Vista Trail remains near the meandering river, approaching it one last time before climbing to the left. Plod up a 0.4-mile ascent that soon crests an oak-dominated ridge. With

Chapman Falls along the Eightmile River

the hammering of woodpeckers and the chorus of scarlet tanagers in the air, follow a short spur straight to a ledge with bucolic views of nearby forested hillsides.

Head back to the main path and turn right. Weaving along the ridge, cross two small streams. Beyond the second one, arrive at a junction. The Vista Trail proceeds straight, returning to the covered bridge in 0.5 mile. Complete a longer loop by bearing right onto the white-blazed option.

After a brief ascent, hike straight through an intersection where a path exits right to a youth camping area. Once through a pine grove and over a stone wall, the white-blazed trail begins a final 0.5-mile descent along a small babbling brook. Weave through clusters of mountain laurel in the narrowing valley before leveling off. Ahead, an unmarked route leads to a view of Chapman Falls. Follow the trail left across the small stream and quickly return to the covered bridge. Retrace your steps past the falls to complete the journey.

Extend Your Trip: Explore the quieter trails on the park's western side by following the pavement south 0.1 mile from the covered bridge. Just before the picnic area entrance swings right to Hopyard Road, stay straight on the red-blazed Millington Trail. It meanders 0.4 mile to Hopyard Road. Once across, turn left on the yellow-blazed Witch Hazel Trail, which forms a 1.2-mile loop that begins and ends with a steep pitch. Near its halfway point, an undulating, blue-blazed trail departs left to form a separate 2.3-mile circuit past rocky ledges, secluded streams, and a small pond. After completing the Witch Hazel Trail, follow the red blazes back to the picnic area.

8 *Mashamoquet Brook State Park*

Distance: 4-mile loop
Difficulty: moderate
Hiking time: 2 hours
Elevation gain: 675 feet
High point: 710 feet

Management: Connecticut DEEP
Season: year-round
Map: DEEP website
GPS coordinates: 41.85125°, −71.96907°

Getting there: Take exit 41 off Interstate 395 and follow Route 101 west 4.9 miles. Turn left, just before the intersection with Route 44, onto Wolf Den Drive. In 0.7 mile, turn left onto a campground driveway that leads 0.1 mile to a day-use parking area near the state park office building on the right. *Note:* Camping available in the state park.

The famous—some may argue infamous—location where Connecticut's last gray wolf met its ultimate demise, Mashamoquet Brook State Park is a tranquil 900-acre oasis in eastern Connecticut. Today, the park is an amalgam of three previous independent parks, including Wolf Den State Park, first protected by the Daughters of the American Revolution in 1899. This family-friendly 4-mile loop slithers up rocky slopes, visits stately forests, and explores diverse wildlife habitats.

The Blue Trail begins south of the parking area near a small sign. This grassy route quickly swings right between pine trees. Veer left, cross the stone wall, and begin the first of many short climbs on the hike's first 1.5 miles. While this is the most difficult section of the hike, it is also the most interesting. Follow the path as it navigates the rolling terrain, passing one quirky geologic feature after another, signs of how the most recent ice age shaped the landscape.

One mile from the parking area, cross a horse trail. Stay on the blue-blazed route as it rises 0.1 mile to Indian Chair, a small seat-shaped rock perched atop a wooded ledge. Soon after, a

Connecticut's historic Wolf Den

red-blazed option enters from the right. Over the next 0.4 mile, the two trails coincide. After crossing a small bridge, the trail climbs quickly and reaches the Wolf Den on the left. Here a plaque commemorates Israel Putnam's 1742 slaying of the state's final wolf. Mr. Putnam proceeded to build upon his lore by becoming a famous major general during the American Revolution. A final ascent leads to a four-way intersection. Check out the short spur that departs right to Table Rock, a large flat boulder reminiscent of a sacrificial altar.

From the Table Rock Spur, the Red Trail continues north. Head west along the Blue Trail, which leads through a parking area and down a dirt driveway. At Wolf Den Drive, turn right and then immediately swing left back onto a narrower path. A relaxing 1.4-mile stroll follows. Gradually descending the hilltop, the trail passes an open field before dropping through a fern-filled forest. The route bends sharply right, crosses a small stream, and reaches a trail junction. To the left, a yellow-blazed path descends 0.2 mile to a campground, a popular picnic area,

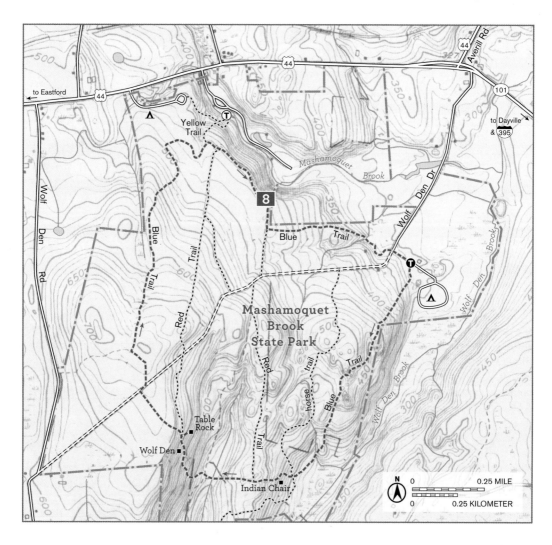

and swimming holes on Mashamoquet Brook, so named by Native Americans because of its excellent fishing. This is an alternative starting point for the hike at the state park's main entrance.

Continue right and follow the trail as it remains on the rim high above a steep slope.

With the sounds of picnickers echoing below, press on and stay left at two intersections with the Red Trail. After the second one, the blue-blazed route parallels stone walls and eventually reaches Wolf Den Drive one last time. Cross the road and follow the driveway 0.1 mile ahead to the parking area.

Connecticut Forest & Parks Association

This membership-based organization is dedicated to connecting people to the land to protect forests, parks, walking trails, and open spaces in Connecticut for future generations. They provide many services, including environmental education, land conservation, and the maintenance of the state's extensive 825-mile blue-blazed hiking-trail network.

9 Breakneck Pond

Distance: 7.4-mile loop
Difficulty: moderate–challenging
Hiking time: 5 hours
Elevation gain: 900 feet
High point: 1010 feet

Management: Connecticut DEEP
Season: year-round
Map: DEEP website
GPS coordinates: 41.99855°, −72.12628°

Getting there: Take exit 74 from Interstate 84 in Union. From the south, turn right off the exit and quickly turn right again onto Route 171. From the north, take the first two lefts from the exit, then drive over the interstate and turn right onto Route 171. Drive 2.3 miles south and bear left at a junction with Route 190, remaining on Route 171. In 1.4 miles, turn left into Bigelow Hollow State Park. Drive 0.6 mile to a parking lot on the left near a picnic area. *Notes:* Non-resident fee required. Backcountry campsites available.

Breakneck Pond is surrounded by a 9000-acre conservation area that comprises Bigelow Hollow State Park and Nipmuck State Forest. In Algonquin, Nipmuck describes a land "abounding in small ponds and streams." Aptly named, this thickly forested region is also dissected by a series of long, narrow ridges decorated with lichen-draped boulders, carpets of ferns, and prolific mountain laurels. This recommended circuit in one of eastern Connecticut's largest undeveloped areas is an excellent overview of a natural oasis that demands further exploration.

Begin on the east side of the road near a hiking sign. Up a small bank, the trail splits. Stay right on the East Ridge Trail, which follows an old dirt road. Remain on this white-blazed route as it winds gently 1 mile north.

As you approach the southern tip of Breakneck Pond, the trail swings east into a large opening where multiple routes diverge. Follow the much-narrower Nipmuck Trail that exits left toward the water. Hugging the eastern shore for 1.9 miles, this delightful blue-blazed path visits numerous viewpoints and interesting rock formations while tunneling through mazes of

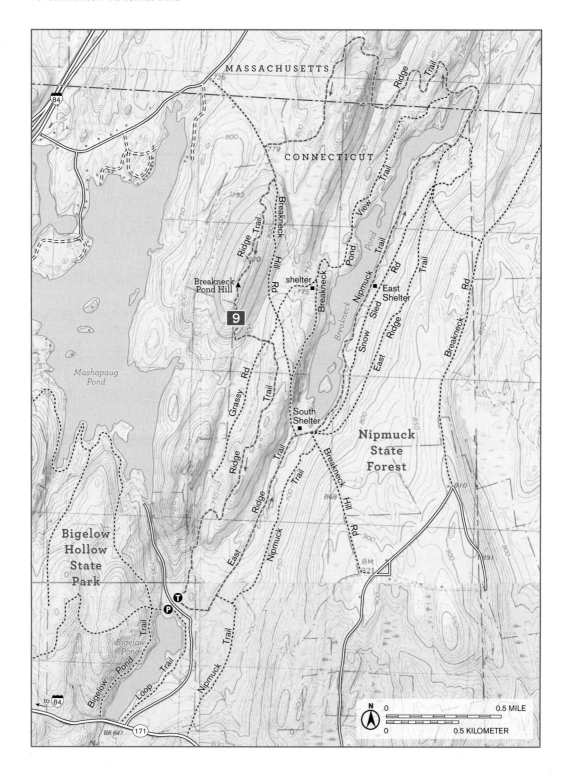

MASSACHUSETTS

CONNECTICUT

Ridge Trail

Pond View Trail

Breakneck Ridge Trail

Breakneck Hill Rd

Breakneck Pond Hill

shelter

Breakneck

Breakneck Pond

Nipmuck

Snow Sled Rd

East Ridge Trail

East Shelter

Breakneck Rd

9

Mashapaug Pond

Grassy Rd

Trail

South Shelter

Ridge

700 Trail

Ridge

Nipmuck State Forest

Breakneck Hill Rd

BM 921

Bigelow Hollow State Park

East

Nipmuck

910

Trail

Loop

Bigelow Pond

Bigelow Pond Trail

Nipmuck Trail

T
P

to 84

BR 547

171

N

0   0.5 MILE

0   0.5 KILOMETER

mountain laurel and scrambling up a series of small inclines. Near the halfway point, pass East Shelter, a small lean-to available for overnight use. The route eventually joins a dirt road before entering Massachusetts.

Swing left on the Breakneck Pond View Trail at the wetland's northern edge and take in the final reflections off its blue water. Upon crossing a small stream, ascend to a junction and branch sharply right onto the blue-and-orange-blazed Ridge Trail. Heading up a small but steep incline, the rustic path winds 1 mile over ledges, around a large beaver pond, and through a hillside labyrinth of impressive boulders. Rise 0.2 mile to the top of a forested ridge with modest views of surrounding hillsides.

Beyond the high point, the trail drops quickly before meandering 0.5 mile to Breakneck Hill Road. Follow this dirt road southeast past a small gate and then bear right onto a second road. Up the hillside, the Ridge Trail quickly departs sharply right and heads south along a narrower pathway. Climbing gradually over the forested

The calm waters of Breakneck Pond along the Nipmuck Trail

top of Breakneck Pond Hill, the journey eventually winds down to a grassy road crossing in 0.9 mile. For the final 1.5 miles, the path traverses the narrowing ridgeline, descends abruptly to a small stream, and soon ends at the parking area.

Shorter Options: Instead of following the Ridge Trail back, head south along the Breakneck Pond View Trail and loop around the entire pond. Return on the East Ridge Trail to complete a 5.8-mile hike. Alternatively, complete either the 1.3-mile loop of Bigelow Pond or the 4.8-mile circuit to Mashapaug Pond; both begin south and west from the parking area.

10 *Talcott Mountain*

Distance: 4-mile loop
Difficulty: moderate
Hiking time: 2–3 hours
Elevation gain: 650 feet
High point: 940 feet

Management: Connecticut DEEP
Season: year-round
Map: DEEP website
GPS coordinates: 41.83839°, −72.78490°

Getting there: From the junction of Routes 202 and 44 in Avon, drive north on Route 202. In 2.9 miles, turn right onto Route 185. Follow Route 185 for 1.7 miles and then turn left into Penwood State Park. The driveway leads 0.1 mile to a parking area on the right.

Rising above Hartford, Talcott Mountain is a long, narrow ridge that stands above the gentler Connecticut River valley landscape to the east. While its natural appearance is not unique in the region, Talcott stands apart from its neighbors thanks to the 165-foot Heublein Tower that rises atop its summit. Built in 1914 by a Hartford resident, German-born hotelier and restaurateur

Rocky bluff atop King Phillip Mountain

New England colonists for two bloody years, this blue-blazed route is also part of the larger New England Trail that meanders from Long Island Sound to southern New Hampshire. Ascend gradually, hike under a powerline, and reach a red-blazed trail departing left in 0.5 mile—this Metacomet Bypass route provides a longer, quieter option to reach the summit. Stay straight on the Metacomet Trail as it swings north before climbing a series of switchbacks. As the terrain levels, turn abruptly left onto a narrower and more interesting landscape. Weave along the ridge over numerous ledges, one offering pleasant western views near the top of King Phillip Mountain.

Soon, the Metacomet Trail intersects and coincides with the more popular Tower Trail. Continue left 0.1 mile to the white monolith on the summit. Maintained by a nonprofit, the Heublein Tower is well worth exploring when it is open (visit Friends of Heublein Tower's website for hours of operation). On a clear day, visitors can view much of Connecticut as well as destinations to the north, including New Hampshire's Mount Monadnock. Hartford's skyline is especially impressive from this aerial location.

Be sure to check out the tower's many displays. Its history includes two noteworthy guests in the early 1950s: World War II hero and future president Dwight D. Eisenhower, as well as head of the Screen Actors Guild and president-to-be Ronald Reagan. Hike 0.1 mile south of the tower to a picnic area near a rocky bluff that provides sweeping views, whether the tower is open or not.

For the return trip, follow the Tower Trail north. The wide pathway drops gradually for 0.8 mile. For the most scenic descent, pick up the narrower route that parallels the Tower Trail to

Gilbert Heublein, the tower provides one of the finest views in the Nutmeg State.

From the parking area, walk south to Route 185 and take your time crossing the road to a sign for the Metacomet Trail. Named for a seventeenth-century Wampanoag sachem who battled

New England National Scenic Trail

The New England National Scenic Trail is a 215-mile hiking trail comprised of the historical Mattabesett and Metacomet Trails in Connecticut as well as the Metacomet–Monadnock Trail in Massachusetts. Although often from a distance, the route parallels the Connecticut River from the New Hampshire border to Long Island Sound.

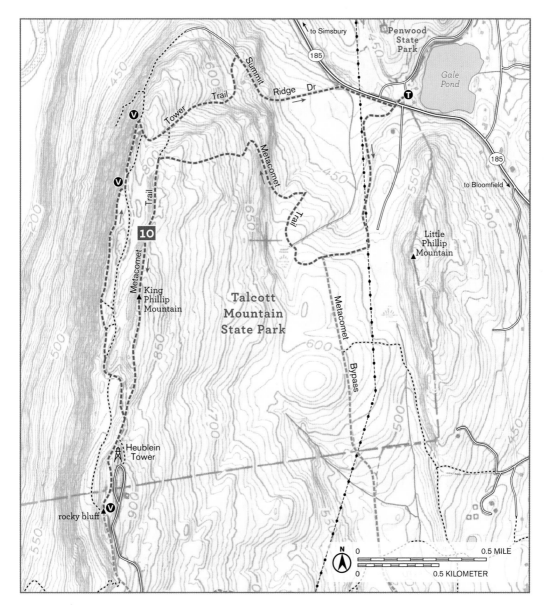

the left for most of its course. There are multiple connectors between the two. This more dramatic path follows closer to the mountain's ledges. Watch your step along the way and beware of the many precipitous edges. Rejoin the Tower Trail at a final viewpoint and descend steeply 0.4 mile to a large parking area.

Turn right and follow the paved park road back to Route 185. Turn right again to quickly complete the circuit.

Extend Your Trip: To extend your hike or for a future trip in the area, explore Penwood State Park on the north side of Route 185. The Metacomet Trail and other paths traverse this 800-acre preserve, visiting rocky vistas and pleasant, forested surroundings.

11 *Sleeping Giant State Park*

Distance: 5.8-mile loop
Difficulty: challenging
Hiking time: 4 hours
Elevation gain: 1650 feet
High point: 739 feet

Management: Connecticut DEEP
Season: year-round
Map: DEEP website
GPS coordinates: 41.42120°, −72.89894°

Getting there: From the junction of Route 10 and Route 40 in Hamden, drive 1.4 miles north on Route 10 and then turn right onto Mount Carmel Avenue. Continue 0.3 mile to the state park entrance and parking area on the left (across from Quinnipiac University).
Note: Non-resident fee required.

Featuring a mountain with towering cliffs and numerous peaks that resemble a sleeping giant from a distance, this state park is one of Connecticut's most popular hiking destinations. While most stick to the gradual, well-manicured Tower Trail, the park features miles of less-traveled paths crisscrossing the forested slopes and rocky ridges. Choose this challenging loop for a greater appreciation of Sleeping Giant's rugged beauty, and discover its more hidden rewards.

The recommended circuit remains on two distinct paths—the Quinnipiac Trail and the Orange Trail—with one brief exception. At the northern end of the loop road, find the Blue Trail. It descends 0.1 mile to a junction near the banks of the Mill River.

Follow the wide path right. After crossing a small tributary, veer slightly left at a junction with a red-blazed trail and begin a challenging 3.4-mile trek along the Quinnipiac Trail. Along the way, there are countless intersections. Follow

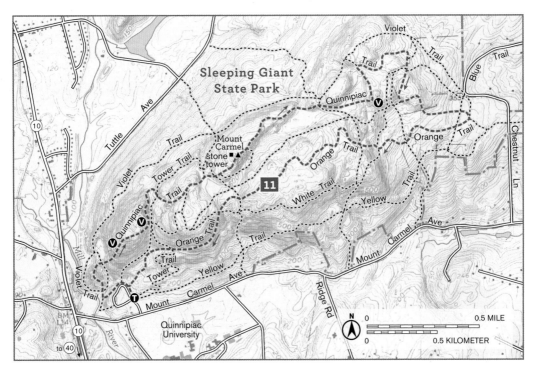

the route's abundant blue markings at every bend.

Ascend rapidly 0.1 mile up a small knoll for the day's first views—scenes of rocky slopes rising above a quarry. After a brief, very steep drop, tackle the hike's most difficult section, an aggressive 0.3-mile ascent. Scramble up the ledge-covered slope and check out the views south, where New Haven's skyline rises above Long Island Sound. The trail eventually eases before skirting along the edge of a precipitous cliff that showcases dramatic views east—watch your step near the edge. A rocky 0.1-mile descent soon follows. Level off near an intersection with the Tower Trail.

Now, 1 mile from the start, head across the popular Tower Trail and continue along the Quinnipiac Trail. Up and over a wooded summit, cross the Tower Trail again in 0.3 mile. A final 0.2-mile rise leads to the base of the summit's historic stone structure atop 739-foot Mount Carmel. From the tower's top floor, marvel at 360-degree scenery, but be prepared for a lot of company.

Rejoin the Quinnipiac Trail as it departs to the northeast. After passing short spurs leading to precarious vistas, the trail drops rapidly into a scree-filled saddle. Swing right and scramble 0.2 mile up to the day's fifth distinct peak. From this quieter locale, find secluded rock perches that lie beneath the soaring wings of turkey vultures.

Another 0.2-mile descent is followed by a circuitous rise of a similar length to the journey's sixth summit. Shrouded in boulders, this peak offers shots looking back to the tower. The hike rambles 0.7 mile to a seventh bump. Continue along the Quinnipiac Trail as it drops rapidly to flatter ground and reaches a four-way junction with the Orange Trail in 0.5 mile.

Although the parking area is still 2.3 miles away, the most difficult terrain is behind you. Head right on the Orange Trail. Level at first, it

Ledgetop views near the western end of Quinnipiac Trail

soon traverses a series of less-pronounced ups and downs while winding around rocks, passing secluded vernal pools, and exploring quiet forest surroundings. Take your time, as the footing is rough in places, and scan the surrounding landscape for resident avian life. The final climb is followed by a steady descent. Cross the Tower Trail and wind back to the parking area.

Other Options: If you are looking for a more moderate end to the hike, follow the Yellow or Violet Trails rather than the Orange. The Violet Trail is a couple of miles longer, while the Yellow is the same length. Both options are accessible near the eastern end of the Orange Trail. Those seeking a more relaxing excursion should stick to the 1.3-mile Tower Trail both ways. Check out the detailed map on the state park's website.

12 *Peoples State Forest*

Distance: 5.1-mile loop
Difficulty: moderate
Hiking time: 4 hours
Elevation gain: 975 feet
High point: 1120 feet

Management: Connecticut DEEP
Season: year-round
Map: DEEP website
GPS coordinates: 41.94259°, −73.00713°

Getting there: From the junction of Routes 44 and 181 in Barkhamsted, follow Route 181 north 1.1 miles. Stay on Route 181 by turning right to cross the Farmington River. Immediately turn left onto East River Road and drive 2.4 miles to the parking area on the left.

The American Legion State Forest and Peoples State Forest form an impressive block of conservation land along both sides of the Wild and Scenic Farmington River. Connecticut acquired the first portions of both forests in the mid-1920s. The American Legion Forest was donated to the state with the hope of demonstrating proper forest management. Around the same time, the Connecticut Forest and Park Association spearheaded an effort to assemble the Peoples Forest. Today, visitors flock to the area for swimming, fishing, and exploring the more than 10 miles of hiking trails that weave throughout. This 5.1-mile loop showcases stands of impressive old trees, scenic ledges, and tranquil wetlands.

Begin on the Jessie Gerard Trail, near a large kiosk on the opposite side of the road. Immediately take the left fork onto the Falls Cutoff Trail. It climbs steeply up stone steps past tumbling water before cresting the ridge in 0.2 mile. Bear left, rejoining the Gerard Trail, and hike through the mountain laurel understory. Climb steadily to the first of two viewpoints, the Grand Vista, an impressive perch high above the Farmington River valley. The path levels off and soon reaches Chaugham Lookout, which offers a different perspective of the winding river. Ahead, the Gerard Trail cuts between the large Veeder Boulders before swinging east and ending at Greenwoods Road.

Turn right and follow the road through the Big Spring picnic area. In a few hundred feet, the Charles Pack Trail descends left to a Civilian Conservation Corps fire pond, one of hundreds

built in the area. Follow the trail down through a towering stand of hemlocks. In 0.5 mile, turn left on Beaver Brook Road. Cross the rushing stream and then turn right into a picnic area.

The Pack Trail continues east and for 1.5 miles winds up and over many slopes and crosses a

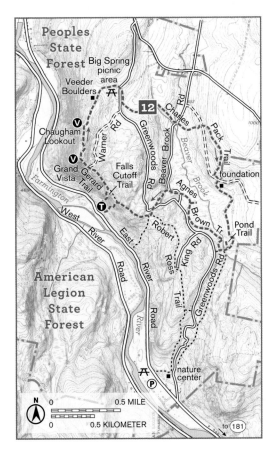

handful of forest roads. After dropping toward a large marsh where an old foundation remains, the route makes its way to Beaver Brook. Check out the 0.1-mile Pond Trail that exits here to a peaceful spot on the secluded water body, then proceed across the bridge and beyond to an intersection.

Turn right on the Agnes Brown Trail. Follow the orange-and-blue-blazed path across level terrain near the shoreline. In 0.3 mile, a path diverges right to a boardwalk that leads into the heart of the pond—a great place to spot waterfowl and other birds. The main trail soon reaches a road. Turn right and walk along the pavement a few hundred yards, until the hiking route veers left. Climbing over a low ridge, the Brown Trail continues straight across another road and soon arrives at a four-way intersection.

Follow the blue-blazed Robert Ross Trail right. After passing a modest viewpoint, the path wraps around rugged ledges and in 0.4 mile reaches a junction with the Gerard Trail.

Taking a break on the Pond Trail

Turn left and hike 0.4 mile down the weaving switchbacks to complete the circuit. The final stretch winds through the former site of a Native American settlement known as Barkhamsted Lighthouse.

Other Options: Some hikers may find the lower sections of the Jessie Gerard Trail to be too steep, and in winter, these sections can be icy. Consider altering the loop by beginning at the forest's nature center, which is located on East River Road 0.5 mile south of the Jessie Gerard trailhead. Follow the Robert Ross Trail to the loop and use the Agnes Brown Trail to return to the start. This is also a good option if the Gerard Trail parking is full.

13 *Hidden Valley Preserve*

Distance: 3.8-mile loop
Difficulty: easy–moderate
Hiking time: 2 hours
Elevation gain: 525 feet
High point: 830 feet

Management: Steep Rock Association (SRA)
Season: year-round
Map: SRA website
GPS coordinates: 41.65648°, −73.31801°

Getting there: From the junction of Route 47 and Route 109 in Washington Depot, follow Route 47 north. Drive 1.2 miles to the parking area on the right, just before crossing the Shepaug River. *Notes:* Additional parking on Route 47 on the north side of the river. Dogs must be leashed.

The Steep Rock Association has a long and storied past that began in 1889 with the protection of 100 acres along the Shepaug River in Washington Depot. Today, this membership-based land trust welcomes visitors to explore more than 2000 acres of conservation land featuring nearly 50 miles of recreational trails. For a wonderful introduction to their work, complete the Van Sinderen Loop's tour of the Hidden Valley Preserve by touring former carriage paths along a peaceful river, through a historical quartz mine, and to pastoral vistas of the surrounding hillsides.

Follow the orange-blazed President's Trail along the side of the Shepaug River and quickly arrive at the Thoreau Bridge. The suspension bridge offers pleasant views of the river and features quotes from the famous nineteenth-century New England writer. Remain on the river's south side and enjoy intimate views of the rushing water around a bend in its channel. In 0.6 mile, the route ends at a three-way intersection.

Turn left to join the yellow-blazed Van Sinderen Loop, which you have been paralleling thus far. The loop was named in honor of the family that donated this preserve to the trust in 1963. Remain on this well-marked route for the rest of the hike. Note that portions of this circuit are also available for equestrians and mountain bikers.

Thoreau Bridge showcases quotes from the famous writer.

Over the next 0.5 mile, the wide trail stays close to the Shepaug River. Pass a footbridge providing access to paths on the other side of the water, skirt the left edge of a small field, and then arrive at a four-way intersection, where the Van Sinderen Loop turns sharply right. To the left, a spur leads to a quaint spot on the river.

Head away from the water. In 0.1 mile, swing left toward the base of the property's nineteenth-century quartz mine. The trail uses switchbacks to climb through the remains, with white rock pebbles at your feet and intact ledges on the side. Rise out of the narrow chasm to a wider footpath above.

Begin a modest ascent of the hillside as the trail bends left and then right at consecutive intersections. The route soon levels off and stays high on the ridge over the next 1.2 miles with minor ups and downs. Along the way, enjoy inviting scenery from the Hidden Valley Lookout and across a small meadow. At the end of the ridge, a blue-blazed trail enters from the left and soon exits left as well. Briefly join this path up a short incline to Hidden Valley Pinnacle, the preserve's finest vista.

Retrace your steps back to the Van Sinderen Loop and turn left. Over the next 0.4 mile, the route meanders easily down the steep hemlock-draped hillside. A final bend in the trail leads back to the parking area.

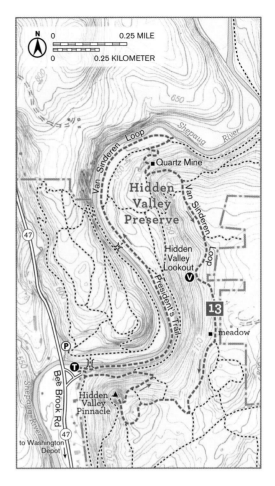

Extend Your Trip: If you are itching for more adventure, check out the paths on the north side of the Thoreau Bridge, or visit another of the nearby Steep Rock Association's preserves.

14 *Macedonia Brook State Park*

Distance: 6.4-mile loop
Difficulty: moderate–challenging
Hiking time: 5 hours
Elevation gain: 1825 feet
High point: 1357 feet

Management: Connecticut DEEP
Season: year-round
Map: DEEP website
GPS coordinates: 41.76110°, −73.49377°

Getting there: From Route 7 in Kent, follow Route 341 west 1.8 miles. Turn right onto Macedonia Brook Road. In 0.8 mile, stay left at the fork. Drive 0.7 mile more and just beyond the bridge crossing Macedonia Brook, turn left into the small parking area.

Macedonia Brook snakes through a scenic valley in western Connecticut. Bordered by steep ridges, the brook forms the core of a 2300-acre park that began with a 1552-acre donation to the state in 1918. While most hikers opt for the less-than-1-mile ascent of scenic Cobble Mountain, this 6.4-mile loop provides greater variety, solitude, and more wildlife-viewing opportunities. With camping sites in the park and lodging nearby, a trip to this beautiful corner of Connecticut can easily be extended with other adventures to nearby Kent Falls or excursions along the Appalachian Trail.

Follow the Blue Trail west up a steep slope, and pass the first of many blue blazes marking the entire loop. It is hard to imagine the more industrial activities that once took place here, including cider, grist, and sawmills as well as an iron forge. A couple of switchbacks lead to a small brook crossing. Bear right and emerge atop an ever-increasing series of open outcrops. As you continue climbing, each step offers more expansive views of the valley below. Return to the shady forest canopy and proceed over minor ups and downs. A steadier climb leads to an intersection with the White Trail, 1.6 miles from the start. Stay left and ascend the rocky slope that ends atop Cobble Mountain, with 180-degree views encompassing New York's Catskill Mountains and the Taconic Range extending north toward Massachusetts.

Level at first, the loop proceeds north and soon descends rapidly to the top of an impressive ledge. Take your time and watch your footing on the very steep, rocky section that follows. The path drops into a saddle and a junction with the Green Trail. Stay left and follow the blue blazes up to another view of Macedonia Brook valley. Once over the ridge, the trail winds gradually down to a wide corridor at a junction with the Orange Trail.

Turn left and in about 100 yards, go straight across a dirt road onto a grassy lane. In 0.4 mile, head north along Weber Road. Before reaching Hilltop Pond, the route quickly crosses to the other side and heads up a steep hemlock-covered slope near the park's northern boundary. Descend

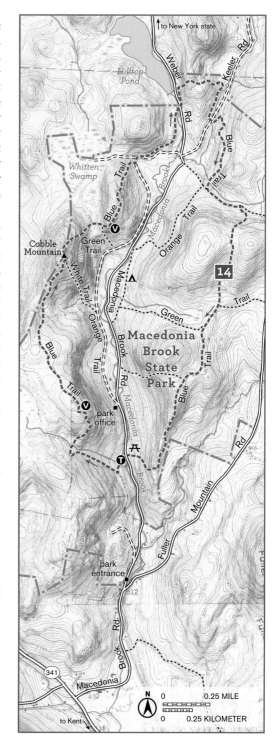

A spring day along Macedonia Brook

past stone walls and through dense ferns to make your way to a small pond before paralleling the inviting banks of the park's namesake brook.

Go left on a dirt road, cross a bridge, and then immediately swing right, back into the forest. The gradual terrain of the loop's eastern section begins to dominate. After veering left and hiking up a forested road, the blue-blazed route heads south. A steady climb is followed by a more relaxing stretch across an undulating ridgeline for nearly 2 miles. The final descent begins through semi-open oak forests, but as the trail falls northwest a final time, the canopy closes. A few more steps, and the gurgling sounds of Macedonia Brook can once again be heard. Follow the paved road right to complete your journey.

Shorter Options: There are many ways to shorten the described route using the various paths that intersect the blue-blazed loop. Leaving from the park's office, consider a scramble to the summit of Cobble Mountain combining the Orange, Green, Blue, and White Trails. Complete this 2.4-mile loop in a counterclockwise fashion to hike up the steep section of the Blue Trail, rather than descending it.

15 *Bear Mountain and Sages Ravine*

Distance: 7.9-mile loop
Difficulty: challenging
Hiking time: 6 hours
Elevation gain: 2050 feet
High point: 2316 feet

Management: Connecticut DEEP
Season: year-round
Map: No official online map
GPS coordinates: 42.02879°, −73.42889°

Getting there: From the junction of Routes 41 and 44 in Salisbury, take Route 41 north 3.3 miles to the parking area on the left. *Note:* Backcountry campsites available.

Under a canopy of towering hardwood trees and through a labyrinth of mountain laurel, this 7.9-mile excursion follows beaten-down paths to quaint campsites, hidden cascades, and spectacular vistas. Enjoy the melodious tunes of colorful songbirds, the hammering rhythm of resident woodpeckers, and the graceful flight of circling raptors while exploring diverse habitats along the way. Although it is challenging, this loop is a must-visit hiking adventure to Connecticut's highest summit and one of Massachusetts's most alluring natural treasures.

Begin on the Undermountain Trail as it leads west through the shady forest. Weaving moderately up the slope, the path reaches Brassie Brook in 1 mile. Follow the trail right and climb

Mount Everett (left) and Mount Race (right) rise to the north of Bear Mountain.

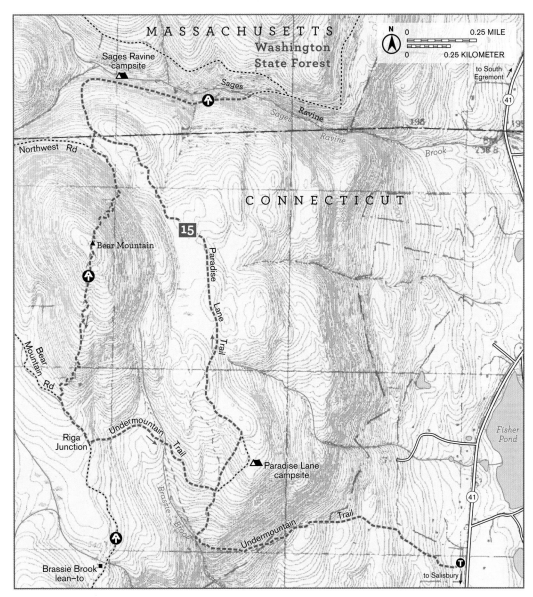

more aggressively 0.2 mile to two intersections. The first leads north to a group campsite. A few steps later, take the second one right onto the Paradise Lane Trail. After a 0.3-mile climb, another path departs right to the camping area. Stay straight and enjoy more-relaxing grades over the next 1.6 miles. The blue-blazed trail rises over many bumps on the high plateau and skirts the edge of numerous wetlands, occasionally offering views of Bear Mountain's summit. After carving through a dark hemlock grove and entering Massachusetts, descend to a junction with the Appalachian Trail (AT).

The loop continues left, but for now turn right and descend into Sages Ravine. Reach the banks of Sages Ravine Brook in 0.1 mile, and follow the tumbling water downstream. A spur leads left to an inviting campsite, but the water crossing might be difficult with high water. Continue into the narrowing chasm, where the brook falls over increasingly higher drops. Lush with mosses and green vegetation, the ravine receives cascading streams from all angles. Make your way to a series of stone steps leading to the other side. Here the river drops out of view to the east and the AT continues north to scenic Mount Race (see Hike 26).

Retrace your steps 0.8 mile back to the Paradise Lane junction. This time, stay straight and follow the AT south across a small saddle, where the unmarked Northwest Road departs west. Rising to the left, the white-blazed path soon reaches the base of a long, steep pitch—by far the most difficult section of the hike. Catch your breath before tackling the punishing 0.4-mile climb. Before long, reach your well-deserved reward—sweeping 180-degree views from Bear Mountain's immense summit rock pile.

The hike continues south along the AT. Descending steadily 0.8 mile, the ledge-covered trail passes numerous vistas, sinks into the dense understory, and arrives at Riga Junction. For those interested in spending a night on the mountain, the Brassie Brook lean-to is straight ahead on the AT in 0.6 mile. To return to the parking area, turn left and rejoin the Undermountain Trail. The path drops off the ridge and quickly moderates, crosses Brassie Brook, and in 0.7 mile reaches the Paradise Lane intersection. Remain on the Undermountain Trail for the final 1.2 miles of the day's exhilarating travels.

Shorter Options: Skip the side excursion into Sages Ravine to complete a 6.3-mile loop. For a more straightforward hike, follow the Undermountain Trail and the AT—5.4 miles roundtrip, out and back.

Opposite, top: Hopper Trail begins in fields with views of Mount Greylock.

Opposite, bottom: Bay Circuit Trail weaves through Borderland State Park.

Massachusetts: The Bay State

Though Massachusetts is home to large urban areas, New England's most populated state also has a long and proud tradition of land conservation. Today, the state offers hundreds of miles of trails spread out across more than 450,000 acres of parks and reservations. Complementing these state-managed gems are national wildlife refuges, historic sites, and a world-class seashore, as well as innumerable land trust properties.

Many of Massachusetts's conservation areas are connected along the Bay Circuit, Midstate, Metacomet–Monadnock, and Appalachian Trails, four long-distance routes featuring a breadth of day hiking opportunities. From the sand dunes of Cape Cod and the rolling hills of Greater Boston to the traprock ridges of the Pioneer Valley and the rugged peaks of the Berkshires, the state offers hikers plenty to explore throughout the year, often near quintessential New England towns as old as the nation.

16 *Great Island*

Distance: 6.8-mile loop	**Management:** Cape Cod National
Difficulty: challenging	Seashore
Hiking time: 5 hours	**Season:** year-round
Elevation gain: 300 feet	**Map:** NPS website
High point: 60 feet	**GPS coordinates:** 41.93274°, −70.06910°

Getting there: From Route 6 in Wellfleet, 1.4 miles north of the lookout tower, turn west onto Main Street toward Wellfleet Center. In 0.7 mile, bear left on Holbrook Avenue. Continue 0.1 mile and turn right on Chequessett Neck. Drive 2.5 miles to the parking area on the left. **Notes:** Seasonal dog restrictions. For easier travel, explore during low to mid tides, as portions of the route can be submerged under water. Take your time, as trail signs are sporadic, unofficial routes are common, and intertidal portions of the trail can change over time.

The Cape Cod National Seashore features impressive beaches, family-friendly bike paths, and a hiking-trail network spanning the sandy peninsula's diverse coastal habitats. Once home to Native American settlers, European whalers, and small abandoned structures long since swallowed by the stormy seas, Great Island in Wellfleet Harbor is an alluring landscape of shifting sand dunes and pitch pine forests that is home to the seashore's wildest and most challenging hiking route.

From the parking area, a well-groomed path descends gently 0.1 mile to the water's edge. Here, the Gut, a small bay adjacent to Wellfleet Harbor, provides a scenic backdrop. Veering right, the trail leads 0.4 mile toward the sand dunes and the first of two beach access points. Turn right, cut through the wind-sculpted sands, and emerge upon a seemingly endless beach. From April to August, keep an eye out for diminutive piping plovers. The National Park Service fences off nest sites to protect these endangered shorebirds, and dogs are prohibited during this time.

Follow the shoreline south 1.8 miles. Just past the base of Great Beach Hill, look for a small gap in the dunes that leads inland. South of this point, it is possible to explore the sandbar for another mile or so. Jeremy Point, which

View toward Great Beach Hill

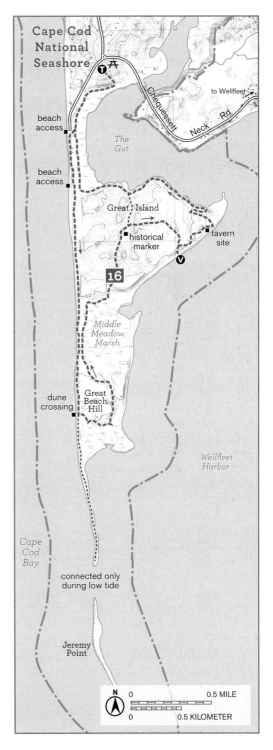

used to be permanently connected, is only accessible during low tide. While exploring this area, be aware of the changing tides and watch carefully for additional shorebird nesting sites—the territory-defending least tern and the orange-billed American oystercatcher often rear their young here.

From the beach, the inland route heads east. As you walk, armies of fiddler crabs scurry along the path, darting into tiny holes. Before reaching the shores of Wellfleet Harbor, turn north and ascend through the heart of the pine-shaded hillside. The path quickly descends to and then circles 0.5 mile around Middle Meadow Marsh. Be sure to remain on the trail to minimize potential contact with ticks and poison ivy.

Turning sharply left, the trail heads up a small incline. Level off and journey through the pleasant forest surroundings. Beyond a historical marker on the right (a Mayflower descendant once lived here), reach a trail junction. Turn right and follow the narrow path as it rises gently 0.3 mile to a short, unmarked spur that ends at a striking viewpoint of the harbor. The main trail meanders 0.3 mile northeast to a spot where a tavern once served customers from 1690 into the 1740s.

The route proceeds north 0.1 mile to a grassy opening high above the Gut. Swing right and descend to the beach. Follow the shoreline left 0.6 mile back to the main trail. Join the path as it meanders west and then parallels the sand dunes north, before returning to the parking lot in 1.2 miles.

Nearby Options: If you have time, visit the nearby Marconi observation area (located in Wellfleet on the opposite side of the Cape Cod peninsula), or venture south to the National Park Service's Salt Pond Visitor Center in Eastham to learn about other recreational opportunities within the seashore.

17 *Borderland State Park*

Distance: 7.8-mile loop	**Management:** Massachusetts DCR
Difficulty: moderate	**Season:** year-round
Hiking time: 5 hours	**Map:** DCR website
Elevation gain: 450 feet	**GPS coordinates:** 42.06257°, −71.16476°
High point: 335 feet	

Getting there: Take exit 17 from Interstate 95 in Foxborough. Drive 2.3 miles on South Main Street toward Sharon and then turn right onto East Foxboro Street. In 1 mile, stay left on Lakeview Street. Continue 1.4 miles to an intersection with Massapoag Avenue. Turn right and drive 1.7 miles to the state park entrance on the left. **Note:** Entrance fee required.

Spreading out over 1773 acres and including more than 20 miles of well-marked trails, Borderland State Park is the perfect destination for nature enthusiasts of all ages. The park's maturing forests, intriguing geologic features, ubiquitous wetlands, and historical elements provide a delightful backdrop throughout the year.

This comprehensive journey begins along the Bay Circuit Trail (BCT), a long-distance route that coincides with numerous paths as it traverses the park from south to north. Pick up the BCT near the park's visitor center as it follows the Pond Walk, by descending 0.1 mile to the scenic shores of Leach Pond.

Staying close to the water's edge, continue 0.1 mile north to reach the West Side Trail (BCT). This intersection and most others are clearly marked, often with maps. Bear left and follow the BCT north over the next 2.5 miles as it turns right onto the French Trail, left onto the

Secluded pond on Morse Loop

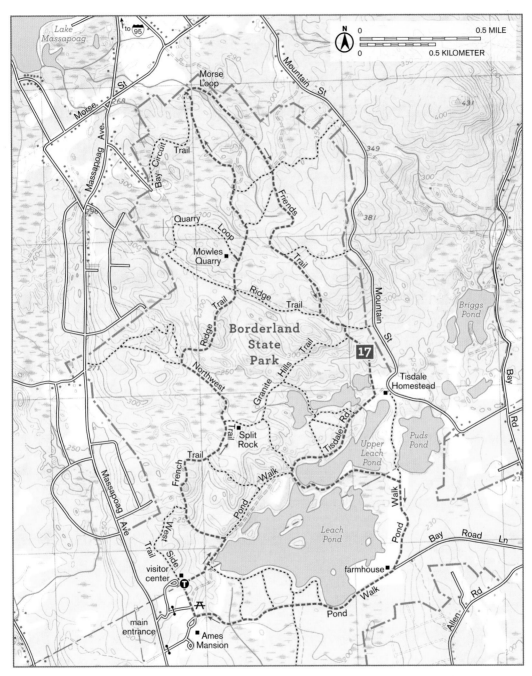

Northwest Trail, right on the Ridge Trail, straight on the Quarry Loop, and straight on the Morse Loop. There are numerous features to admire along the way, including a quick diversion on the Split Rock Trail to the base of an enormous boulder that is hard to miss. Check out the short spur along the Northwest Trail that leads to a perch above a sprawling wetland. Finally, before joining the Morse Loop, follow the Quarry Loop left to quickly arrive at the remains of Mowles Quarry.

Near the northern tip of the Morse Loop, the BCT exits left. Stay right and parallel the park's northern boundary to the shores of a secluded pond. Cross its outlet stream and then follow the path southeast along a wide corridor. In 0.4 mile, join the Friends Trail as it diverges left. This pleasant path meanders 0.7 mile over gently rolling terrain. Before ending, the route splits, with one option heading over a small ledge and the other wrapping around it.

Turn left onto the Ridge Trail and quickly descend to a large boulder. Bear right and follow the narrower corridor to a junction with the Granite Hills Upper Loop, which leads left 0.2 mile to a grassy field. Ahead, find a gate and views of Upper Leach Pond, near the remains of the former Tisdale homestead.

Follow the Tisdale Road west. This easy path winds 0.5 mile to a junction with the Pond Walk. While the visitor center lies straight ahead in 0.6 mile, take the Pond Walk left for a longer and more scenic end to the hike. Dissecting Upper Leach and Leach Ponds, the gentle trail offers multiple views of both, as well as the abundant waterfowl that congregate here. In 0.6 mile, stay right and hike 0.3 mile south through fields that have been maintained for more than three hundred years.

The final mile of the journey begins at a gate. Proceed past an old farmhouse to reach Leach Pond's southern shore and then the Ames Mansion, an immense stone structure built in 1910 for botanist Oakes Ames and his wife, Blanche, an artist and suffragist. The Ames Estate occupied much of Borderland State Park through the 1900s. Turn right and pass through the picnic area to conclude the circuit.

Shorter Options: There are multiple ways to shorten the described hike. Many visitors limit their travels to the 2.9-mile loop along the Pond Walk. For slightly longer adventures, combine the Pond Walk with portions of the Granite Hills Trail.

Bay Circuit Trail

Covering more than 230 miles, the Bay Circuit Trail forms a semicircle around Greater Boston and visits some of eastern Massachusetts's most beautiful landscapes. The trail is managed by partners, including the Appalachian Mountain Club and the Trustees of Reservations. Many of its sections are accessible via public transportation.

18 Great Blue Hill

Distance: 2.8-mile loop
Difficulty: moderate
Hiking time: 2 hours
Elevation gain: 900 feet
High point: 635 feet

Management: Massachusetts DCR
Season: year-round
Map: DCR website
GPS coordinates: 42.21409°, −71.09313°

Getting there: Take exit 3 off Interstate 93 in Milton. Drive north on Blue Hill River Road for 0.5 mile, and then turn right onto Hillside Street. Continue 0.6 mile to the parking area on the right (across from the reservation headquarters). Additional parking is available near Houghtons Pond, 0.3 mile to the south.

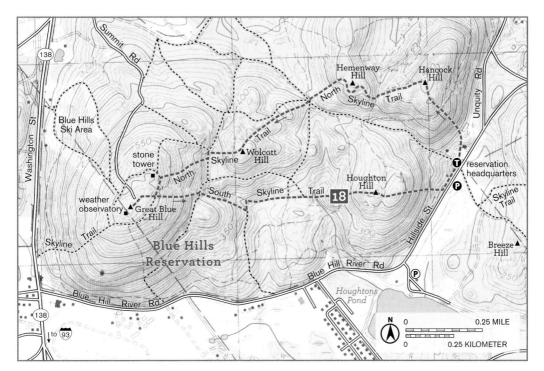

As the highest point in the 7000-acre Blue Hills Reservation, Great Blue Hill offers expansive views east to the Atlantic Ocean, north to the Boston skyline, and west across the hills and ponds of southeastern New England. The Blue Hills, named by European sailors who spotted their rolling silhouettes on the horizon, were home to generations of Indigenous inhabitants known as the "people of the great hills." Today, the popular reservation, less than 10 miles from downtown Boston, offers more than 125 miles of hiking trails. This 2.8-mile loop is a rocky, challenging introduction to an area that begs further exploration.

After carefully crossing Hillside Street, head up the paved road to the reservation headquarters. Here, you can purchase a map of the area clearly outlining the elaborate maze of trails in the reservation. While on this described hike, the map may help pinpoint your exact location at the many intersections encountered; however, having the map is not essential, as the entire loop follows the well-marked, blue-blazed Skyline Trail.

Follow the dirt road past the headquarters. Soon, the North Skyline Trail veers right onto a steep, rocky slope and rises to the first of many outcrops atop Hancock Hill. Under the shadow of jets approaching Logan Airport, continue over the rounded high point and drop into a small depression. Swinging right, the path scales the mostly wooded summit of Hemenway Hill, but then drops more rapidly down a ledge-covered ridge. Watch your footing as you make your way to a major trail intersection.

Continue to follow the blue blazes straight and easily up tree-covered Wolcott Hill. Another tricky descent leads to a forested wetland. Catch your breath for the final push to Great Blue Hill's summit area. Aided by rock steps, the initial climb slowly eases through a shady grove of evergreens. Emerge onto a series of ledges that lead to a stone bridge, picnic area, and stone observation tower. A curling flight of stairs winds to an impressive view of Boston's skyline.

Follow the blue blazes south across the bridge to a stone marker for the South Skyline Trail. Proceed a little farther to reach the summit weather observatory. Sitting on the 635-foot high point of Great Blue Hill, the observatory has a gift shop and museum that welcome visitors for a small fee.

Return to the South Skyline stone marker and begin a steep, rocky descent. Pass numerous viewpoints as the trail winds over ledge back into a denser forest. The route levels off after bending right on a wider corridor. Follow the blue blazes as they turn sharply left and then right. The narrowing path cuts through a noteworthy boulder near a small stream. After a brief climb, drop to another marshy wetland. The day's final ascent follows. Rise to very limited views from Houghton Hill before carefully making your way down the steep section that leads back to Hillside Street. Cross the road and parallel it left to the parking area.

A young hiker scrambles up Hancock Hill.

Extend Your Trip: Consider exploring nearby Houghtons Pond, where an easy trail loops a mile around its shores. To explore more scenic vistas, follow the Skyline Trail east 1 mile to Buck Hill's mostly open summit. Just beyond its high point, a red-blazed trail leads a similar distance back to Houghtons Pond. For an even more challenging adventure, continue past Buck Hill another 3.7 miles along the blue-blazed Skyline Trail to its eastern terminus in Quincy. Since this route ends at a distant parking lot, you will need to arrange transportation back. The rugged trail offers many views across the reservation's rocky ridgeline from multiple peaks.

19 *Battle Road*

Distance: 10.3 miles roundtrip	*Management:* Minute Man NHP
Difficulty: easy–moderate	*Season:* year-round
Hiking time: 5 hours	*Map:* NPS website
Elevation gain: 525 feet	*GPS coordinates:* 42.45856°, −71.32213°
High point: 290 feet	

Getting there: Take exit 46B off Interstate 95 in Lexington and head west on Route 2A. Drive 2.7 miles and stay right on Lexington Road. Continue 0.7 mile to the Meriam's Corner parking area on the right. *Note:* Multiuse trail popular with bicyclists.

A great way to appreciate and better understand the sacrifices of the brave soldiers who took up arms against the British in the spring of 1775 is to walk in their footsteps along Battle Road from Concord to Lexington. This crushed-stone path is lined with historical houses, productive farmland, stone memorials marking signature events, diverse wildlife habitats, a visitor center to provide additional context, and ample opportunity to immerse yourself in the Revolutionary War's earliest confrontation.

Today's Battle Road is a combination of the original route and newer sections that fill in pieces claimed by subsequent development. From the parking area, head left to quickly arrive at Meriam's Corner and an impressive colonial building. Here, on April 19, 1775, colonial militia faced off with seven hundred British soldiers. While minor skirmishes had already taken place, this was the American forces' first organized offensive, as the British redcoats retreated to Boston. Time to discover the chapters that followed.

Walk 0.1 mile back to the parking area, continue east, and encounter the first of many fields. These rich soils were some of the earliest agricultural lands established by European settlers. Although the landscape is more forested today, the route passes pockets of productive croplands over the next 0.8 mile.

Swing left to explore a 0.7-mile stretch that begins and ends on wooden boardwalks. In between, walk along the side of Lexington Road, learn about the arrival of colonial reinforcements who aided the battle, and gaze across a vast wetland expanse once drained and used as hayfields.

Back on dry land, the route rises 0.4 mile to Bloody Angle, where the British infantry was susceptible to heavy crossfire. It is difficult to imagine the battlefield chaos in today's idyllic forested setting. The path swings right and then left (near a junction with the Vernal Pool Trail) before proceeding straight 0.3 mile to Hartwell Tavern, a good place to tour a historical building where volunteers are often present in period clothes.

Continue east 0.4 mile as you pass the remains of a burned-out tavern on the left, learn how residents witnessed the frantic battle, and visit an impressive period structure, the Captain William Smith House. Hike through a tunnel and reach the Paul Revere capture site in another 0.5 mile. While British soldiers thwarted his legendary efforts to reach Concord, one of his lesser-known companions successfully completed the task, setting the stage for the day's conflict.

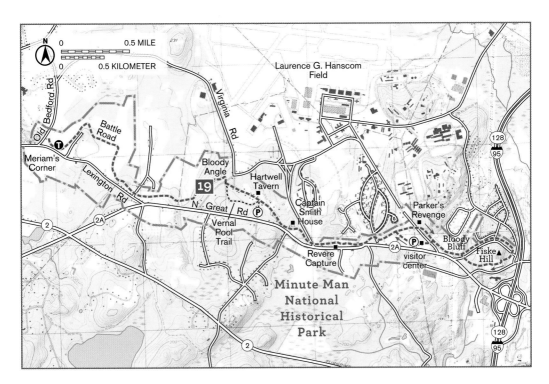

Hartwell Tavern, near the center of Battle Road

Over the next 1.3 miles, the trail visits numerous signs, graves, foundations, and historical buildings. Be sure to check out a short spur left that describes Parker's Revenge, and a plaque located at the base of Bloody Bluff, two sites where the enemy combatants exchanged gunfire.

Once under the powerlines, begin a 1-mile loop around Fiske Hill by staying left on Battle Road. It rises gently before dropping to the trail's easternmost point, where signs describe the challenge of taking care of the wounded.

Continue the loop west as it wraps around the hill's south side before descending across an open field to a parking area.

Cross the road, retrace your steps 0.3 mile west, and then follow the crosswalk left. This path continues 0.1 mile to the National Park Service's informative visitor center and 0.2 mile farther to a large parking area. Rejoin Battle Road and hike 4 miles back to Meriam's Corner. For a little variety, consider exploring the Vernal Pool Trail near Hartwell's Tavern. It adds 0.3 mile to the journey.

Shorter Options: Park at the visitor center or near Hartwell Tavern and limit your exploration to the trail's eastern half, from Bloody Angle to Fiske Hill. This is the heart of the trail with the most-interesting historical features.

20 *Mount Watatic*

Distance: 3.7-mile loop
Difficulty: moderate
Hiking time: 3 hours
Elevation gain: 825 feet
High point: 1832 feet

Management: Massachusetts DCR
Season: year-round
Map: No official online map
GPS coordinates: 42.69662°, −71.90450°

Getting there: From the junction of Routes 101 and 119 in Ashburnham, drive west on Route 119 for 1.4 miles to the parking area entrance on the right, near the intersection with Old Pierce Road. ***Notes:*** Parking lot fills quickly. Overflow parking is prohibited on Route 119 but allowed on portions of Old Pierce Road.

Located at the southern end of the 21-mile Wapack Trail and the northern terminus of the 92-mile Midstate Trail, Mount Watatic provides sweeping 360-degree views of eastern Massachusetts and southern New Hampshire. With the mountain destined to become another telecommunications facility in early 2000, members of the Ashby and Ashburnham Conservation Trusts joined forces to permanently protect the summit from the proposed development. Today, the mountain's high point is the centerpiece of more than 1000 acres of conservation land.

Join the Wapack and Midstate Trails as they head north on Old Nutting Hill Road. The path descends to a small beaver pond and follows wooden planks across the outlet stream. After a short climb, reach a trail junction 0.2 mile from the start.

Remain on the Wapack and Midstate Trails by veering right onto a narrower corridor. Over a small ridge and around a bend, descend 0.1 mile to a brook crossing. The path carves through a large rock split in two and then begins a steady, sometimes steep 0.5-mile climb up the hemlock-shaded slopes. Where the well-trodden path widens, try to remain in the center to reduce further erosion. At the base of a small ledge, the trail swings left, then circles to the top of a rock face with views of Mount Monadnock. Ahead lies Nutting Ledges, a scenic vista featuring shots of Wachusett Mountain.

The final 0.3-mile climb is less difficult, though not flat. Reenter the evergreen forest and wind through the rocky landscape before emerging on the semi-open summit. On a clear day, the Boston skyline is visible on the eastern horizon. To the southeast, follow a spur that drops 0.1 mile to the top of East Watatic. Although lower, this vantage point affords unobstructed views as well as better picnic spots.

From the high point, follow the Wapack and Midstate Trails. They descend briefly on an old service road before bearing left near a wildlife sanctuary sign. The route parallels a long stone wall throughout, the remnant of a time when pastureland spread across the now heavily forested landscape. After leveling off, scale and traverse Nutting Hill's rocky but mostly viewless summit. Reach a trail junction following a brief descent.

Stay straight and hike 0.4 mile along the old road to the New Hampshire border. Here, the Wapack Trail continues for nearly 20 miles over a series of panoramic peaks, ending on the Granite State's Pack Monadnock Mountain (see Hike 53). Turn left and follow the border a few

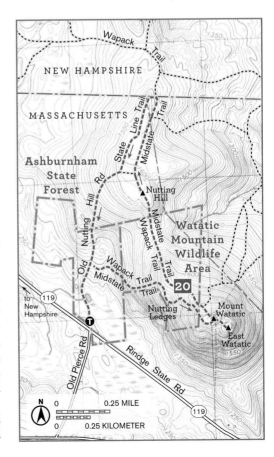

Early morning mist filters sunlight below Mount Watatic summit.

hundred feet to reach a stone plaque marking the northern terminus of the Midstate Trail. From here, head south on the State Line Trail. It meanders 0.4 mile along a low ridge before intersecting Old Nutting Hill Road. Turn right for the final 0.7-mile leg of the journey. While the road is eroded in places, the corridor is wide and easy to follow.

21 *Wachusett Mountain*

Distance: 4.3-mile loop
Difficulty: moderate–challenging
Hiking time: 3 hours
Elevation gain: 1050 feet
High point: 2006 feet

Management: Massachusetts DCR
Season: year-round
Map: DCR website
GPS coordinates: 42.50412°, −71.88809°

Getting there: Take exit 92 off Route 2 in Westminster. Turn south onto Route 140. Drive 2.3 miles and turn right onto Park Road/Mile Hill Road. In 0.5 mile, turn right onto Bolton Road and then immediately turn left toward the ski area. Drive 0.2 mile into the ski area parking lot. Look for a large kiosk on the right, near the middle of the parking area.

Wachusett Mountain, the highest peak in southeastern New England, is at the heart of a 3000-acre state reservation with more than 17 miles of hiking trails and extensive areas of old-growth forests—some as old as 350 years. A great destination for hikers of all ages, the mountain provides four seasons of exploration with panoramic summit views, including Boston's skyscrapers, New Hampshire's Monadnock Region, Vermont's Green Mountains, and the Berkshires.

The hike begins along the Balance Rock Trail, which coincides with the yellow-blazed Midstate Trail (MT), a long-distance route that uses many different paths while winding through the Wachusett Mountain Reservation. Rise steadily

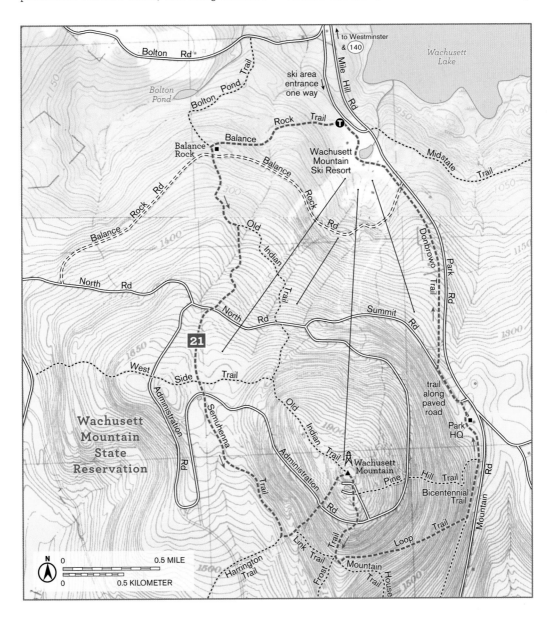

0.4 mile to a trail junction near the base of Balance Rock, a large boulder sitting atop another that has miraculously stood since the last ice age.

Follow the Old Indian Trail (MT) left as it crosses a dirt road and climbs to an intersection in 0.2 mile. Bear right to ascend the Semuhenna Trail (MT). Through shady forests, this path wraps around ski slopes, crosses the paved summit road, and meets the West Side Trail (MT). Stay straight on the blue-blazed Semuhenna Trail. Past a picnic area and over the paved summit road, it circles a small pond. Drop into a stand of towering trees and discover yellow birch and red oaks that are hundreds of years old. Continuing below the rocky summit slopes, the Semuhenna Trail ends at a signed junction.

Turn left on the red-blazed Harrington Trail to begin the final 0.3-mile ascent, a challenging scramble up ledge. Beyond a viewpoint spur and across the paved road one last time, the trail leads easily to the base of the summit tower. Check out the viewing platform with signs describing sights in all directions. The summit is often busy, but there are many places to spread out and enjoy the scenery.

Head south down the Mountain House Trail (MT). This blue-blazed route wraps around a tiny summit pond before heading across a parking area. Descend 0.2 mile down the wide path and stay left when the Frost Trail and Link Trail (MT) depart right. At the next intersection, in 0.1 mile, stay left on the Loop Trail. Dropping gradually

The summit tower rises above the small summit pond.

0.4 mile through a pleasant hardwood forest, this route passes an eastern vista before ending.

Take the Bicentennial Trail left and hike 0.3 mile down to the reservation's headquarters and visitor center. Follow the driveway out to the summit road, bear left, and walk 0.2 mile along the pavement to a parking area on the right. Here, pick up the Donbrowo Trail, a route that descends gradually 0.6 mile to the base of the ski area. Make your way past the ski lodge to the parking lot to complete the journey.

Shorter Options: Begin at the reservation's visitor center to enjoy a shorter 2.5-mile circuit along the Bicentennial, Pine Hill, Mountain House, and Loop Trails. You can also complete a fun 3.8-mile loop from the ski area trailhead by following the described route to the summit and then descending along the Old Indian Trail.

Midstate Trail

Supported by a committee of volunteers, this 92-mile route offers numerous day hike opportunities on public and private lands in eastern Massachusetts. The trail's signature yellow-triangle blazes lead hikers from Douglas State Forest on the Rhode Island border across the Worcester Hills to Mount Watatic on the state's boundary with New Hampshire.

22 *Tully Lake and Jacobs Hill*

Distance: 10.5 miles roundtrip
Difficulty: moderate–challenging
Hiking time: 6 hours
Elevation gain: 950 feet
High point: 1100 feet
Management: The Trustees of

Reservations (TTOR), Army Corps of
Engineers
Season: year-round
Map: TTOR website
GPS coordinates: 42.65074°, −72.20681°

Getting there: Take exit 75 off Route 2 in Athol and head north on Route 32. Follow
Route 32 signs closely in downtown Athol, where the road makes sharp turns. In 6.5
miles from Route 2, turn right off Route 32 onto Doane Hill Road. Drive 0.9 mile to the
parking area on the right (overflow parking at boat launch across the street). *Notes:* TTOR
campground near trailhead. Bikes allowed on a small portion of described route.

The region's centerpiece is the 22-mile Tully Trail, a loop that connects a mosaic of state, federal, and private conservation areas. This 10.5-mile trek uses a portion of the long-distance route to form two hikes in one. The first ventures to picturesque Spirit Falls and Jacobs Hill's scenic summit ledges, while the second explores roaring Doanes Falls before circling around Tully Lake's wildlife-rich habitat. (Note: Parts of Tully Lake Trail may be underwater during spring or after heavy rain.)

Cross Doane Hill Road to join the Tully Trail near the boat-launch entrance. Here, the yellow-blazed path coincides with a bike route.

Spirit Falls is a series of small cascades.

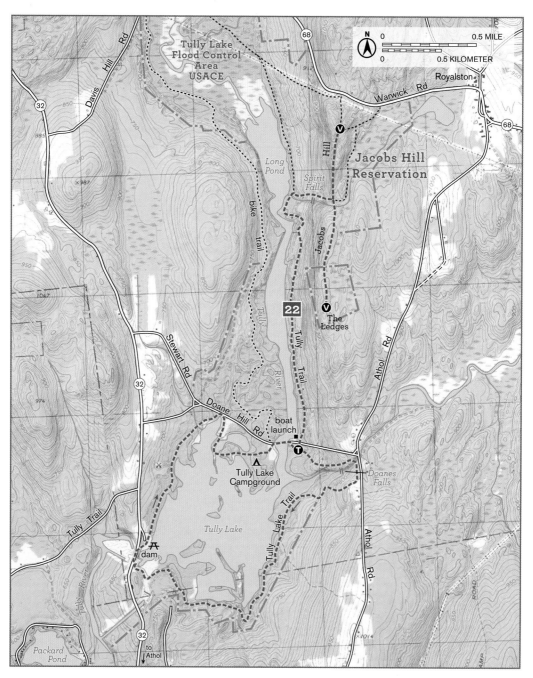

Follow the wide corridor as it parallels Tully River from a distance. Approach the water in 0.5 mile and then rise from the shore once again. Return to the water's edge just south of Long Pond before hugging the side of the widening water body. Reach a junction 1.7 miles from the start.

Turn right on the Tully Trail. It crosses a small stream and begins a steep ascent through a hemlock forest. Halfway up, the 0.3-mile climb arrives at the base of Spirit Falls, an impressive series of small cascades that tumble down the rocky landscape. The trail eventually levels off at a four-way intersection within the Trustees of Reservation's (TTOR) Jacobs Hill property.

Before heading back to the trailhead, check out two nearby vistas. The Ledges is the more scenic one. It is located 0.6 mile to the south on a spur that ends with views of Tully Lake and the hills surrounding the Quabbin Reservoir. To the left, the Tully Trail rises 0.5 mile to an inviting viewpoint near the summit of Jacobs Hill. Then retrace your steps to Doane Hill Road to complete the first hike—5.6 miles roundtrip.

Begin the second adventure on the Doanes Falls Trail, which leads gradually 0.3 mile to Lawrence Brook before aggressively climbing 0.4 mile through the TTOR reservation. Climb past one impressive fall after another, remaining on the trail and watching your step near the water's edge. Upon reaching Athol Road, follow the pavement right 0.1 mile.

Pick up the Tully Lake Trail, which winds gradually 0.5 mile down the steep hillside and levels off as it approaches the expansive lake. Follow the well-blazed path over mostly flat terrain as it hugs the shore for the next 1.5 miles. There are numerous spots to capture photos and scan for waterfowl and other wildlife. Once through a habitat restoration area and past a disc golf course, climb to the top of an earthen dam.

After dropping down the staircase aside the dam, the route cuts through riprap and makes its way across a picnic area to a parking lot. To the right, pick up the Tully Trail as it enters the woods at a sign pointing to Doanes Falls. For 1 mile, the yellow-blazed trail winds past various spurs leading to shoreline picnic spots. While mostly level, there are occasional inclines and the footing is uneven in places.

Approach Doane Hill Road, swing south along a narrow peninsula, and then hike east to a few final intimate locations on the lakeshore. In 0.6 mile, arrive at the entrance to TTOR's Tully Lake Campground, an overnight facility popular with hikers, anglers, and paddlers. Turn right onto Doane Hill Road and hike 0.2 mile to end the 4.9-mile circuit.

Trustees of Reservation

For more than a century, the Trustees of Reservation has been protecting special places, managing natural areas, offering engaging programs, and sharing their expertise with people across Massachusetts. Today, the public is invited to explore this membership-based organization's more than one hundred properties around the state—many featuring hiking trails.

23 *Holyoke Range*

Distance: 7.6 miles roundtrip
Difficulty: moderate–challenging
Hiking time: 5 hours
Elevation gain: 1950 feet
High point: 1106 feet

Management: Massachusetts DCR
Season: year-round
Map: DCR website
GPS coordinates: 42.30515°, −72.52852°

Getting there: From the eastern junction of Routes 9 and 116 in downtown Amherst, take Route 116 south 4.9 miles into the Notch. Turn left into the Notch Visitor Center parking lot. There is overflow parking on the opposite side of the road.

Enjoying views atop Rattlesnake Knob

In the heart of Mount Holyoke Range State Park, Mount Norwottuck is one of several scenic summits connected by an undulating section of the Metacomet–Monadnock (MM) Trail. This introduction to one of the Pioneer Valley's most-prominent mountain ridges includes bucolic vistas, inviting forest surroundings, and attractive geologic features, such as impressive caves used by Shays's Rebellion protagonists in 1786.

The entire hike follows sections of the white-blazed MM Trail (a 108-mile route that winds from the Massachusetts-Connecticut border to New Hampshire's Mount Monadnock), the orange-blazed Robert Frost Trail (a 33-mile route that links many natural features in the Amherst region), or both. While you will encounter countless other marked and unmarked paths, these two routes are easy to navigate.

Pick up the multi-blazed (orange, white, and blue) trail that departs east from the visitor center. Descending quickly, it leads around a large quarry, proceeds under powerlines, and reaches an intersection in 0.5 mile. With the Robert Frost Trail diverging left, turn right and follow the MM Trail as it rises steeply up the hardwood-covered slope.

Cresting the ridgeline in 0.2 mile, the route swings east and offers an occasional glimpse through the dense vegetation. Ascend the rocky landscape 0.5 mile to reach Norwottuck's summit. Gazing north, enjoy modest views beyond the University of Massachusetts skyline to the Green Mountains' southern peaks. Just beyond the high point, the trail drops to a more impressive perch showcasing scenes of forested hills to the east.

Leaving the summit area, the trail descends rapidly over loose soil. In 0.3 mile, reach the top of the Horse Caves and watch your step while squeezing through the gap in the rock to the base of the massive overhanging ledge. Here, in the nooks and shadows, disgruntled farmers who were aligned with Daniel Shays sought cover. Their rebellious actions undermined the Articles of Confederation, contributing to the evolution of the nation's present-day Constitution.

From the caves, hike 0.3 mile along gentler terrain to a junction with the Robert Frost Trail. Continue east on the now-joined trails as they rise past a town marker. In 0.2 mile, at a sharp bend, an unmarked spur departs left to Rattlesnake Knob. Check out this short diversion that leads to a pair of scenic ledges, each with pastoral views of the countryside.

Return to the main trail and stay left to begin the 1.7-mile trek to Long Mountain. Though it drops rapidly at first, the route quickly levels off. Follow the white and orange blazes as the trail swings left, then right, and left again. Rise gradually over an unnamed peak and then descend into a narrow col. The winding trail eventually climbs steeply to Long Mountain's open summit ledge. Just below the forested high point, enjoy western views across the Holyoke Range.

Retrace your steps to where the Robert Frost Trail and the MM Trail last parted ways, west of Rattlesnake Knob. Avoid a return climb over Norwottuck by staying right on the Robert Frost Trail. The orange-blazed path descends the ridge and in 0.1 mile turns sharply left before beginning a relaxing 1-mile stroll through a stately forest filled with scattered boulders. Cross a small stream and rise south 0.2 mile to rejoin the MM Trail.

Follow both paths right to return to the parking area. For variety, explore the blue-blazed Laurel Loop toward the end. It is slightly longer and visits a few patches of its namesake plant en route to the visitor center.

Shorter Options: Skip Long Mountain and limit your stops to Mount Norwottuck, Horse Caves, and Rattlesnake Knob. These three destinations make for a less-demanding 4.2-mile loop.

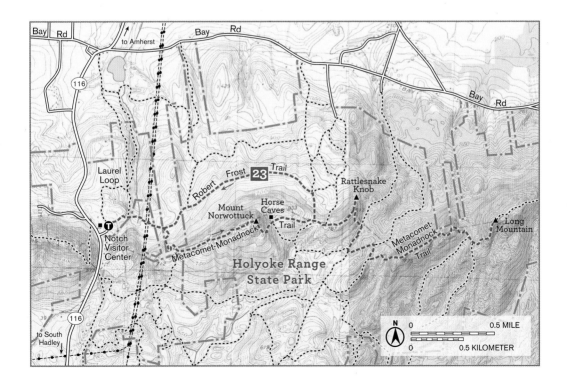

24 *Sugarloaf Mountain*

Distance: 4.7 miles roundtrip
Difficulty: moderate
Hiking time: 3 hours
Elevation gain: 1300 feet
High point: 792 feet

Management: Massachusetts DCR
Season: year-round
Map: DCR website
GPS coordinates: 42.46786°, −72.59507°

Getting there: In Deerfield, take exit 35 from Interstate 91. From the south, turn right off the exit. From the north, turn left. Follow Route 5 north 0.2 mile and bear right at the traffic light. Drive east on Route 116. In 1 mile, turn left at the light and immediately arrive at the Mount Sugarloaf State Reservation parking lot (just beyond the entrance to the summit road). **Note:** Parking fee required.

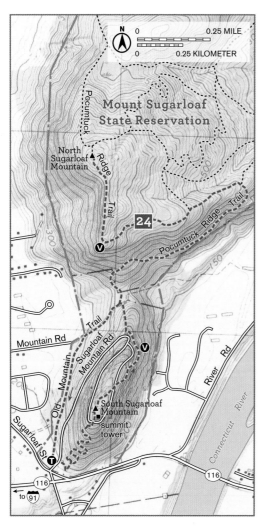

Sugarloaf Mountain's two summits sit low on the horizon, but both rise abruptly from the flat, fertile farmlands abutting the Connecticut River in the heart of Massachusetts's Pioneer Valley. The first stop along this half-day excursion is the scenic summit of the lower peak, where an auto road enhances its popularity. Leaving the crowds behind, the hike continues north to less dramatic vistas and quieter forest surroundings.

From the parking area, join the Pocumtuck Ridge Trail. It heads up the stairs, crosses the auto road, and winds through a picnic area to the base of the mountain. While a steep slope awaits, the 0.4-mile route uses a series of a dozen or so switchbacks to lessen the incline. Reach the first of many aerial shots of the river before reaching the auto road. Cross the pavement to the summit tower and enjoy sweeping views south to the Holyoke Range and Mount Tom.

The hike continues north past picnic tables.. Look for the trail exiting from the right edge of the parking area. It quickly drops to a quaint bench with views of Mount Toby rising above the Connecticut River. Continue dropping near the side of the auto road, where eventually the path leaves the pavement behind and proceeds to a saddle on the ridge.

To the left, the Old Mountain Trail leads back to the start. Venture farther north along the Pocumtuck Ridge Trail to Mount Sugarloaf's higher summit. Along the way, you will encounter a handful of unmarked intersections. Follow the blue blazes closely throughout.

The Connecticut River is the centerpiece of multiple South Sugarloaf viewpoints.

The route drops a bit more, swings left, and then climbs sharply to the right. Under a canopy of towering oaks, wind under the north peak's wooded summit ledges before dropping rapidly to more-level ground. Heading in an easterly direction, the blue-blazed path takes advantage of a mostly gradual course to ascend the rugged slopes. In 0.5 mile, stay left at a rock cairn and continue rising gently, now in a westerly direction.

In 0.4 mile, reach the first of a handful of rocky outcrops offering views south and west. Just before this first outcrop, an unmarked spur diverges left to a tiny cave beneath the vista. Swing north and follow the blue blazes another 0.3 mile to the other viewpoints and the north peak's wooded summit.

While the Pocumtuck Ridge Trail continues another 12 miles north to Greenfield, retrace your steps back to the Old Mountain Trail to complete the hike. This wide route drops gently to the edge of the state reservation. Be alert; multiple routes exit right to nearby housing developments. Stay on the main path as it turns left. Hike 0.4 mile near the powerlines to reach the trailhead parking.

25 *Mount Tom Reservation*

Distance: 7.6-mile loop
Difficulty: challenging
Hiking time: 5 hours
Elevation gain: 1900 feet
High point: 1201 feet

Management: Massachusetts DCR
Season: year-round
Map: DCR website
GPS coordinates: 42.26885°, −72.61657°

Getting there: From the south, take exit 15A from Interstate 91. Turn right off the exit and then left onto Route 5. Drive north 3.9 miles to Reservation Road on the left. From the north, use exit 23 off Interstate 91 and turn right. Follow Route 5 south 3.5 miles to Reservation Road on the right. Follow Reservation Road into the Mount Tom State Reservation and turn left into the Lake Bray parking area in 0.5 mile. **Note:** Entrance fee required.

Accessible along a network of more than 20 miles of diverse trails, Mount Tom's rugged traprock ridge showcases dramatic views from multiple promontories. Explore the 2082-acre state reservation that bears its name to discover precipitous cliffs facing west and subtler forested mountain slopes to the east that are home to 75 percent of Massachusetts's reptile and amphibian species (including timber rattlesnakes). This 7.6-mile excursion visits the reservation's most scenic spots, with an option to extend your trek on the northern end of the challenging loop.

Pick up the Universal Access Trail that begins just north of Lake Bray, a small pond surrounded by picnic tables. The wide path winds 0.2 mile to the start of the Kay Bee Trail. Follow this blue-blazed route as it rises steadily 0.8 mile to Keystone Junction. Proceed straight through this four-way intersection and join the Keystone

The Connecticut River forms an oxbow north of Dry Knoll.

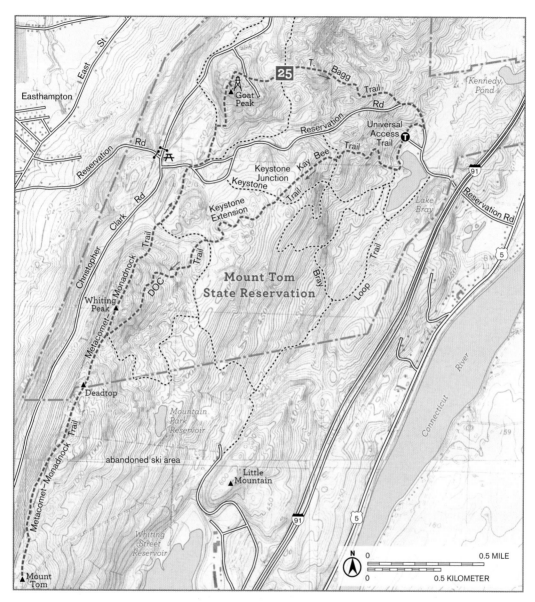

Extension, an orange-blazed 0.6-mile trail that gently swings over low rocky hillsides and past diminutive wetlands.

At a well-marked intersection, proceed straight on the DOC Trail. Here, a more aggressive climb begins. With increasingly rocky footing, the path levels, offering limited views. Circle around the high point of Whiting Peak before reaching the Metacomet–Monadnock (MM) Trail, also called the New England Trail.

Turn left onto the MM Trail and reach the first of many spectacular vistas on the ridge's western flank. Perched high above Easthampton, the rocky outcrop offers 180-degree views of western Massachusetts. The 1.3-mile journey south to Mount Tom's summit includes consecutive, and often more dramatic, vantage points. The most picturesque cliff face is only 0.3 mile from the DOC Trail junction, near the summit of Deadtop. While gaining little overall elevation, this section of trail contains frequent minor ups and downs and uneven walking surfaces, but the payoff is well worth the effort. Note, however, that the final section to Mount Tom is on private land, and while the summit offers views, it is covered in communications towers.

After reaching Mount Tom, return to the DOC Trail junction and then continue hiking north along the MM Trail. Ascend the southern side of Whiting Peak and pass yet more scenic viewpoints on the left. The route descends abruptly, at first down a narrow, natural rock staircase and then along a shady, forested slope. As steepness gives way to level ground, continue straight through yet another four-way intersection, and in 0.3 mile, reach Reservation Road.

Follow the pavement right 0.1 mile and then swing left back into the woods. The MM Trail makes its way easily at first before veering right and rising to a viewpoint near the top of Goat Hill. Here, a short spur leads to the peak's summit tower, a popular location for fall hawk-migration enthusiasts.

Remain on the main trail to descend the forested hill. After crossing a service road, proceed over mostly level terrain to the edge of a large vernal pool and two trail junctions. If you have not had enough, continue north along the MM Trail to a scenic vista atop Dry Knoll (0.3 mile) and the historical remains of the Eyrie House (0.7 mile), an elaborate ridgetop hotel built in the nineteenth century. Otherwise, turn right at the second junction.

The 0.8-mile T. Bagg Trail is a pleasant route off the ridge, descending steadily down ledge-covered slopes. Be sure to look for the red blazes, as the route makes an occasional abrupt twist and turn before ending at Reservation Road. Follow the pavement to the left and hike 0.1 mile back to the Lake Bray parking lot.

Shorter Options: There are countless ways to shorten the described hike. Many hikers begin their journey near the intersection of the MM Trail and Reservation Road. For an even more relaxing journey, explore the less-rugged paths that surround Lake Bray.

26 *Race and Everett*

Distance: 10.9 miles roundtrip	**Management:** Massachusetts DCR
Difficulty: challenging	**Season:** year-round
Hiking time: 7 hours	**Map:** DCR website
Elevation gain: 3400 feet	**GPS coordinates:** 42.08988°, −73.41115°
High point: 2608 feet	

Getting there: From the junction of Routes 41 and 23 in Egremont, follow Route 41 south for 5.2 miles. Turn right into the small parking area on the west side of Route 41 in Sheffield. **Note:** Backcountry campsites available.

The highest peak in the southern Berkshires, Mount Everett, and arguably the state's most scenic summit ridge, Mount Race, are attractive destinations on their own. This rigorous hike adds Race Brook's impressive series of long cascades and Guilder Pond's picturesque laurel-filled shoreline to complete a challenging but rewarding trek in southwestern Massachusetts.

The 1.9-mile Race Brook Trail begins at a large kiosk. Pass a field and continue west under a dark evergreen canopy to a small sign. To the right, a path slopes gently to the base of Lower

Take in the views from Mount Race's summit ridge.

Race Falls in 0.4 mile. Stay left and hike to a river crossing, which can be a mixed blessing: it's difficult during high water, but the falls shrink to a trickle during dry periods. Once across, begin a steady ascent and pass two junctions with trails departing right. They form a short loop with a spur leading to a viewpoint above Lower Race Falls. The main path swings north and climbs to the base of the Upper Falls, where water careens down a large rock face.

Cross the brook and make your way up the ledge-covered slope. Beyond a small viewpoint, the trail returns to Race Brook and begins a pleasant 0.5-mile journey, paralleling the brook's course through a moss-covered grove. Hike past a tent-site area and quickly arrive at the Appalachian Trail (AT). Here the hike forms a T, with the first stop being scenic Mount Race.

Turn left and head south along the AT. The well-trodden path winds over the rocky landscape while rising steadily 0.9 mile to the mostly open 2365-foot summit. While there are excellent western views from the high point, continue south 0.2 mile. Here the trail emerges to an open ridgeline with dramatic cliffside vistas. Hike another 0.4 mile along the ridge, visiting one scenic vantage

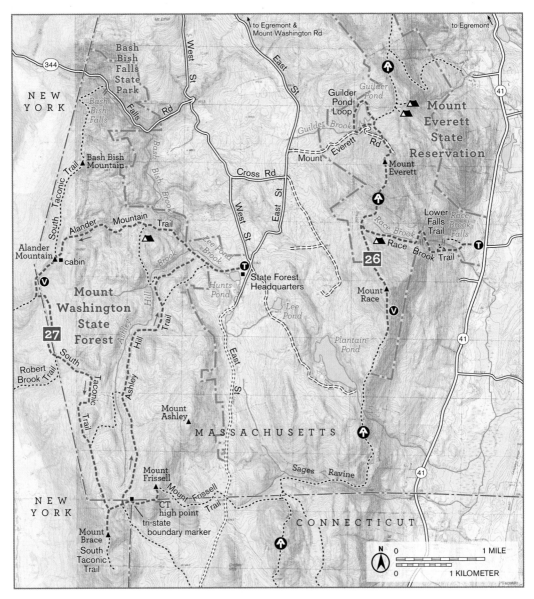

point after another and stop when the route sharply swings right, into the woods.

Retrace your steps 0.6 mile, ascend 250 feet back to Mount Race's high point, and drop 0.9 mile to the junction with the Race Brook Trail. This time, head north from the intersection. After a brief descent, the terrain levels off before becoming more rugged. In places, wooden steps assist the aggressive climb up the challenging terrain.

With each step, there are fewer and shorter trees, affording limited views of nearby peaks.

In 0.8 mile from the junction, reach the base of the former summit tower and limited views above the stunted vegetation. The AT proceeds east a few hundred feet where a spur departs left to a ledge with attractive views of Mount Greylock and nearby wetlands. The well-marked route continues north. After steadily dropping nearly 600 feet in a little more than a half mile, cross a dirt road. One last descent leads to a small picnic area near Guilder Pond. Accessible by cars, this spot is a shorter alternative starting point from the town of Mount Washington (see Shorter Options).

Complete an enjoyable circuit of the pond by following the AT north 0.1 mile. Here a trail exits left and soon visits the shore, a perfect spot for viewing mountain laurels blooming in early summer. The well-marked path winds around the pond and, although scenic, it remains away from the water until approaching the end. Near the pond's outlet, arrive at a dirt road and follow it left 0.1 mile to the AT. Retrace your steps to Route 41.

Shorter Options: Limit your travels to Mount Race, including the mountain's scenic ridgeline. It is 6.8 miles roundtrip, out and back from Route 41. Alternatively, start your hike at Mount Everett Reservation's Guilder Pond (road is seasonally gated). Looping around the pond and visiting Mount Everett is a more relaxing 2.4-mile adventure. If beginning from East Street because the gate is closed, add roughly 2 miles roundtrip.

27 *Alander Mountain*

Distance: 12.6-mile loop
Difficulty: challenging
Hiking time: 8 hours
Elevation gain: 2500 feet
High point: 2380 feet

Management: Massachusetts DCR
Season: year-round
Map: DCR website
GPS coordinates: 42.08634°, −73.46219°

Getting there: From the junction of Routes 41 and 23 in Egremont, follow Route 41 south. Drive 0.1 mile and turn right on Mount Washington Road. Continue 4.4 miles, then stay left on East Road. In 0.8 mile, bear left, remaining on East Road. Drive 3.6 miles and turn right into Mount Washington State Forest. The entranceway swings right to a parking area. **Note:** Backcountry campsites available.

Located in the Mount Washington State Forest, this ambitious circuit in Massachusetts's southwest corner showcases breathtaking vistas from promontories located in three states. Take advantage of mostly moderate terrain as you enjoy the cascading streams, and scan the surrounding landscape for resident wildlife, including the boisterous rufous-sided towhee and the more reclusive timber rattlesnake.

The blue-blazed Alander Mountain Trail winds 0.5 mile through fields and forests before descending gradually to a brook crossing. Continue straight 0.2 mile to the start of the day's loop. Veer right, remaining on the Alander Mountain Trail as it descends into a deep valley to the confluence of the Ashley Hill and Lee Pond Brooks.

Through hemlock groves and fern patches, the trail rises moderately 0.8 mile to a path departing left to backcountry campsites. In another 0.5 mile, the incline becomes more pronounced and the corridor narrows. Parallel an intermittent stream and climb steadily 0.6 mile to a small rustic cabin. Although it is not an inviting campsite, its location 0.1 mile from Alander's 2241-foot summit is ideal. Just beyond, the trail swings right. Scramble up ledge and stay left at a junction with the South Taconic Trail before emerging onto the rocky high point. There are sweeping views south and west, dominated by New York's Catskill Mountains on the distant horizon.

Time to explore a portion of the 21.3-mile South Taconic Trail, a white-blazed route that connects

South Taconic Trail visits multiple rocky perches south of Alander Mountain.

peaks along the New York–Massachusetts border. The initial 0.3-mile descent is one of the trail's most scenic sections as it traverses a mostly open landscape, visiting outcrops with stunning views across the valley. Beyond the final pinnacle, watch your footing on the steep, 0.5-mile drop that follows.

At a well-marked junction, stay left on the South Taconic Trail, which largely follows an old road lined with stone walls. After an initial climb, the trail moderates. In 2.2 miles, a route leading left provides a shortcut to the Ashley Hill Trail. Beyond this junction, the path passes unmarked spurs departing right to viewpoints before reaching an intersection with the Mount Frissell Trail in 0.8 mile.

The loop continues left, but for now stay straight on the South Taconic Trail. Hike easily 0.4 mile to New York's Mount Brace, where open meadows surrounding the north summit cairn provide extensive views in most directions. The path continues easily to the mostly forested south summit and beyond. Instead, retrace

your steps north and turn right onto the Mount Frissell Trail.

Tunnel through the ubiquitous mountain laurel and intersect the Ashley Hill Trail in 0.3 mile. This red-blazed path leads back to the trailhead, but another diversion is in order. Remain on the Mount Frissell Trail 0.4 mile to its namesake summit in Massachusetts. The journey to the wooded peak passes a tri-state boundary marker, scrambles an exposed ledge with impressive western views, and arrives at a small cairn marking the high point of Connecticut. Although it is not the mountain's top, at 2380 feet, it is the highest spot in the Nutmeg State.

Return to the Ashley Hill Trail and head right. This wide route follows the remains of an old road much of its way and gradually descends 1.4 miles to a junction. Over the next 2 miles, your travels will follow Ashley Hill Brook, initially near its banks but soon high above it. Remain on the red-blazed corridor until it ends at a junction with the Alander Mountain Trail. Retrace your steps 0.7 mile back to the start.

Shorter Options: Hike out and back along the Alander Mountain Trail; it is 5 miles roundtrip to the summit. To complete a shorter, 9.6-mile loop, skip Mounts Brace and Frissell by using the signed but unnamed route connecting the South Taconic and Ashley Hill Trails.

28 *Monument Mountain*

Distance: 2.8-mile loop
Difficulty: moderate
Hiking time: 2 hours
Elevation gain: 725 feet
High point: 1642 feet

Management: The Trustees of
Reservations (TTOR)
Season: year-round
Map: TTOR website
GPS coordinates: 42.24301°, −73.33516°

Getting there: From downtown Great Barrington, head north on Main Street (Route 7). In 0.5 mile, stay right on Route 7 and drive 3.5 miles to the parking area on the left. Or from downtown Stockbridge, follow Route 7 south 3.1 miles to the parking area on the right. *Note:* Fee required for non-members to the parking area on the right.

Monument Mountain is one of Trustees of Reservations' (TTOR) most popular destinations, and for good reason. This 503-acre parcel that surrounds its uniquely shaped peak has been a sacred site for the Mohican people. Their tradition of leaving stone offerings

Gazing out across the Devils Pulpit

of prayer as a "monument" on the mountain inspired today's name. In the 1850s, the summit attracted Nathaniel Hawthorne and Herman Melville, whose travels here helped inspire the writing of *Moby-Dick*. While most others enjoy less-note-worthy memories of their Monument Mountain experiences, this iconic Berkshire landmark is a must-see destination.

Begin north along the Hickey Trail. The relatively level path leads to a junction where a trail that begins at an alternative parking area enters from the right. Begin a steady ascent to the northwest. After passing a large boulder on the left, continue along a seasonal stream to a small wooden bridge. Once across, the route swings by a large cave and quickly reaches Inscription Rock. Commemorating the original land transfer that protected the mountain in 1899, the smooth rock sits near a three-way junction.

Join the Peeskawso Peak Trail, which leads south along the narrowing ridgeline. Up a series of rock steps, the scenic path skirts many eastern viewpoints and quickly reaches the 1642-foot summit. Perched high atop the lichen-covered, white-rocked peak, you can take in tremendous views of the surrounding hillsides: Mount Everett and its Taconic neighbors to the southwest, and the towering saddle-shaped Mount Greylock to the north. Watch your step while exploring the summit area and its many different cliffside perches.

Descending south along the ridge, the path reaches a spur left to a scenic vista. Follow this short trail to a view of Devils Pulpit, an area of jagged quartzite cliff formations. Beyond the spur, the route drops steadily and methodically down the ledge-covered slopes and soon ends at a junction with the Mohican Monument Trail.

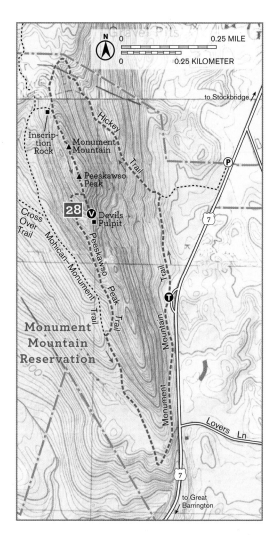

Turn left onto more-level terrain. The wide trail eventually approaches Route 7. Before reaching the busy highway, swing north onto a fairly rustic path. Parallel the road back to the trailhead.

Extend Your Trip: Take advantage of the Cross Over and Willow's Trails to visit nearby Flag Rock. This extension adds roughly 4 miles to the hike and ends atop an open ledge with sweeping views of the Housatonic River and southern Berkshires. Flag Rock is also accessible from a nearby trailhead on Route 183.

Also consider visiting two of TTOR's other destinations in the region: Tyringham Cobble, southeast of Stockbridge, and Bartholomew's Cobble, south of Sheffield near the Connecticut border. Both offer scenic views of the surrounding landscape.

29 *Hoosac Range*

Distance: 5.6 miles roundtrip	**Management:** Massachusetts DCR,
Difficulty: moderate	Berkshire NRC
Hiking time: 3 hours	**Season:** year-round
Elevation gain: 900 feet	**Map:** BNRC website
High point: 2570 feet	**GPS coordinates:** 42.69654°, −73.06465°

Getting there: From the junction of Routes 8 and 2, east of downtown North Adams, follow Route 2 east. Drive up the steep hillside, continue through the hairpin turn, and arrive at the parking lot on the right in 3.8 miles. **Notes:** If you find the parking lot full upon arrival, consider starting your journey at the nearby state forest, where the Busby Trail provides alternative access to the scenic 2570-foot peak (see Shorter Options).

A donor-funded organization, Berkshire Natural Resources Council manages more than fifty preserves, many with hiking trails where the public can experience the incredible beauty that the region has to offer. Their Hoosac Range Trail winds through a 944-acre property that includes a portion of the famed Mohican-Mohawk Trail, a historical travel corridor once used by the Indigenous people who settled here many centuries ago. Today, this high-elevation trailhead provides convenient access to a series of scenic vistas, including ledge-covered Spruce Hill in Savoy Mountain State Forest.

The red-and-white-blazed trail rises gradually 0.5 mile to a junction. Stay left and make your way through the northern hardwood forest. It leads east and then swings south to reach Sunset Rock in 0.3 mile. This pleasant picnic spot is aptly named, featuring views west over the Hoosac River valley to the Taconic Range in the distance.

Just beyond Sunset Rock, arrive at a second intersection. To the right, the trail leads 0.8 mile back to the parking area. You will use this route on the way out, but for now continue hiking south on the Hoosac Range Trail. The well-marked corridor ascends the wooded summit of Whitcomb Hill before proceeding over mostly level ground to a sign marking the halfway point between the parking lot and Spruce Hill.

Meandering around lichen-covered ledges and past gnarled yellow birches, the trail arrives at a mileage sign in 0.6 mile. To the left, a spur

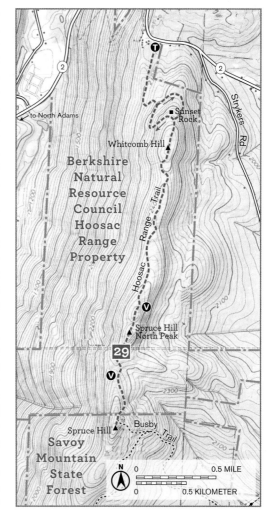

Hoosac Range Trail provides inviting access to Spruce Hill.

leads easily to a small perch showcasing scenes of the forested hills and valleys lying to the east. Back on the main trail, the route swings around the north peak of Spruce Hill; follow the trail carefully as it twists and turns 0.4 mile to another mileage sign. Here a spur departs right a few dozen steps to an open ledge and views of Mount Greylock.

The final 0.3-mile push to the summit is a gradual ascent through the thinning forest, where blueberry bushes become more prolific and offer a great midsummer snack. At a junction with the Busby Trail, stay right and scramble up the rock. A brief trek through stunted trees ends on Spruce Hill's summit ledge. Enjoy spectacular views of Massachusetts's highest mountain, as well as distant shots of the Berkshires trailing to the south and Vermont's Green Mountains rising to the right. When you have had your fill, return 2 miles north. Just before Sunset Rock, stay left at the junction and hike 0.8 mile back to the start.

Shorter Options: For a quick 1.6-mile jaunt, limit your travels to a loop around Sunset Rock. Or access Spruce Hill from Savoy Mountain State Forest: follow the Busby Trail 3 miles roundtrip to the summit. The State Forest features many other trails to explore as well.

30 *Mount Greylock*

Distance: 11.4 miles roundtrip
Difficulty: challenging–strenuous
Hiking time: 8 hours
Elevation gain: 3200 feet
High point: 3491 feet

Management: Massachusetts DCR
Season: year-round
Map: DCR website
GPS coordinates: 42.65555°, −73.20525°

Getting there: From Route 2 in Williamstown, follow Route 43 south 2.5 miles, then turn left onto Hopper Road. Drive 1.3 miles and stay left on Hopper Road. Continue 0.7 mile to the Haley Farm parking area on the right. **Note:** Backcountry campsites available by reservation at Sperry Campground.

Accessed by a paved road and frequented by many visitors, Mount Greylock can feel overwhelming to hikers seeking tranquility. Fortunately, the highest summit in southern New England is blessed with a network of trails that leads adventurers to quieter promontories, serene ridgelines, hidden waterfalls, and wildlife-filled hollows. This challenging daylong excursion captures each of these features while forming a double loop.

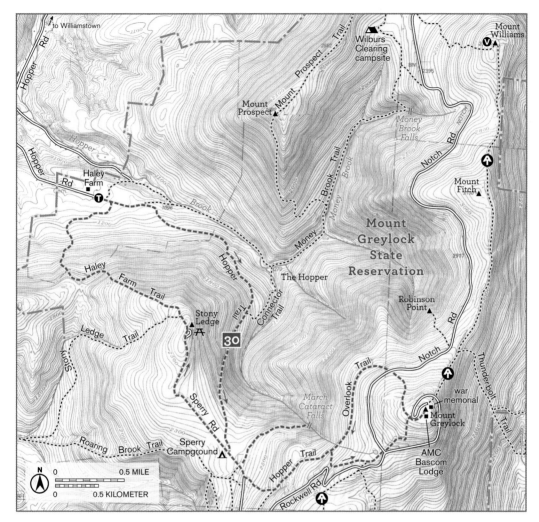

Begin on a shady farm road. In 0.2 mile, just beyond the Haley Farm Trail junction, turn right onto the Hopper Trail. At first, the path traverses gently rising terrain, and then it slowly enters the Hopper, a large steep-walled ravine carved deep in Greylock's western side. Although the route is straightforward, the increasingly difficult climb plods up the mountain slope. The trail eventually levels before intersecting Sperry Road (vehicles prohibited) at a state reservation campground 2.3 miles from the start (visit the DCR website to reserve a campsite).

Turn left and follow the dirt road 0.1 mile to a path that leads left and travels a little more than a half mile to March Cataract Falls. Check out this spur before proceeding up the mountain. It winds through towering sugar maples and yellow birch as it descends to the secluded falls.

Return to Sperry Road, hike 0.1 mile southeast, and then bear left onto the Hopper Trail's upper section. The terrain grows rockier after the trail swings left at a T intersection in 0.2 mile. Hike another 0.5 mile to a junction with the Overlook Trail—the start of the hike's upper loop. Remain on the Hopper Trail as it rises toward and then parallels Rockwell Road before ending at an Appalachian Trail (AT) junction in 0.4 mile.

Secluded March Cataract Falls

Hike north on the white-blazed path and follow it 0.5 mile past a quaint pond, across the paved road, and finally up to the busy summit. The grassy high point is surrounded by parking lots and buildings, including the Appalachian Mountain Club's Bascom Lodge (overnight accommodations available by reservation), and is punctuated with a war memorial. When open, the memorial's tower provides stunning 360-degree views of five states; otherwise, the summit area features unobstructed scenes east and partial views in other directions.

From the summit, retrace your steps south less than 0.1 mile before veering right onto the Overlook Trail. Winding around a utility building, the path enters the forest and drops steadily 0.5 mile to Notch Road. Head across the pavement to rejoin the trail as it leads 1.2 miles with modest elevation change before ending at the Hopper Trail. Just beyond its halfway point, a small ledge provides bucolic views across the valley to the Taconic Range.

Follow the Hopper Trail back to Sperry Road and turn right. Remain on Sperry Road as it passes the lower section of the Hopper Trail. Proceed past numerous campsites and hike 1 mile to the Stony Ledge picnic area, where impressive views of the Hopper and Mount Greylock await.

The final leg of the day's journey starts on the Stony Ledge Trail. In 0.2 mile, be sure to turn right onto the Haley Farm Trail (heading straight leads to a different trailhead). Enjoy a mostly gradual descent over the next half mile, which includes a pleasant vista north across Williamstown. Dropping more steeply into the impressive hardwood forest, the trail takes advantage of switchbacks over the next 1.2 miles before emerging into a field. Hike through the tall grasses to the junction below. Turn left to quickly reach the parking lot in 0.2 mile.

Other Options: To complete a shorter 7.6-mile adventure, consider limiting the hike to the lower loop by hiking up the Hopper Trail, visiting March Cataract Falls, heading over to Stony Ledge, and then descending the Haley Farm Trail. For a longer adventure, follow the AT north to Mount Williams and complete a 12.2-mile circuit by using the Money Brook Trail.

Opposite, top: Silver Lake sits in the heart of the Mooselamoo National Recreation Area.

Opposite, bottom: Pico Peak dominates southern scenes from Deer Leap.

Vermont: The Green Mountain State

The hiking centerpiece of Vermont is the 272-mile Long Trail. Dubbed the "footpath in the wilderness," the Long Trail was developed between 1910 and 1930 and runs the length of the state, from Massachusetts to Quebec. It is the nation's oldest long-distance trail and the inspiration for the much-longer Appalachian Trail (the two coincide for 100 miles). Though it is famous as a backpacking destination, it also joins with more than 166 miles of connecting trails that offer countless day hikes as well.

Vermont, New England's least-populated state, is home to the 385,000-acre Green Mountain National Forest, numerous state-owned lands, and more than 600,000 acres of land trust–conserved properties. While its sweeping mountain ridges, long flowing rivers, and verdant Champlain Valley are most alluring in autumn, when prolific maple forests are aglow in bright reds and oranges, the region's only land-locked state is a wonderful year-round destination for hikers of all skill levels.

Water careens down Lye Brook Falls.

31 Lye Brook Falls

Distance: 4.6 miles roundtrip
Difficulty: moderate
Hiking time: 2.5 hours
Elevation gain: 975 feet
High point: 1580 feet

Management: Green Mountain NF
Season: year-round
Map: GMNF website
GPS coordinates: 43.15883°, −73.04126°

Getting there: From Manchester, take exit 4 off Route 7. Follow Route 30 east and turn right in 0.4 mile onto East Manchester Road. Turn right again in 100 feet to stay on East Manchester Road. Drive 1.1 miles, then bear left on Glen Road. In 0.1 mile, continue straight on Glen Road. Follow the dirt surface 0.3 mile to the circular parking area.

This well-trodden path to the base of a 125-foot waterfall, one of Vermont's highest, is the perfect introduction to the Green Mountain National Forest's 15,680-acre Lye Brook Wilderness. Today, Lye Brook is the centerpiece of a wild, resilient expanse of forests, wetlands, and hidden natural beauty that reveals few signs of the century-old bygone era of intense logging, railroads, sawmills, and charcoal kilns that once flourished here.

The Lye Brook Trail begins on the parking area's eastern side. Walk a few hundred feet to a large kiosk featuring a map and area description. Following an old woods road, the path leads across mostly level terrain to start. In 0.2 mile, veer left onto a narrower path before quickly rejoining the old road near a trail register. Enjoy the easy grade 0.2 mile to the wilderness boundary.

Upon entering the Lye Brook Wilderness, a more modest climb ensues. Watch your footing; there is uneven terrain in places as the ascent grows steadily near the trail's halfway point. Higher up the deepening valley, the forest transitions to evergreens and the surface becomes increasingly inviting. With the rushing sounds of Lye Brook far below, reach a trail junction and sign pointing to the falls—1.8 miles from the start.

To the left, the main route becomes narrower and more difficult to follow as it leads into the heart of the wilderness. There are no significant points of interest on that route prior to reaching backcountry campsites at scenic Bourne Pond in 5.3 miles or Stratton Pond in 7.2 miles.

Instead, stay right to tackle the final 0.5-mile stretch to the falls. The spur is easy at first, meanders through a rockslide, and then slowly descends to the edge of the water. Located on a tributary, Lye Brook Falls is not a single waterfall

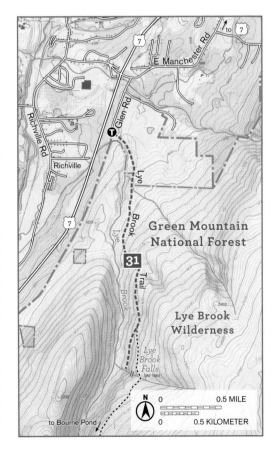

but a series of cascades. There are two excellent vantage points. The main route ends at a large boulder near the base of the falls. Check out the unmarked spur that rises left to a less obstructed perch. Watch your step and resist the temptation to scramble higher up the side of the falls, as the footing is very slippery. Retrace your steps 2.3 miles to return to the trailhead.

Nearby Options: If you are looking for a mountain adventure, check out the trails that wind through the Equinox Preservation Trust's 914-acre conservation property located just west of downtown Manchester. There are many trails to choose from, including a challenging route to the scenic summit of the preserve's namesake peak.

32 *Haystack Mountain*

Distance: 4 miles roundtrip
Difficulty: moderate–challenging
Hiking time: 3 hours
Elevation gain: 1050 feet
High point: 3425 feet

Management: Green Mountain NF
Season: year-round
Map: GMNF website
GPS coordinates: 42.89972°, −72.91074°

Getting there: From Route 9, 1.1 miles west of Wilmington, head north on Haystack Road. Drive 0.3 mile, then stay right on Haystack Road. In 1 mile, bear left onto Chimney Hill Road and then turn right onto Binney Brook Road in 0.2 mile. Climb this windy route 1.1 miles before turning right onto Upper Dam Road. Stay left in 0.1 mile and continue 0.2 mile to the trailhead on the right. Park along the right side of the road; do not block nearby driveways. ***Note:*** Access to Haystack Pond is prohibited.

Haystack Mountain's distinctive pinnacle-shaped high point rises prominently above the Deerfield River and the Harriman Reservoir in the southeast corner of Vermont's Green Mountain National Forest. This popular excursion explores an inviting northern hardwood forest, cuts through rock ledges, and winds to the summit's evergreen-shaded rock perch with pleasant views across the Connecticut River valley.

At a small kiosk, begin the hike on municipal land. The wide route quickly enters the Green Mountain National Forest as it initially coincides with a gated dirt road that provides access to Haystack Pond. After a steady climb, arrive at a well-marked junction in 0.5 mile. The road that continues straight to the local water source is not open to the public.

Turn sharply left on the Deerfield Ridge Trail, which drops briefly before crossing Binney Brook. Rise gradually to the south 0.3 mile before

Birch and maple line the lower portions of Deerfield Ridge Trail.

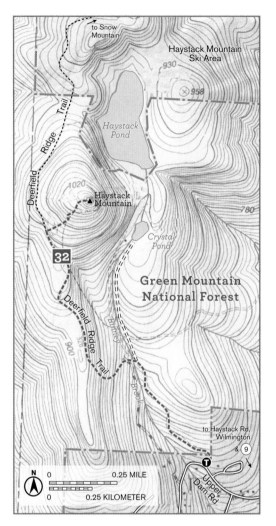

swinging right. Catch your breath and begin a more aggressive 0.5-mile ascent up the wide rock-covered path. Fortunately, there are plenty of opportunities to stop and admire maturing yellow birches along the way, as well as carpets of wildflowers adding splashes of color to the forest floor.

As you approach the ridgeline, the trail narrows and becomes less steep. Along with the increased elevation, notice the growing number of conifers in the surrounding forest. The evergreens take advantage of the shallower soils, where exposed ledge and large boulders become more prevalent. Take advantage of the paths that diverge right to avoid wetter sections of the original route. A steady climb soon leads to a trail sign.

The Deerfield Ridge Trail continues straight and winds more than 3 miles across the ridge. This lightly used route ends with modest views from atop the Snow Mountain ski area. For today's hike, turn right to reach Haystack Mountain's 3425-foot summit.

The 0.3-mile spur rises across roots and through the moss-covered boreal forest. A final pitch leads to an open ledge, highlighted with views of Haystack Pond tucked below the summit, Mount Ascutney rising to the north, and Mount Monadnock dominating the eastern horizon. To the left, a short, unmarked path leads to the wooded high point. Before retracing your steps back to the trailhead, check out the unmarked spur that leads right a few dozen feet to a perch overlooking Harriman Reservoir.

Nearby Options: Located just east of downtown Wilmington, Molly Stark State Park offers overnight camping and a delightful 1.7-mile loop to the top of Mount Olga. Here, a tower showcases sweeping views of southern Vermont and neighboring states.

33 *Stratton Pond and Mountain*

Distance: 5.6 miles roundtrip
Difficulty: challenging
Hiking time: 8 hours/2 days
Elevation gain: 2400 feet
High point: 3940 feet

Management: Green Mountain NF
Season: year-round
Map: GMNF website
GPS coordinates: 43.06113°, −72.96769°

Getting there: From the town of Stratton, follow Stratton Arlington Road west 3.4 miles to a parking area on the right. Alternatively, beginning in East Arlington, pick up Kelly Stand Road in the village of East Kansas and drive east 10.5 miles to the trailhead on the left. Access in the winter is only from the east. (Winter parking is 0.7 mile east of the trailhead.) ***Note:*** Backcountry campsites available.

This classic Green Mountain hike includes the largest lake on the Long Trail and the summit where James P. Taylor first visualized the creation of Vermont's so-called "footpath in the wilderness." In 1917, his dream came true, and today Stratton Pond and Mountain are not only a key link along the Long Trail's 272-mile journey from Massachusetts to Canada, but prominent features on the Appalachian Trail's much-longer route from Georgia to Maine. This circuit features moderate terrain throughout, ideal for an overnight backpack or a more vigorous one-day adventure.

The 3.8-mile climb to Stratton Mountain begins gradually, heading north along the Appalachian Trail/Long Trail (AT/LT). With little elevation change, follow the white-blazed route 1.4 miles to the International Paper (IP) Road. Once across this multiuse trail, the AT/LT climbs more steadily. Wind around Little Stratton Mountain and reach a saddle 2.7 miles from the start. Continue up modest grades to the forested high point and 70-foot summit tower. The highest mountain in southern Vermont, Stratton offers hikers 360-degree views of four states from its summit tower.

The 3.2-mile hike to the pond descends rapidly to the northwest through spruce-fir forests. As the terrain eases and the forest turns to northern hardwoods, cross the IP Road again. The path drops to a wooden bridge, ascends a low hill, and then drops quickly to a junction with the Stratton Pond Trail. Stay right on the AT/LT and hike 0.1 mile down to the pond's grassy shore, an

Pausing at a secluded stream east of Stratton Pond

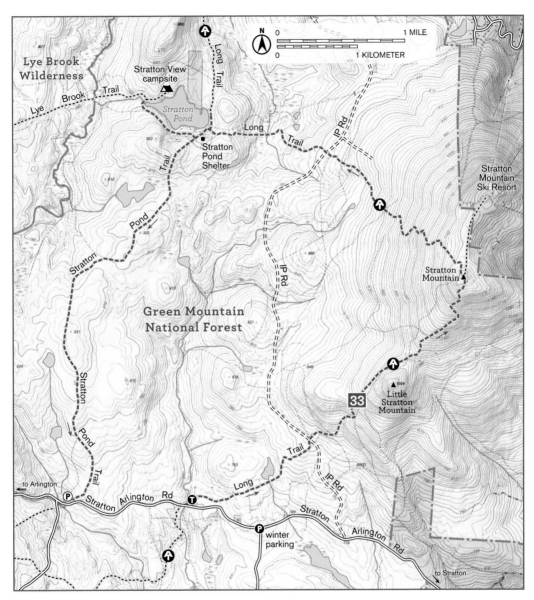

idyllic resting spot for picnicking and wildlife observation.

After retracing your steps back to the Stratton Pond Trail, bear right and hike 0.1 mile to a spur that leads left to an overnight shelter. This popular camping spot, as well as a tent site on the pond's western shore, are managed by the Green Mountain Club. Both are available for a small fee on a first-come, first-served basis. Overnight camping near the pond is prohibited outside of these two designated areas.

Continue south on the Stratton Pond Trail and immediately arrive at a junction with the Lye Brook Trail on the right. Explore this path as it meanders to a quieter corner of the pond and pleasant shoreline views, including sights of Stratton Mountain from atop a wooden boardwalk. At an intersection with a spur that leads right to the Stratton View tent site, the wilderness path continues left. Turn around here and hike 0.6 mile back to the Stratton Pond Trail.

To complete the circuit, hike 3.5 miles south over the gentle, rolling terrain. The landscape is wet and muddy in places, but the trail features occasional boardwalks to ease the way. A final descent leads to Stratton Arlington Road and the Stratton Pond Trailhead parking area. Follow the road east 1 mile to complete the loop.

Shorter Options: The pond and the mountain are each pleasant, shorter day hikes on their own: 7.4 miles and 7.6 miles roundtrip, respectively.

Green Mountain Club

Vermont's Green Mountain Club has been building and maintaining hiking trails for more than a century. The mission of this membership-based organization is to make the Vermont mountains play a larger part in the lives of the people by protecting and maintaining the Long Trail system and fostering, through education, the stewardship of Vermont's hiking trails and mountains. They maintain more than five hundred miles of trails in the Green Mountain State.

34 *Mount Ascutney*

Distance: 6 miles roundtrip	**Management:** Vermont DFPR
Difficulty: moderate–challenging	**Season:** year-round (except mud season;
Hiking time: 4 hours	see Notes)
Elevation gain: 2200 feet	**Map:** VDFPR website
High point: 3144 feet	**GPS coordinates:** 43.42680°, −72.46625°

Getting there: From Interstate 91 in Weathersfield, take exit 8 and follow Route 131 west 3.2 miles. Turn right onto Cascade Falls Road and then in 0.1 mile, stay left on High Meadow Road. Follow the dirt surface 0.4 mile. The road swings right near a private residence and ends at a parking area. **Note:** The trail is closed during mud season, generally mid-April through late May.

Mount Ascutney, which gets its name from a series of Algonquin words meaning "mountain of the rocky summit," is the centerpiece of more than 3000 acres of conserved land featuring over 25 miles of recreational trails. This out-and-back excursion along the Weathersfield Trail visits quaint cascades before climbing steadily to a series of picturesque vistas, including a breathtaking panorama from atop the summit tower.

Beginning under a canopy of imposing maple trees, the path swings right and crosses the top of Little Cascade Falls in 0.4 mile. Here the water tumbles gently down a small ledge. Climbing more quickly up switchbacks, recross the stream at the base of a deep flume and ascend a wooden ladder. Passing semi-open outcrops with views south across the pastoral landscape, the trail winds 0.4 mile over a small incline before descending to a junction with the Falls Bypass. Stay left and drop 0.1 mile to a scenic ledge, where Crystal Cascade Falls plummets out of sight below—watch your step!

The route continues upstream along the east bank and then swings right. Up a hemlock-covered ridge, parallel the water from a more

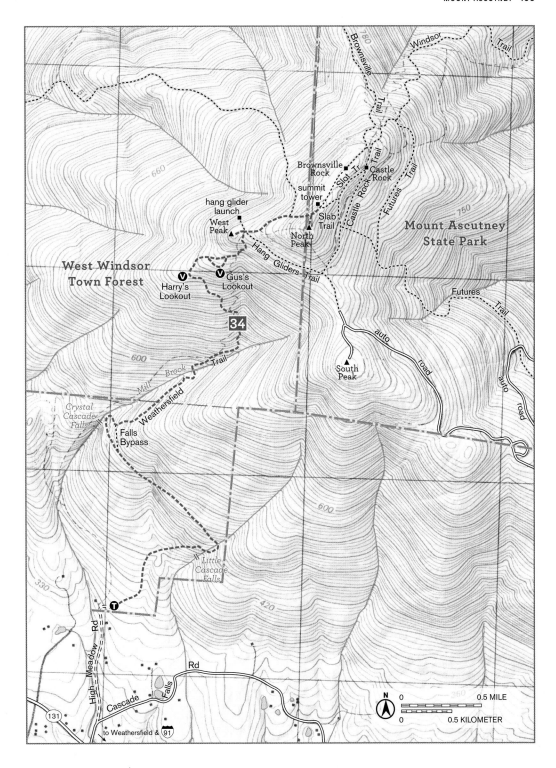

Brownsville Trail

Windsor Trail

Brownsville Rock

Slot Tr.

Castle Rock

summit tower

Castle Rock Trail

Futures Trail

Slab Trail

West Peak

hang glider launch

North Peak

Mount Ascutney State Park

Hang Gliders Trail

West Windsor Town Forest

Harry's Lookout

Gus's Lookout

Futures Trail

34

auto road

auto road

South Peak

Mill Brook

Weathersfield Trail

Crystal Cascade Falls

Falls Bypass

Little Cascade Falls

T

High Meadow Rd

Cascade Falls Rd

131

to Weathersfield & 91

N

0   0.5 MILE

0   0.5 KILOMETER

Fall foliage adds color toward Killington Peak from Brownsville Rock.

distant location before returning to its side. Hop across to where the path intersects an old woods road. At a sign marking Halfway Brooks, 1.7 miles from the start, catch your breath—the difficulty is about to ratchet up. Scale the steep slope and follow the turns and bends that eventually lead to the ridgeline and Harry's Lookout, which honors a long-time trail maintainer.

The route winds through the evergreen forest, reaching a spur that leads right to Gus's Lookout. Named for a 1967 charter member of the Ascutney Trails Association, this vantage point offers excellent views into western New Hampshire. Rejoin the main trail in a few hundred feet and continue climbing to a small saddle, where a path winds 0.1 mile left to West Peak's scenic

rocky top. This saddle also includes an intersection with a hang gliders' trail that leads east to a parking area and west to a launching pad.

Remain on the main trail another 0.3 mile as it rises to a spur leading right to the high point, just below the base of the summit observation tower. Built in 1989, the sturdy structure provides breathtaking views of southern Vermont, glimpses of the White Mountains, and distant scenes west to New York State. Before returning to the parking area the same way you came, follow the wide path south that leads anticlimactically to the mountain's North Peak, its high point. The surrounding communications towers shield the scenery, but you cannot come this far without touching the top.

Extend Your Trip: Consider heading north to enjoy scenic views from Brownsville and Castle Rocks by completing a 0.7-mile loop using the Brownsville, Windsor, Castle Rock, and Slot Trails.

35 *Baker Peak and Griffith Lake*

Distance: 8.8-mile loop
Difficulty: challenging
Hiking time: 6 hours/2 days
Elevation gain: 2350 feet
High point: 2790 feet

Management: Green Mountain NF
Season: year-round
Map: GMNF website
GPS coordinates: 43.31263°, −72.98684°

Getting there: From Emerald Lake State Park in Dorset, follow Route 7 north for 2.3 miles and turn right on South End Road. Drive 0.5 mile to the parking area on the left.
Note: Backcountry campsites available.

This 8.8-mile loop cuts through the heart of the 6723-acre Big Branch Wilderness and is a gratifying daylong journey or a more relaxing two-day jaunt, with an overnight stay near the shores of a secluded high-elevation pond. Enjoy many rewards along the way, including commanding views from Baker Peak's white-rocked summit and more-subtle beauty beside McGinn Brook's cascading water.

The Lake Trail climbs gradually to start. Cross a small stream and then enter private property in 0.4 mile. Remain on the well-marked path as it parallels the stream's east side 0.3 mile. The route swings sharply left and rises gently 0.4 mile,

reentering the Green Mountain National Forest at a Big Branch Wilderness sign.

The climb becomes more aggressive up the former carriage road that once led to the Griffith Lake House, a private home of Vermont's first millionaire, lumber baron Silas Griffith. A mile and a half from the parking lot, carefully cross a metal bridge cut into the side of a ledge as small gaps in the forest offer glimpses of the Taconic Range to the west. The trail curves right and becomes narrower as it approaches McGinn Brook. With rocky ledges rising on the right and the running water cascading to the left, climb steadily 0.3 mile to a stream crossing. Reach a

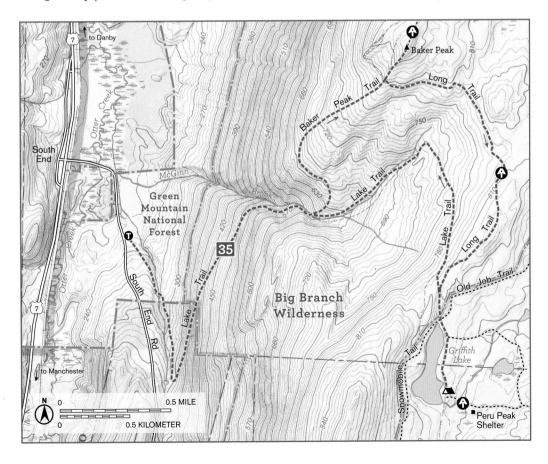

Baker Peak provides exceptional views of the Taconic Range.

trail junction and the start of the loop on the other side.

The hike proceeds left on the 0.9-mile Baker Peak Trail. Take your time on the aggressive but straightforward 800-foot ascent. Eventually birch and maple give way to spruce and fir. Through the changing forest, make your way up the rugged landscape to an intersection with the Appalachian Trail/Long Trail (AT/LT), just 0.1 mile south of Baker Peak's summit-area ledges.

Turn left and immediately reach a junction where a blue-blazed bad-weather route diverges right. Continue straight and head up the more rugged, white-blazed trail. Watch your step and scramble up the exposed rock to expanding views—the surface can be very slippery if wet. Before the trail reenters the forest, find a 180-degree vista that is especially impressive south to Mount Equinox and west to Dorset Peak.

Carefully retrace your steps back down to the Baker Peak Trail junction, then stay left. Follow the well-trodden AT/LT south 1.7 miles. While there is little overall elevation change, the undulating trek is not flat as it rises over a series of small ridges. Continue 0.1 mile past the upper end of the Lake Trail and descend to a junction where the Old Job Trail departs left and a snowmobile route exits right.

Enjoy your first views of Griffith Lake before hiking straight. The AT/LT leads 0.2 mile over boardwalk to a Green Mountain Club tenting area—available for a small fee on a first-come, first-served basis. Near the campsite, a spur right leads to the lake's shore. (For a different perspective of the water body, head back to the Old Job Trail junction and turn left onto the snowmobile trail. This wide corridor quickly leads to the lake's western shore and pleasant picnic spots.)

Begin the final leg of the circuit by backtracking 0.1 mile north along the AT/LT to the Lake Trail. Follow this blue-blazed route left 1.3 miles. It descends gradually at first, crossing a series of small tributaries. As you approach McGinn Brook, the trail drops more aggressively; watch your step on the uneven terrain. Upon reaching the Baker Peak Trail intersection, cross the brook before hiking 1.9 miles back to the start.

36 *Little Rock Pond*

Distance: 4.8 miles roundtrip
Difficulty: easy–moderate
Hiking time: 3 hours
Elevation gain: 350 feet
High point: 1860 feet

Management: Green Mountain NF
Season: May–Nov
Map: GMNF website
GPS coordinates: 43.37282°, −72.96269°

Getting there: From Route 7 in Danby, drive east on Mount Tabor Road for 1 mile to Big Branch. From here, Mount Tabor Road becomes Forest Service Road 10 and is not maintained in winter. Continue 2.3 miles to the parking area on the right. *Note:* Backcountry campsite available.

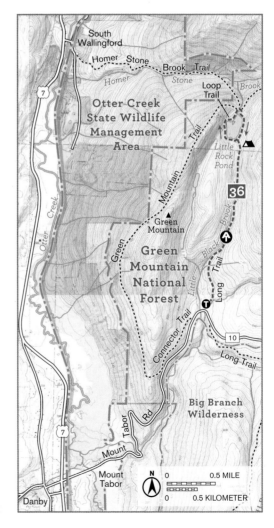

The reflective surface of Little Rock Pond lures hikers of all ages to explore the water body's picturesque setting deep in the Green Mountain National Forest. Along the way, get lost in the chorus of diverse songbirds announcing their territory in the spring, marvel at the abundant wildflowers and mushrooms adding color to the forest floor throughout the summer, and photograph the lush canopy of maples, beech, and birch that present a vibrant palette of reds, oranges, and yellows in the heart of autumn.

Follow the Appalachian Trail/Long Trail (AT/LT) north; the two white-blazed long-distance trails coincide for a little more than 100 miles from the Massachusetts border to just beyond Killington Peak. This 2-mile stretch to Little Rock Pond is one of the more popular sections. Well used by backpackers and day hikers alike, it rises less than 350 feet along its route to the secluded pond.

Easy to start, the path crosses Little Black Brook in 0.6 mile and recrosses a second time shortly after. The white-blazed route features numerous boardwalks throughout, helping to ease the way across the wet landscape. Take advantage of the gradual climb to scan the forest for resident flora and fauna. With a little patience, you might spot an ovenbird or black-throated blue warbler singing from a low-hanging perch in the understory.

Upon arriving at Little Rock Pond's southern shore, begin a 0.7-mile circuit around the scenic water body by heading left on the Little Rock

Little Rock Pond lies nestled beneath the slopes of Green Mountain.

Pond Loop Trail. This more rugged path remains close to the water's edge, visiting picnic spots along the way. Reach the Green Mountain Trail in 0.3 mile and turn right. After crossing the pond's outlet stream, intersect the AT/LT.

Complete the circuit around the pond by bearing right. Head south 0.3 mile along the pond's eastern shore. There are numerous vantage points that feature attractive views of nearby Green Mountain's ledge-covered slopes that often reflect upon the tranquil water below. Pass a spur trail that exits left to a Green Mountain Club campsite with a multi-person lean-to and tenting area. Both are available for a small fee on a first-come, first-served basis. Once the loop is complete, retrace your steps 2 miles south to the trailhead.

Extend Your Trip: If you are looking for a more adventurous 6.7-mile itinerary, instead of returning south along the AT/LT, consider heading up and over the summit of Green Mountain. From Little Rock Pond, the Green Mountain Trail rises steadily at first, levels off, and descends gradually. Swing left on a connector trail to reach the parking area. While mostly forested, this route leads to scenic ledges atop the ridge. For a quieter trip to the pond that is available all year, follow the 2.3-mile Homer Stone Brook Trail from South Wallingford.

37 *Killington Peak*

Distance: 7.6 miles roundtrip
Difficulty: challenging
Hiking time: 6 hours
Elevation gain: 2500 feet
High point: 4235 feet

Management: Vermont DFPR
Season: year-round (except mud season; see Notes)
Map: Trail Finder website
GPS coordinates: 43.61924°, −72.87691°

Getting there: From the junction of Routes 4 and 7 in Rutland, follow Route 4 east. Drive 5 miles and turn right onto Wheelerville Road. Continue south 4 miles to large parking area on the left. **Notes:** Backcountry campsite available. The trail is closed during mud season, generally mid-April through late May.

Famous for its alpine ski slopes, Vermont's second-highest peak is sometimes overlooked by hikers more attracted to the state's northernmost 4000-foot mountains. However, this excursion in the 16,166-acre Coolidge State Forest will not disappoint. Once on the mountain's rocky pinnacle, enjoy striking scenery that includes neighboring New Hampshire and New York as well as the state's Green Mountain range trailing off to the north.

The 3.5-mile Bucklin Trail begins easily under a stand of tall white pines. Immediately intersect the Catamount Cross-Country Ski Trail, as the two routes coincide briefly. Hike past a large kiosk in 0.1 mile and cross a bridge that spans Brewers Brook. The Catamount Trail departs left as the hiking trail swings right. Continue up the valley and in 0.2 mile, turn sharply left away from the brook. Over gently rolling terrain, the route is still paralleling the water but from a distance.

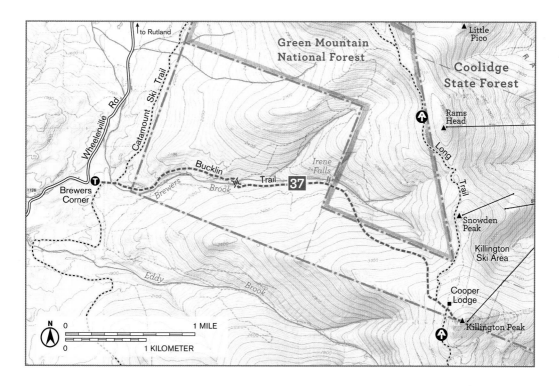

Pico Peak dominates the views north from Killington's summit.

Follow the blue blazes closely as unmarked corridors depart left. Eventually, the trail swings right and descends rapidly to Brewers Brook, 1.4 miles from the start.

Cross the bridge and turn left. The Bucklin Trail parallels the brook 0.8 mile with minimal elevation change, but the footing becomes a bit rougher. As the valley narrows, reach a short spur that departs left to Irene Falls, a small cascade. Shortly after, the Bucklin Trail swings sharply right and begins an aggressive 1.3-mile ascent to the ridgeline. This stretch combines steep grades with occasional moderation. While the climb is difficult, the terrain is straightforward and easy to navigate. Rising higher up the slope, the hardwood forest slowly transitions to evergreens. Before long, arrive at a wooden sign and a junction with the Appalachian Trail / Long Trail (AT/LT).

Turn right and follow these two famous long-distance routes. Marked with white blazes, the AT/LT rises moderately 0.1 mile to Cooper Lodge, a very rustic building that provides bunks for backpackers. Nearby, there are more-appealing sites for pitching a tent at this high-elevation camping area. This is a good location to catch your breath before the final stretch.

Just after the Cooper Lodge, the AT/LT bears right. Stay straight and join the Killington Spur. Don't underestimate its 0.2-mile length; this is the hike's most demanding section. Scramble up the steep ledges through the thinning forest. Soon the hard work pays off as the trail emerges atop the mostly open 4235-foot summit with nearly 360-degree views. Before retracing your steps back to the trailhead, enjoy a nice picnic lunch while gazing upon the mountains and ridges that include the Adirondacks to the west, the Green Mountains to the north, and New Hampshire's White Mountains towering to the east.

38 *Deer Leap*

Distance: 3.2-mile loop
Difficulty: moderate
Hiking time: 2 hours
Elevation gain: 1000 feet
High point: 2770 feet

Management: Green Mountain NF
Season: year-round
Map: GMNF website
GPS coordinates: 43.66363°, −72.83277°

Getting there: From the junction of Routes 7 and 4 near downtown Rutland, drive east on Route 4 toward Killington. Reach the top of Sherburne Pass in 9.1 miles and turn right into the large parking area. There is also a smaller lot on the other side of the road—on the east side of the inn that is located there.

Although the breathtaking views from Deer Leap's scenic overlook are the highlight of this moderately challenging circuit in Central Vermont, hikers of all ages will also discover maturing northern hardwood forests decorated with random boulders, carpets of wildlflowers, and lichen-covered ledges. Take your time exploring the changing habitats as you listen for the flute-like call of the hermit thrush, Vermont's state bird.

To reach the Sherburne Pass Trailhead, use extreme caution crossing Route 4. The traffic moves quickly here in both directions, and it is not easy to see cars coming from the west. Once safely across, find the trailhead to the right of the inn. A path leads left to rock-climbing routes. Stay on the blue-blazed Sherburne Pass Trail. This well-trodden route wastes little time rising under Deer Leap's rugged lower slopes. The incline eases a bit as the sound of the highway fades into the distance. A final push leads to a well-marked intersection with the Appalachian Trail (AT).

To the right, the AT leads 1 mile to Gifford Woods State Park—an alternative starting place for the hike. It offers overnight camping and features impressive old-growth trees. Stay left and quickly reach the eastern junction of the Deer Leap Trail. For now, remain straight and follow the white blazes. The AT strolls 0.7 mile through beech and birch to Deer Leap Trail's western terminus.

With the long-distance route's southern journey proceeding ahead to Georgia, turn left to begin an aggressive 0.5-mile climb up Deer

Leap Mountain. While mostly forested, the blue-blazed route offers a few limited views north toward the main ridge of the Green Mountains. Level off and swing around the 2782-foot high point before beginning a steady 0.2-mile descent to a small brook. A brief 0.1-mile climb follows. Scramble up a rock ledge to reach a junction with the Deer Leap Overlook spur.

Dropping 0.1 mile south, the popular path weaves through a dense evergreen forest. After

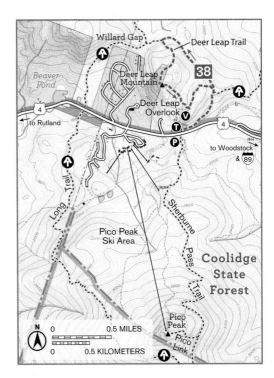

descending a wooden staircase, make your way to the prominent rock outcrop. The views of nearby Pico Peak towering above and New York's Adirondack Mountains rising in the distance are breathtaking. Take a few moments to enjoy the spectacular scenery.

Return to the main route and keep right. The remaining 0.4-mile section of the Deer Leap Trail is mostly level at the start and gradually descends. Swing past a large boulder, then arrive at a junction with the AT. Bear right to head back to Sherburne Pass.

Extend Your Trip: Follow the Sherburne Pass Trail south from the parking area. It rises aggressively 2.5 miles to the 0.4-mile Pico Link. Hike out and back on these two routes to complete a challenging trek to the summit of 3967-foot Pico Peak, where expansive views await from its open ski slopes.

Enjoying late-afternoon sunlight atop Deer Leap Overlook

39 *Moosalamoo National Recreation Area*

Distance: 6.7 miles roundtrip
Difficulty: moderate
Hiking time: 4 hours
Elevation gain: 925 feet
High point: 1330 feet

Management: Green Mountain NF
Season: year-round
Map: GMNF website
GPS coordinates: 43.90038°, −73.06429°

Getting there: From the junction of Routes 73 and 53 in Forest Dale, follow Route 53 north 5.4 miles to a large parking area on the right. Alternatively, from the junction of Routes 7 and 53 south of Middlebury, follow Route 53 east 3.8 miles toward Branbury State Park. Drive 0.3 mile past the state park entrance to the parking area on the left.
Notes: Backcountry campsites available. Multiuse trail also used by mountain bikers.

Lying in the shadows of taller peaks to the east, the 20,000-acre Moosalamoo National Recreation Area in the Green Mountain National Forest is often overlooked by outdoor adventurers seeking higher summits. Those drawn to its family-friendly trail network will discover dramatic cascades, dense forests, tranquil water bodies, and sweeping ledge-top vistas. Check out this recommended trek as an introduction to a place demanding future exploration.

Near a large kiosk, the Silver Lake Trail ascends a rock staircase and soon swings right on a wider corridor. The inviting route climbs gradually 0.3 mile to an opening where the Silver Lake Penstock descends steeply. Originally constructed in 1917 and upgraded in 1935, this long pipeline is part of a hydroelectric project that supplies electricity to more than eight hundred homes.

Hike 0.1 mile ahead and look for unofficial routes leading left to aerial views of the Falls of Lana. Watch your step along the edge of the chasm. Named in honor of General Wool, a Mexican-American War veteran nicknamed Lana (the Spanish word for wool), the falls carve a deep channel in the bedrock. In another 0.1 mile, the main trail reaches a major junction.

Turn sharply right, remaining on the Silver Lake Trail. Open to mountain bikers, the wide multiuse route gradually ascends the slope with an occasional switchback. Stay on the main trail as a handful of unmarked options depart right. Level off near a forested wetland and, in 0.8 mile,

arrive at a signed junction with the Lenny's Lookout Trail on the right. Check out this 0.2-mile spur that meanders up a utility corridor to a ledge with pleasant scenes west toward the Adirondacks.

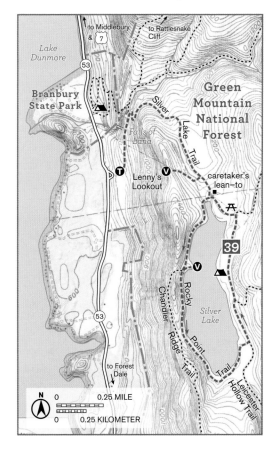

Silver Lake Trail draped in fallen leaves

Back at the Silver Lake Trail, bear right to complete its final 0.2 mile. The trail ends at the entrance to the Silver Lake Recreation Area. Managed by the National Forest Service, this hidden locale surrounds its namesake water body and features picnic spots, a campground with fifteen overnight sites, and the interpretive Rocky Point Trail. The campground caretaker's lean-to on the left and large kiosk straight ahead welcome visitors.

The best way to explore Silver Lake is to complete the 3-mile loop around its shores. From the large kiosk, head west along the Rocky Point Trail. It crosses an earthen dam with views of the lake. On the far side, the path swings left near the first of many interpretive signs describing the area's history and natural features. Hike 0.5 mile and stay straight where the Chandler Ridge Trail

exits right. Just beyond, a short spur on the left leads to scenic Rocky Point.

Over the next 1.2 miles, the Rocky Point Trail hugs the shoreline through an evergreen forest draped in ledges and fern-covered boulders. The footing is uneven in places, but there is little elevation change. Wrapping around the lake's southern shore, the route swings sharply left at an intersection with the Leicester Hollow Trail.

Now heading north, and at a greater distance from the shore, follow the wider corridor past a series of campsites and large boulders before swinging left in 0.8 mile. Cross an aqueduct and arrive at a large picnic area near a sandy beach. The circuit proceeds through the picnic area and ends in 0.2 mile. Retrace your steps 1.5 miles along the Silver Lake Trail to complete your journey.

Extend Your Trip: While it is closed to protect nesting peregrine falcons from March 15 to August 1, Rattlesnake Cliffs is a must-see addition to the described hike or an alternative destination on a different day. To make your way to the cliffs, pick up the North Branch Trail at its junction with the Silver Lake Trail near the Falls of Lana. Along with the Aunt Jenny and Rattlesnake Cliffs Trails, the three paths form a 4-mile loop to Rattlesnake Cliffs, where breathtaking views of the Green Mountains, the Lake Champlain Valley, and the High Peaks of New York await. For a shorter extension, explore the Branbury State Park paths that descend west from the North Branch Trail. The main path visits an alluring ledge-top vista before dividing in two. Both options lead to Route 53; follow the road left to complete the hike.

40 *Vermont's Presidential Range*

Distance: 13.6-mile loop
Difficulty: challenging–strenuous
Hiking time: 10 hours/2 days
Elevation gain: 3800 feet
High point: 3780 feet

Management: Green Mountain NF
Season: May–Oct
Map: GMNF website
GPS coordinates: 44.04075°, −72.95363°

Getting there: Beginning in Lincoln, follow East River Road 1.1 miles east and turn right onto South Lincoln Road. Cross the New Haven River in 4.1 miles, then bear left onto Forest Road 201. Drive 0.3 mile to the parking area—the dirt road begins on private property. *Note:* Backcountry campsites available.

Located in the heart of the sprawling 24,986-acre Breadloaf Wilderness, this remote traverse of New England's lesser-known Presidential Range is a perfect multiday backpacking destination or a rigorous daylong adventure featuring an occasional high-elevation vista. Choose this hike to explore fern-draped ridges, lush hardwood forests, and moss-covered rocks that shelter wild creatures ranging in size from ubiquitous eastern toads to reclusive black bears and many others in between.

The 3.1-mile Cooley Glen Trail leaves the parking area and parallels the New Haven River 0.4 mile to a bridge crossing. After entering the Green Mountain National Forest's largest wilderness area, the route never strays far from the water while rising gently for 1 mile. Near a confluence of tributaries, swing left and make your way up a narrower valley. Beyond a series of small stream crossings, the steady climb ends at a junction with the Long Trail.

The loop continues to the right, but first, head north and immediately pass the Cooley Glen

Shelter. Maintained by the Green Mountain Club, this is one of two camping locations along the hike that are available on a first-come, first-served basis. Proceed past the wooden structure and tackle the 0.9-mile ascent of Mount Grant, a 3623-foot peak named in honor of the nation's eighteenth president and US Civil War hero. The trail winds steadily through the evergreen forest. Just before reaching the high point, a small ledge offers intimate views south and more-distant scenes east to the White Mountains.

Retrace your steps and hike south from the Cooley Glen Shelter. The Long Trail scrambles up a short steep pitch, but the incline soon eases. Crest Mount Cleveland's wooded high point in 0.5 mile and pause briefly to reflect on the only person to be elected to two nonconsecutive US presidential terms, despite winning the popular vote in three straight elections.

Descend steadily 0.6 mile into a saddle on the ridge, the trek's most remote section. The trail meanders 2.1 miles up and over the wooded summit of Little Hans Peak and scales the

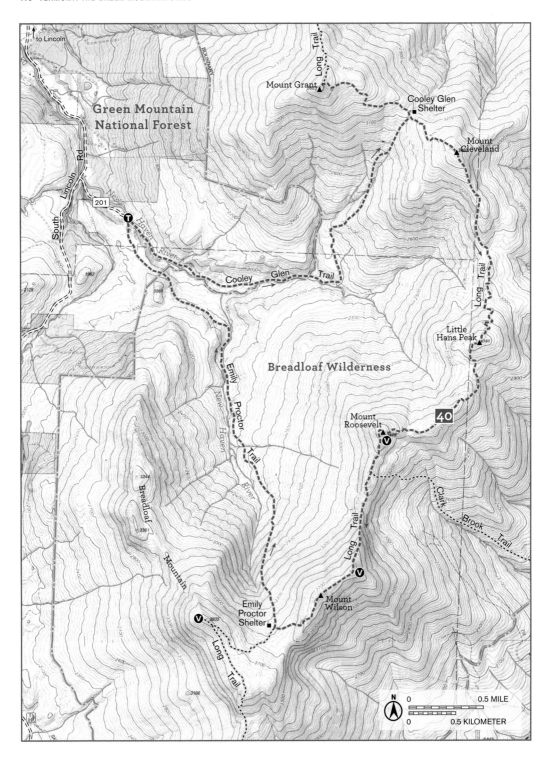

to Lincoln

Green Mountain
National Forest

BOUNDARY

Long Trail

Mount Grant

Cooley Glen
Shelter

Mount
Cleveland

Long Trail

South Lincoln Rd

201

T

New Haven River

Cooley Glen Trail

Little
Hans Peak

Breadloaf Wilderness

Emily Proctor Trail

New Haven River

Mount
Roosevelt

V

40

Clark Brook Trail

Breadloaf Mountain

Long Trail

Long Trail

V

Emily
Proctor
Shelter

Mount
Wilson

V

N

0   0.5 MILE

0   0.5 KILOMETER

Mount Roosevelt provides sweeping views near the loop's halfway point.

increasingly rocky slopes of Mount Roosevelt. Before reaching the wooded high point, emerge atop a summit ledge with breathtaking views south to Killington Peak. This is a great place to enjoy a midday snack and recall Teddy Roosevelt's enduring conservation legacy.

To warm up for the journey's final climb, descend 0.4 mile south to a junction with the Clark Brook Trail. Continue straight to the col and then head 0.5 mile up the steep, rocky slopes of Mount Wilson. Although the incline remains steady, the footing becomes more forgiving near the mountain's eastern summit, where a short spur leads left to a small vista.

The trail proceeds 0.5 mile with minimal elevation change while passing over the mountain's wooded 3780-foot high point, named for America's twenty-eighth president and architect of the League of Nations—precursor to the United Nations. Descend rapidly 0.3 mile to the Emily Proctor Shelter, the second welcoming overnight destination along the route. To the left, the Long Trail leads to summit ledges atop Breadloaf Mountain—an optional 1.2-mile roundtrip extension that is worth the extra effort.

Begin the final leg north on the blue-blazed Emily Proctor Trail. At first, this 3.5-mile path drops steadily, and the footing is rough. In 0.9 mile, cross a small stream and begin a more gradual descent along increasingly welcoming terrain. Hike 1.1 miles to a crossing of the New Haven River. Over the final 1.5 miles, the hike is relatively level with a few minor ups and one final drop to the parking area.

Shorter Options: Two shorter adventures to consider are out-and-back treks on either the Cooley Glen or Emily Proctor Trails. The roundtrip hike to Mount Grant is 8 miles, and the journey to Breadloaf Mountain and Mount Wilson is 9.8 miles. Although it begins at a distant trailhead, the 3-mile Clark Brook Trail provides a convenient route to Mount Roosevelt.

41 *Mounts Abraham and Ellen*

Distance: 12.3 miles roundtrip
Difficulty: challenging–strenuous
Hiking time: 9 hours / 2 days
Elevation gain: 4100 feet
High point: 4083 feet

Management: Green Mountain NF
Season: year-round
Map: GMNF website
GPS coordinates: 44.11276°, –72.96361°

Getting there: From the town of Lincoln, drive north 0.6 mile on Quaker Street and then turn right onto Elder Hill Road. Stay right in 1.4 miles, left in 0.6 mile, and arrive at the parking area on the left in 0.1 mile. **Note:** Backcountry campsites available.

Connected along one of Vermont's highest ridgelines, Mounts Abraham, Ellen, and the many less-prominent peaks between them feature exquisite views of three states from multiple scenic perches along the way. While this strenuous hike requires an out-and-back along the same trail, there are options to explore more terrain by continuing north to nearby trailheads to complete a one-way hike if you have the ability to spot cars or arrange a ride (see Other Options). Conversely, turn around at Mount Abraham for a much-shorter but still rewarding trek.

Most hikers who make their way to Mount Abraham begin from Lincoln Gap, the highest

String lining Long Trail protects Mount Abraham's fragile summit vegetation.

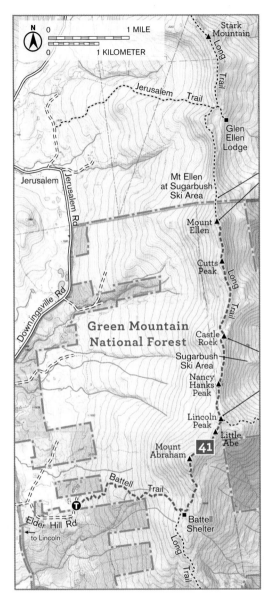

hardwoods and around ledges to start. Beyond the halfway point, the forest abruptly transitions to spruce and fir. Soon after, the route ends at a junction with the Long Trail.

Stay straight and follow the white blazes 0.1 mile to the Battell Shelter, a popular overnight campsite maintained by the Green Mountain Club that is available on a first-come, first-served basis for a small fee. Continuing north, ascend 900 feet over the next 0.8 mile. At first, the trail is straightforward, but soon it becomes steeper and rockier. Carefully scramble up exposed ledges. With ever-increasing scenery, there are numerous spots to catch your breath. The shrinking vegetation gives way to wider views of the Adirondacks, Lake Champlain, and the Green Mountains south to Killington Peak. Eventually reach Abraham's wide-open 4006-foot summit, where scenes extend east to the White Mountains and north to Mount Ellen. Please stay out of the roped-off areas to protect the fragile alpine plants that have been slowly reclaiming the summit after years of trampling.

There are numerous ups and downs on the 3.5-mile journey north along the ridge, but the trail never falls below 3700 feet. The initial 0.7-mile stretch winds gently over Little Abe's windswept forested summit before a short, steep pitch ends on Lincoln Peak. Enjoy panoramic views from a wooden platform and from the open ski slopes descending east.

The Long Trail swings left to reenter the evergreen forest and embarks on a 1.2-mile trek to the Castle Rock Ski Lift. Along the way, a scenic ledge near Nancy Hanks Peak features sweeping views of Mount Washington. Just beyond Castle Rock's wooded top, the path swings right to reach modest views from its namesake ski lift.

Meandering along the moss-covered ridgeline, the path rises to an open vista on Cutts Peak in 1 mile. Plod ahead another 0.6 mile to reach the wooded summit of 4083-foot Mount Ellen. Continue a few more feet to nearby ski slopes, where there are views in most directions, including Camels Hump and Mansfield towering to the north. Retrace your steps from here to complete the hike.

paved road along the Long Trail. The Battell Trail is a great alternative that is also accessible during the winter. Named in honor of Colonel Joseph Battell—a conservationist who donated more than 30,000 acres of mountainous terrain to Vermont, the federal government, and Middlebury College in 1911—the 1.9-mile Battell Trail maintains a steady ascent throughout. Climb a series of short switchbacks through northern

Other Options: If you can leave a second car or arrange a pickup at a different trailhead, continue your hike north on the Long Trail. You can either head down the Jerusalem Trail or remain on the Long Trail to Appalachian Gap. The former is a 10-mile trek, and the latter is a more challenging 11.5-mile adventure that traverses attractive scenery across Stark Mountain. For a shorter half-day adventure, hike 5.8 miles roundtrip to Mount Abraham via the Battell Trail.

42 Spruce Mountain

Distance: 4.4 miles roundtrip
Difficulty: moderate–challenging
Hiking time: 3 hours
Elevation gain: 1200 feet
High point: 3037 feet

Management: Vermont DFPR
Season: year-round (except mud season; see Notes)
Map: Trail Finder website
GPS coordinates: 44.23488°, −72.37795°

Getting there: From Route 2 in downtown Plainfield, head east on Main Street. In 0.5 mile, stay right on East Hill Road. Drive 3.8 miles, then turn left on Spruce Mountain Road. This narrowing dirt road winds 1 mile to a large parking area. **Note:** The trail is closed during mud season, generally mid-April through late May.

Spruce Mountain showcases panoramic views in all directions from its historical summit lookout tower. The pointy peak is the centerpiece of the 642-acre L. R. Jones State Forest, Vermont's

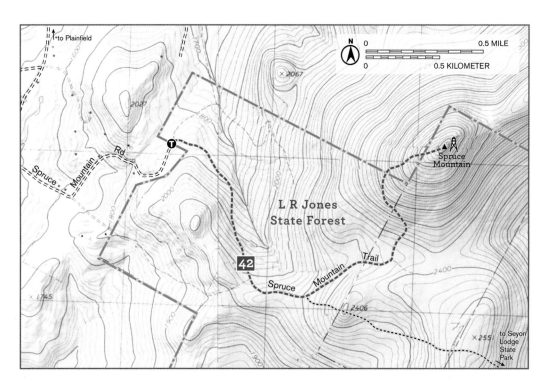

A summit ledge features scenes east toward the White Mountains.

oldest. This family-friendly hike winds through changing forest habitats across land acquired by the state beginning in 1909.

At a large kiosk and gate, the Spruce Mountain Trail begins easily on a wide corridor. Enjoy the modest elevation gain and good footing over the first half of the journey. This is a great section to loosen up and get ready for the more challenging terrain ahead. There is also ample opportunity to admire ferns and wildflowers growing beneath the northern hardwood canopy. The lush surroundings form attractive habitat for songbirds and more-reclusive wildlife.

The trail levels off and arrives at a junction 1 mile from the start. To the right, a more rustic path meanders 3.8 miles to nearby Seyon Lodge State Park. Remain left on the Spruce Mountain Trail. Over the next 0.5 mile, the incline remains gradual, but the trail narrows and grows rougher, especially near the shores of a small marshy wetland.

After swinging left, the path tackles the final 0.7-mile stretch. Take your time, as the footing is uneven in places and an occasional ledge might be slippery. While weaving through the higher elevation, notice the mountain living up to its name. The thin soils provide optimum conditions for spruce, as well as verdant carpets of moss and an occasional birch.

Reach the summit fire tower, where five flights of stairs lead to the cozy cabin and breathtaking views in all directions, including the nearby Hunger Range and the main ridge of the Green Mountains rising farther to the west. Below the tower, an open ledge provides scenes of Groton State Forest and the White Mountains to the east. Retrace your steps 2.2 miles to complete the hike.

Nearby Options: A great companion destination to Spruce Mountain is nearby Groton State Forest, which is home to campgrounds, state parks, and family-friendly hiking trails that ascend small peaks and circle sprawling wetlands. Drive east of Plainfield on Route 2 for 8 miles and then turn right on Route 232 to reach the forest boundary five minutes later.

43 Camels Hump

Distance: 7.6-mile loop
Difficulty: challenging–strenuous
Hiking time: 6 hours
Elevation gain: 2700 feet
High point: 4083 feet

Management: Vermont DFPR
Season: year-round (except mud season; see Notes)
Map: VDFPR website
GPS coordinates: 44.31629°, −72.84957°

Getting there: Take exit 10 from Interstate 89 in Waterbury, and head southwest on Route 100. At the traffic circle, take the second right and head southeast on Route 2. Drive 0.2 mile and then turn right on Winooski Street. In 0.4 mile, bear right onto River Road. Turn left on Camels Hump Road in 4 miles. Drive 3.1 miles to the Camels Hump View parking on the left (winter parking). The road bends right and climbs steeply 0.4 mile to overflow parking and 0.1 mile farther to the main lot. **Notes:** Backcountry campsites available. The trail is closed during mud season, generally mid-April through late May.

This recommended loop to one of Vermont's most popular destinations features pleasant scenes from the mountain's rugged southern ridge, a scramble across the peak's fragile alpine zone, and a brief diversion to escape the crowds. Be sure to check the forecast before heading out to maximize the panoramic rewards atop Vermont's highest undeveloped mountain, as there is little protection from the elements on the often windswept summit.

The journey begins at the former Couching Lion farm site, which got its name from French explorer Samuel de Champlain's description of the mountain. Originally owned by a Professor Monroe, the forested land was donated to Vermont years ago and added to the existing state

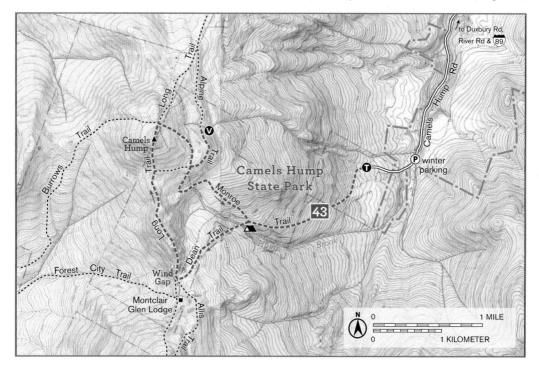

The rocky Camels Hump summit features 360-degree views, including Mount Mansfield to the north.

park, today comprising nearly 24,000 acres. The appropriately named Monroe Trail steadily climbs under beech, birch, and maple to start. In 1.3 miles, reach an intersection.

Stay left on the 1-mile Dean Trail and descend to a bridge leading across Hump Brook. After a spur exits left to a tenting area, a moderate ascent follows and soon reaches a small beaver pond on the right with views of the rugged ridge ahead. The Dean Trail ends 0.3 mile farther at a four-way junction in Wind Gap.

Hike north on the Long Trail and scale the precipitous rocky slope. The route emerges onto open ledges offering spectacular views. In and out of the trees, the climb eases past additional scenic perches. About a mile from the gap, begin a very aggressive ascent to the base of the mountain's sheer southern face. To the right, the Alpine Trail offers a bad-weather option that avoids the summit. It also is home to the eerie remains of a military plane that crashed here in 1944, killing nine of the crew members and severely injuring the tenth.

Head left on the Long Trail and scramble up the uneven terrain to a dramatic vista of Lake Champlain and the Adirondacks. Briefly reenter the forest before resuming the vigorous ascent across the barren landscape. In 0.1 mile, arrive at the 4083-foot summit to breathtaking 360-degree scenery of three states and the province of Quebec. The views north to Mount Mansfield are especially impressive. While enjoying the scenery, avoid the roped-off areas set aside to protect the mountain's fragile alpine plants.

Watch your step on the rugged surface while descending 0.3 mile north on the Long Trail. At a four-way intersection and the former site of a hotel that burned in 1875, turn right to rejoin the

Monroe Trail. The route leads 0.6 mile through the boreal forest to a junction with the Alpine Trail. Head left to check out this lightly used path that winds to a series of viewpoints offering an intriguing perspective of the mountain's summit and expansive scenes to the east. Reach the final vista in 0.3 mile before retracing your steps back to the Monroe Trail.

Turn left and take your time, as the footing is a bit rough over the next 0.4 mile. The trail drops to a crossing of Hump Brook, then briefly parallels it. A more straightforward descent ensues for the next 0.8 mile as the route weaves down the mountain to the Dean Trail junction. Stay straight for the final 1.3 miles.

Other Options: Combine the Monroe and the western section of the Alpine Trail to complete a 6.5-mile journey—best to hike the loop around the summit in a clockwise direction to tackle the steepest section on the ascent. Or, if you can set up two cars or arrange to be picked up at another trailhead, consider a 9.5-mile trek that combines the Monroe Trail with a descent north along the Long Trail to Duxbury Road near the Winooski River. This challenging option is very scenic and much less frequently traveled.

44 *Worcester Range*

Distance: 7.8 miles one-way
Difficulty: challenging–strenuous
Hiking time: 6 hours
Elevation gain: 3050 feet
High point: 3624 feet
Management: Vermont DFPR

Season: year-round (except mud season; see Notes)
Map: Trail Finder website
GPS coordinates: 44.43886°, −72.66779 (Stowe Pinnacle); 44.40253°, −72.67539 (Waterbury Trail)

Mount Hunger's south summit provides spectacular shots of Mount Mansfield.

Getting there: Shuttle drop-off: From the junction of Routes 100 and 108 in Stowe, head north on Route 100 and turn right onto School Street in 0.1 mile. Drive 0.3 mile and veer right on Stowe Hollow Road. In 1.6 miles, stay straight on Upper Hollow Road. Drive 0.6 mile to the Stowe Pinnacle Trail parking area on the left. *Starting point:* To reach the southern trailhead, drive another mile southwest on Upper Hollow Road. Turn left on Stowe Hollow Road and continue 1 mile. Bear left on Waterworks Road. This narrow dirt road is closed in the winter. Reach the Waterbury Trail on the left in 1 mile. *Note:* Portions of this route are closed during mud season, generally mid-April through late May.

By way of a quiet ridge walk along the Skyline Trail, this rigorous 7.8-mile trek visits two of the most popular and picturesque spots on Vermont's rugged Worcester Range: Stowe Pinnacle and Mount Hunger. Beginning and ending at parking areas that are 3 miles apart, the hike is best completed using two cars, but either summit makes for a shorter, enjoyable journey on its own (see Shorter Options).

The Waterbury Trail rises quickly under a canopy of hardwood trees. Swinging through a field of boulders, climb steadily for nearly a mile to the base of a long, tumbling cascade. Cross the stream and catch your breath. The next 1.2 miles involve a steep and relentless 1500-foot ascent over very rocky and uneven terrain.

At the base of the final climb, a trail descends right to White Rock Mountain. While not easy, this is a worthwhile 1.5-mile roundtrip diversion. To reach Mount Hunger, continue straight and scramble up open ledges that afford tremendous views of Vermont's highest elevations. A few dozen steps lead to Mount Hunger's mostly barren south summit, where 360-degree views include New Hampshire's White Mountains, Vermont's Northeast Kingdom, and the Stowe Valley.

The trek continues north 2.3 miles along the Skyline Trail. While the ridge does not have any significant elevation changes, the footing is occasionally rough. Through fern-draped forests, weave between narrow rock clefts and emerge atop occasional scenic ledges. The lightly used trail makes its way around Mount Hunger's wooded northern summit. Drop into a narrow saddle before methodically ascending a rocky, narrowing ridgeline. There are western views near the ridge's unnamed high point before the path drops to a junction.

To the right, the Skyline Trail proceeds 3 miles to Worcester Mountain's open summit. Instead, turn left onto the 1-mile Hogback Trail. After an abrupt descent that includes a wooden staircase, the path levels off. Hike over Hogback Mountain, a small bump on the ridge, and then

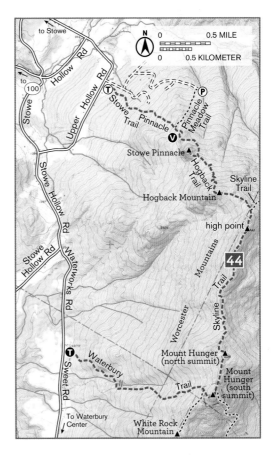

enter an inviting birch forest. Drop steadily 0.5 mile to reach the Stowe Pinnacle Trail.

Bear left and carefully ascend 0.1 mile up the exposed granite through a thinning canopy of evergreens. A final climb crests the rocky pinnacle, where stunning views of Mount Mansfield, Camels Hump, and surrounding peaks await.

To complete the traverse, retrace your steps and stay left on the well-trodden Stowe Pinnacle Trail. The 1.5-mile descent begins easily while wrapping around the peak. Hike across a low sag and swing left. After passing a short spur that leads to a viewpoint, the incline increases significantly. While steep, the path provides solid footing. Stay left at a junction with the Pinnacle Meadow Trail. Maintained by the Stowe Land Trust, Pinnacle Meadow is an alternative access point if the main parking area is full. Continue straight and carefully make your way down the many switchbacks to a grassy field and the trail's end.

Shorter Options: If only one trail interests you, consider the 4.4-mile roundtrip hike to Mount Hunger's south summit (5.9 miles if you add White Rock Mountain) or the 3.4-mile roundtrip trek to Stowe Pinnacle.

45 *Niquette Bay State Park*

Distance: 3.7-mile loop
Difficulty: moderate
Hiking time: 2 hours
Elevation gain: 650 feet
High point: 420 feet

Management: Vermont DFPR
Season: year-round
Map: VDFPR website
GPS coordinates: 44.58956°, −73.18979°

Getting there: From Interstate 89 north of Burlington, take exit 17 and head west on Route 2. Drive 0.9 mile and then exit right toward Raymond Road. Turn left, cross Route 2, and continue 0.2 mile to the park entrance on the left. Proceed 0.1 mile to the gate and then 0.1 mile to the parking area. **Notes:** Entrance fee required. Dogs permitted, but they must be leashed.

A quaint state park only a few miles from Vermont's largest city, Niquette Bay invites hikers to explore its 584 acres on meandering trails that lead to scenic vistas, lakeshore promontories, and a sandy beach. Throughout the nineteenth century, the land was cleared for pastures, but today the park's fertile soils sustain dense forests that shade carpets of wildflowers while attracting thrushes, warblers, and other resident songbirds.

Find the trailhead at the southern edge of the parking area. Enter the forest and immediately reach a four-way intersection. Turn left onto the aptly named Ledges Trail. This 0.9-mile path snakes its way around moss-covered rocks to the top of a forested ridge. Near the halfway point, arrive at the Bay View Vista and enjoy distant views of Lake Champlain through a narrow gap in the trees. Descending quickly, the trail approaches the shoreline and crosses a marshy wetland. Rise atop a pine-covered mound and proceed 0.2 mile to a junction with the Allen Trail.

Stay left and head over a short bridge that crosses Trout Brook. To the left, a spur leads a few dozen feet to a sandy beach on the shores of Lake Champlain. It is the perfect place for a midday picnic or to cool off on a hot summer day.

Beyond the spur, the 0.3-mile Beach Bypass climbs steeply away from the water. Fortunately, the incline is short. Level off and enjoy a relaxing stretch before turning left onto the Burns Trail. Hike south 0.1 mile to a three-way intersection with the Muhley Trail. Stay straight to explore the 0.3-mile Cedar Point Loop. Follow this route

This Lake Champlain beach is a perfect rest stop.

as it circles up and around a scenic peninsula. From atop rocky bluffs, enjoy excellent views of Camels Hump rising above the sprawling lake's distant shore. Near the start of the loop, a short path diverges west to secluded Calm Cove.

Upon looping back to the Muhley Trail, bear left. This 1.3-mile route gradually ascends wooded slopes past rocks and fallen trees. In 0.7 mile, stay left on the Island View Trail. Leading to a bench and scenes of Lake Champlain, this 0.4-mile spur climbs to and then loops over the hike's high point. Return to the Muhley Trail and then descend southeast to the appropriately named Mount Mansfield Vista. The path drops quickly but eases atop a plateau. Parallel Trout Brook's slow-moving waters from above.

After descending toward the running water, swing right onto a wide path that rises gradually 0.2 mile to a signed three-way junction. Turn left on the Burns Trail and drop quickly to a bridge that leads across Trout Brook. A long staircase rises out of the valley to an intersection. Remain on the Burns Trail as it continues left. The final 0.3-mile stretch is easy and a great way to complete this pleasant trek near the shores of Lake Champlain.

Options: The 0.5-mile Allen Trail is the shortest route to the water. This path and the parallel Burns Trail can be used as alternatives for completing shorter loops within the park.

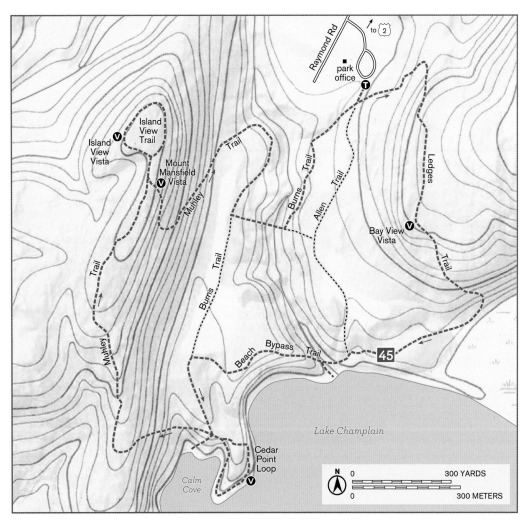

46 *Mount Mansfield*

Distance: 6-mile loop
Difficulty: challenging–strenuous
Hiking time: 5 hours
Elevation gain: 2600 feet
High point: 4393 feet

Management: Vermont DFPR
Season: year-round (except mud season; see Notes)
Map: VDFPR website
GPS coordinates: 44.52923°, −72.84289°

Getting there: From Route 15 in Underhill, follow River Road east 2.5 miles into Underhill Center. Continue straight on Pleasant Valley Road an additional mile and turn right onto Mountain Road. This road dead-ends in 2.7 miles at Underhill State Park. While the park is accessible in the winter, the road may not be plowed the entire 2.7 miles. **Note:** The trail is closed during mud season, generally mid-April through late May.

The Green Mountain State's highest peak boasts Vermont's longest and most scenic high-elevation alpine ridgeline as it meanders more than a mile with 360-degree views throughout. A rewarding outdoor adventure whenever the weather cooperates, hike Mansfield early morning, midweek, or off-season to avoid crowds, which include folks arriving via gondola and the mountain's auto road.

Traditionally, the hike from Underhill State Park began on the Civilian Conservation Corps (CCC) Road. The more direct Eagles Cut Trail offers a shorter, straighter alternative to start. Beyond a gate and kiosk, pick up this route in the parking area. The path climbs steadily 0.3 mile. Turn left and take the CCC Road an additional 0.3 mile to reach a junction with the Sunset Ridge Trail.

Turn right and hike 0.2 mile along the CCC Road to the start of the Halfway House Trail on the left. This 1.1-mile route begins modestly, but soon the terrain becomes steeper and the footing more challenging. Scramble past interesting rock formations, weave up the rugged landscape, and pass an occasional vista before arriving at a cairn atop the ridge.

Catch your breath and then head north along the Long Trail. This scenic path remains above tree line throughout. While the footing is occasionally rough, the scenery is spectacular. Keep in mind that the exposed ridge is not recommended during lightning storms or other severe weather. For the more adventurous, the Subway and Canyon North Trails drop west off the main ridge, allowing for exploration of caves and ledges before returning to the main trail. These challenging alternatives are a good way to find solitude.

Hike over the Upper and Lower Lips, two of the ridge's facial-like features, which from a distance—and with imagination—resemble parts of a human head. Upon reaching an intersection

Mount Mansfield's Chin, the state's highest point, rises to the north.

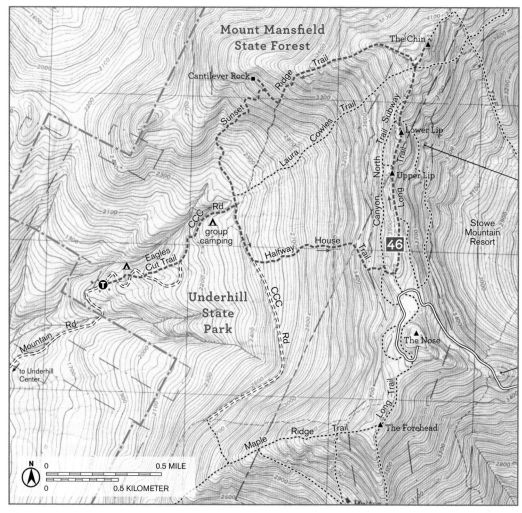

with the Sunset Ridge Trail, proceed straight 0.2 mile to the top of Mount Mansfield's Chin. From this barren 4393-foot pinnacle, Vermont's highest point, enjoy views from Quebec to Killington and Mount Marcy to Mount Washington. While taking in the splendor, watch your step—a carpet of fragile alpine plants is reclaiming large portions of the summit area. This vegetation does not recover easily from hiking boots or paws.

Return to the Sunset Ridge Trail and turn right to quickly reach a junction with the Laura Cowles Trail. Swing north under the summit ledges to reach the top of Sunset Ridge. Descending the mostly open expanse of rock, the trail provides spectacular scenes of Lake Champlain and the Adirondacks. Take your time; although steep, this is the easiest route to descend the mountain. Soon drop into the forest, where a spur exits right 0.2 mile to Cantilever Rock, an interesting geologic formation jutting from the adjoining ledge. Continue another 0.7 mile to rejoin the CCC Road for the final 0.6 mile stretch to the parking area.

Other Options: This trailhead's added advantage is its many options. For a shorter 5.8-mile circuit, use the Sunset Ridge and Laura Cowles Trail. A more challenging and longer choice would be the 8-mile loop ascending the Maple Ridge Trail and heading down Sunset Ridge.

47 Laraway Mountain

Distance: 4.8 miles roundtrip
Difficulty: moderate
Hiking time: 3 hours
Elevation gain: 1675 feet
High point: 2790 feet

Management: Vermont DFPR
Season: year-round
Map: Trail Finder website
GPS coordinates: 44.70843°, −72.71346°

Laraway Mountain's cliffs tower above the Long Trail.

Getting there: From the US Post Office on Route 109 in Waterville, drive north 1.1 miles. Turn right on Codding Hollow Road, cross a covered bridge, and continue east. Stay left at the intersection in 1.3 miles, and arrive at a parking area on the right in 0.9 mile.

Laraway Mountain's towering cliffs and summit-area ledges provide the perfect culmination to a delightful hike along Vermont's storied Long Trail. While one should not underestimate the effort needed to scale this relatively diminutive peak, this half-day adventure invites families and hikers of all ages to revel in many rewards along the way.

From the parking area, head 0.1 mile east along Codding Hollow Road. After crossing Codding Brook, the Long Trail departs south. Stay straight and quickly arrive at a large field. Turn left and head through the opening that provides overflow parking for the hike. At a sign pointing north, the Long Trail rises modestly 0.5 mile along an old road, paralleling and crossing the running water. Near a bend in the trail, a small cascade on the right carves through the rocky landscape.

Leave the brook behind and head up the forested ridgeline. The path winds through the hardwood forest, rising aggressively 0.8 mile. Follow the white-blazed trail as it briefly levels off and swings left. The climb begins in earnest again as the forest shifts to evergreens and the landscape grows more rugged. Over the next 0.3 mile, watch your step and admire the series of towering cliffs rising above. Carpets of bunchberry and other wildflowers add color and texture below the immense ledges as tiny streams of water shower down.

A final scramble leads through spruce and fir to Laraway Lookout, an open promontory with expansive 180-degree views. The scene of Mount Mansfield towering to the south is especially photogenic, and the distant Adirondack peaks rising above Lake Champlain's shores provide an attractive backdrop. This is an ideal location to welcome the sun's rays and enjoy a picnic lunch.

While a bit anticlimactic, continue another 0.4 mile northeast along the Long Trail. Across the undulating moss-covered terrain, the narrow path eventually rises abruptly to Laraway Mountain's 2790-foot summit. A small sign awaits, as well as more limited views through the thick forest canopy. Turn around here and retrace your steps 2.4 miles to the start.

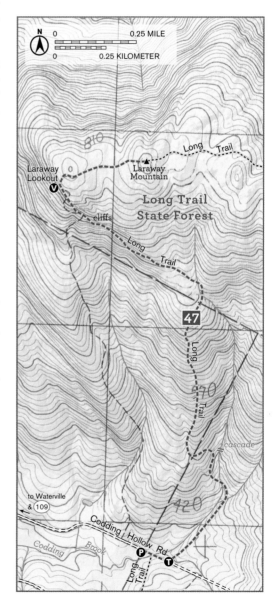

48 Belvidere Mountain

Distance: 5.2 miles roundtrip
Difficulty: challenging
Hiking time: 3 hours
Elevation gain: 2100 feet
High point: 3360 feet

Management: Vermont DFPR
Season: year-round (except mud season; see Notes)
Map: Trail Finder website
GPS coordinates: 44.76392°, −72.58789°

Getting there: From the junction of Routes 118 and 100 in Eden, follow Route 118 north. Drive 4.7 miles and turn right into the Eden Crossing parking area. **Note:** The trail is closed during mud season, generally mid-April through late May.

While not among Vermont's highest peaks, Belvidere Mountain towers over most of its neighbors, providing sweeping views of the Northeast Kingdom and summits along the Long Trail from Jay Peak to Camels Hump. This half-day trek will make you work, but the panoramic scenery from atop the fire tower's lofty heights pays worthy dividends.

The summit fire tower's stairs lead to a breathtaking panorama.

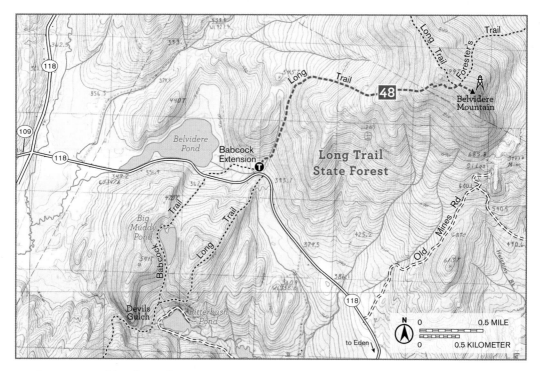

The Long Trail heads north near a sign and private gated road. Stay left of the gate and quickly ascend a low ridge, only to drop briefly to a stream crossing at 0.2 mile. Following an old woods road, the trail parallels the small stream 0.5 mile, rising at a modest grade. Moving away from the water, the white-blazed route swings right and climbs more aggressively through the northern hardwood forest. Over the next mile or so, ascend a series of steep pitches, interspersed with more-moderate inclines. Throughout, the footing is generally forgiving and easy to navigate.

As the surrounding forest transitions to conifers, the terrain becomes wetter and rougher. Watch your step across the uneven surfaces. The trail skirts beneath small ledges and levels off before arriving at a four-way intersection, 2.4 miles from the start. The Long Trail continues left and the Forester's Trail straight—both lead to distant parking areas.

Turn sharply right to reach the day's destination. The narrow path winds 0.2 mile up through an evergreen tunnel before reaching the base of the summit tower. Scale a couple of flights of stairs to get above the forest canopy and be greeted with 360-degree views, including peaks, valleys, and water bodies in three states, as well as the province of Quebec. Not eager to climb the tower? A small ledge offers fine views of Jay Peak to the north, and a larger perch features expansive scenes of Mount Washington and surrounding White Mountain peaks. Retrace your steps 2.6 miles to return to the start.

Other Options: If you are looking to extend your adventure or the day is more overcast than desired, explore the 4.8-mile loop that heads south from the same parking lot. Combine the Long Trail, Babcock Trail, and Babcock Extension to explore wildlife-rich forests, serene wetlands, and the diminutive rock chasm known as Devils Gulch.

49 *Mount Pisgah*

Distance: 4.6 miles roundtrip
Difficulty: moderate–challenging
Hiking time: 3 hours
Elevation gain: 1615 feet
High point: 2751 feet

Management: Vermont DFPR
Season: year-round (except mud season; see Notes)
Map: Trail Finder website
GPS coordinates: 44.74623°, −72.04967°

Getting there: From the junction of Routes 5 and 5A in West Burke, follow Route 5A north 8.5 miles to the trailhead and pull-off on the right. Park parallel to the road. *Note:* The trail is closed during mud season, generally mid-April through late May.

At precarious heights appreciated more often by resident peregrine falcons, Mount Pisgah's heart-stopping summit vistas offer immense rewards for those able to overcome the fear of standing on the edge of precipitous clifftop perches. Enjoy scenes of Vermont's Northeast Kingdom and points beyond from the peak's ledge-scarred slopes that rise 1500 feet above the long, narrow expanse of Lake Willoughby, Vermont's deepest water body.

At a welcome sign to the Pisgah North Trail, rise rapidly from the pavement to a large kiosk and map. Over the next 0.8 mile, the wide route traverses two small streams while gently making its way to a slightly larger one. Swing left, follow the running water up the valley, and then cross it in 0.1 mile.

Ascending more steadily, the trail enters a series of switchbacks. Weave through the northern hardwood forest to an intersection with the Long Pond Trail, 1.5 miles from the start. This is a great place to catch your breath and fuel up. Although not long, the next 0.3-mile climb will get the blood flowing, especially early on. Up rock steps, hike through the shady evergreen forest.

The incline moderates before reaching the first of three spurs over the final 0.3 mile. All three lead right to must-see viewpoints, each offering differing angles and perspectives. The 0.1-mile northernmost spur is the longest. It drops to two vantage points: The lower one leads left to the edge of the cliff—watch your step! From the higher and safer outcrop, enjoy more-expansive views to distant Green Mountain summits and

Quebec's Eastern Township. The middle spur is a short diversion to the west overlook, offering

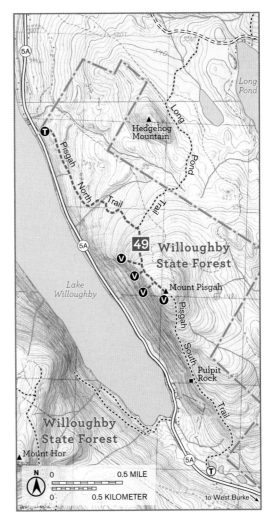

Three summit vistas stand high above Lake Willoughby.

intimate scenes of Lake Willoughby and Mount Hor. Follow the southernmost spur a few hundred feet to a small promontory with equally stunning scenes.

Beyond the final vista, hike over the wooded 2751-foot high point to the start of the Pisgah South Trail, which immediately leads to an open ledge. The least precarious seat on the journey, this viewpoint showcases sweeping shots south to Mount Burke and the White Mountains beyond. Retrace your steps north to complete the hike.

Extend Your Trip: As an alternative 6.9-mile loop, if you do not mind walking along a paved road for 3 miles, continue 1.8 miles along the Pisgah South Trail to its beginning on Route 5A. This inviting route includes a stop at Pulpit Rock, another Mount Pisgah vista.

50 Jay Peak

Distance: 3.4 miles roundtrip
Difficulty: challenging
Hiking time: 3 hours
Elevation gain: 1700 feet
High point: 3858 feet

Management: Vermont DFPR
Season: year-round (except mud season; see Notes)
Map: Trail Finder website
GPS coordinates: 44.91289°, −72.50402°

Getting there: From the junction of Routes 242 and 101 in Troy, follow Route 242 west 6.4 miles to the height of land. Parking is on the left side of the road. **Notes:** Backcountry campsite available. The trail is closed during mud season, generally mid-April through late May.

Named for the nation's first Supreme Court chief justice and the lawyer who paved the way for Vermont's statehood in 1791, Jay Peak rises prominently just south of the state's border with Quebec. This short but challenging jaunt rewards hikers who scale the mountain's prominent rocky pinnacle with breathtaking scenery in all directions.

Carefully cross to the road's north side and join the Long Trail as it enters the forest. In 0.1 mile arrive at the lower branch of the Jay Loop. Descending left, this blue-blazed path leads 0.2 mile to Jay Camp, a small structure available for overnight use. Remain on the Long Trail as it swings right and climbs to the upper branch of the Jay Loop in 0.2 mile. Beyond, the path rises steadily up the slope. While somewhat demanding, the footing is forgiving. Weaving through a forest dominated by birch, beech, and maple, the understory is carpeted with wildflowers and comes alive with a chorus of warbling songbirds.

Just beyond the halfway point, the Long Trail rises into a saddle on the ridge while carving through a dense patch of ferns shaded by conifers. Straight ahead lies the mountain's ski area, somewhat visible through the dense vegetation. Follow the white-blazed trail left as it parallels the alpine ski slope.

Climbing more steeply, take your time on the increasingly rocky terrain. The trail leads up stone steps and over exposed granite, occasionally offering glimpses of distant peaks and ridges. Eventually, the hard work leads to the edge of a ski trail. Use caution crossing over the snowmaking equipment and emerge onto the grassy corridor.

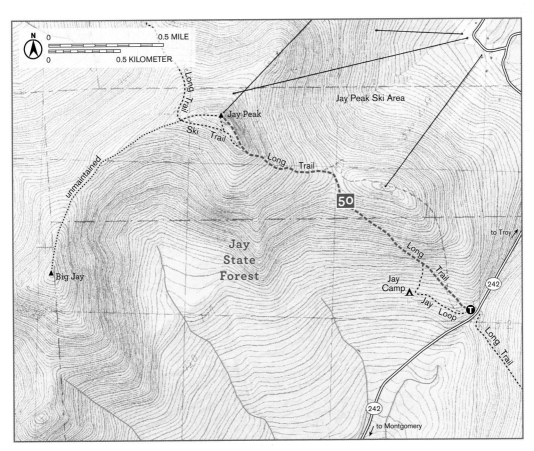

View of Big Jay, which is lower but wider than Jay Peak.

Pick up the Long Trail on the far side to tackle the final 0.2-mile stretch to the summit. A short scramble leads rapidly to an open ridgeline with views stretching in all directions: south along the Green Mountains to Mount Mansfield, east to Mount Washington and the White Mountains, north across Lake Memphremagog and the peaks of southern Quebec, and west over Lake Champlain to Mount Whiteface's pinnacle silhouette. The incline eases as the final steps lead to the barren high point perched above the summit lodge and tramway station.

Retrace your steps to return 1.7 miles to the parking area. For an easier start to the descent, follow the ski trail that parallels the Long Trail. Hike 0.2 mile and be careful not to miss the trail intersection. Turn right to rejoin the route down the mountain.

Extend Your Trip: If you are looking for a longer 5.6-mile adventure and have a good sense of direction, consider a journey across an unmarked herd path to Big Jay. To find it, follow the Long Trail north as it heads west from the high point. Make your way 0.2 mile down a ski slope and reenter the forest near a wooden barrier. Soon after, the unmarked 0.9-mile route exits left. While it is not blazed or maintained, the tread is obvious in most places (although less so at the very beginning). It follows the ridgeline into a saddle and then climbs to scenic ledges. Upon reaching the wooded summit, retrace your steps back to Jay Peak.

Opposite, top: Steep granite ledges on South Baldface

Opposite, bottom: Looking south from Mount Jackson's snowy summit

New Hampshire: The Granite State

New Hampshire is home to the region's premier hiking destination, the White Mountains, with more than 800,000 acres of conserved land and over 1200 miles of diverse hiking trails that attract visitors of all ages twelve months a year. Farther south, scattered across century-old state parks and a growing collection of land trust preserves, the Granite State features short nature walks, challenging rocky peaks, and everything in between.

The state has a proud hiking tradition that began in 1642, when Darby Field was the first to scale New England's highest mountain. This pastime has flourished as the Appalachian Mountain Club and others have continued to enhance outdoor recreational opportunities. New Hampshire features four-season hiking opportunities for all abilities.

51 *Pawtuckaway State Park*

Distance: 9-mile loop
Difficulty: moderate–challenging
Hiking time: 7 hours
Elevation gain: 1800 feet
High point: 1011 feet

Management: New Hampshire SP
Season: year-round
Map: NHSP website
GPS coordinates: 43.10510°, −71.20497°

Getting there: From the southern junction of Routes 43 and 107 in Deerfield, follow Route 107 southeast. Drive 0.7 mile and turn left onto Reservation Road. The road swings right in 1.2 miles. Continue 0.6 mile to the trailhead. Parking is on the left. Space is limited; securing advanced reservations through the state park website is recommended.

Located in a rapidly developing corner of New Hampshire, Pawtuckaway State Park is a vast 5500-acre expanse of conservation land featuring a high concentration of rare species and exemplary natural communities. This ambitious 9-mile circuit visits the park's three principal summits. Together they comprise the remains of an ancient volcano. Along the journey, enjoy attractive forest surroundings, intriguing geologic formations, and diverse wildlife-rich wetland habitats.

Follow the wide path north from the parking area. Beyond a large foundation, the North Mountain Trail meanders 0.5 mile to a junction, where the North Mountain Bypass heads east. Proceed straight up the steep slope, occasionally over ledges with limited southern vistas. The trail eases atop the ridge, reaching the North Mountain summit in 1 mile. Trees obscure any views, so drop 0.3 mile to a bluff showcasing scenes north and east. Over the next 0.6 mile, wind down the steep hillside between boulders and exposed granite. At the base of a second drop, a secluded pond awaits. Continue another 0.4 mile to a junction surrounded by massive rocks and ledges frequented by rock climbers.

Follow the aptly named Boulder Trail left. The mostly flat route proceeds 0.5 mile, never straying far from the abutting wetland. Use caution crossing the uneven surface beneath the overhanging rock near the halfway point, and enjoy views from a high perch near the pond's outlet. Shortly after crossing a small stream, reach Round Pond Road.

Walk left down the dirt road and immediately spot the South Ridge Trail on the edge of the water body. Rising more than 500 feet in a mile, this white-blazed route starts easily along the sprawling wetland before scaling switchbacks. Stay straight at a junction with the Shaw Trail and left where the South Ridge Connector departs right. The challenging ascent weaves across a ledge-covered landscape to South Mountain's 908-foot summit. Check out the peak's fire tower for 360-degree views, or visit a nearby bluff to the west that offers more-limited scenery.

Near the base of the metal structure, descend the 0.4-mile Tower Trail. It wastes little time losing elevation, but the loose footing is forgiving. While it begins on an old jeep road, the route exits right onto a more rustic track before ending at a parking lot.

Venture straight on the dirt road 0.1 mile. Just past a large black walnut tree and the cemetery that serves as the resting place for the family who donated much of the park, find the 1-mile Middle Mountain Trail heading right. This less-traveled way climbs gradually, passes over the wooded high point, and then drops to a semi-open ledge with pleasant views of South Mountain and the Monadnock Region.

Head back to the base of the Tower Trail and turn right onto the Mountain Trail. It skirts a forested wetland before rising to a junction in 0.6 mile. Turn right to quickly access Tower Road. Watch for cars as you follow this corridor left 0.1 mile to an intersection with Reservation Road. Straight ahead a multiuse route ascends steadily 0.2 mile. At an intersection with the Round Pond Trail, bear right on the North Mountain Trail, which weaves 0.7 mile over mostly level terrain to complete the circuit.

Boulder Trail wraps around a large, forested wetland.

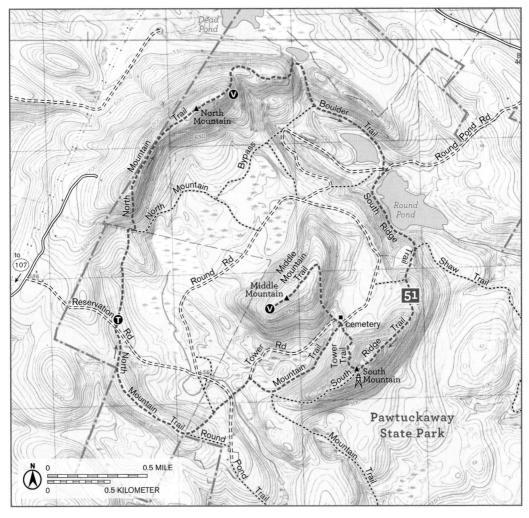

Shorter Options: If you are looking for a less ambitious trek, consider a 5-mile loop using the North Mountain, Boulder, and North Mountain Bypass Trails. Alternatively, park at the start of the Tower Trail, where numerous paths offer opportunities for even shorter loops on South Mountain.

52 *Harris Center*

Distance: 4.6-mile loop
Difficulty: moderate
Hiking time: 3 hours
Elevation gain: 925 feet
High point: 1998 feet

Management: Harris Center for Conservation Education
Season: year-round
Map: Harris Center website
GPS coordinates: 42.97831°, −72.02066°

Getting there: From Route 123 near the town offices in Hancock, head west on Old Dublin Road. Drive 1.4 miles and stay right on Kings Highway. Continue 0.6 mile and turn right into the Harris Center entrance. Parking is available near the Harris Center building. *Note:* Dogs must be leashed and waste carried out.

Connecting people to the natural world through land protection, education, conservation research, and programs that encourage active participation in the great outdoors, the Harris Center for Conservation Education has protected more than 24,000 acres in New Hampshire's Monadnock Region. The center's signature hike is this moderate loop that begins at their headquarters, winds through inviting forests, passes secluded wetlands, and visits two mountaintop vistas.

From the parking area, the Harriskat Trail drops down the hill, crosses the Kings Highway, and enters the forest near one of the property's many bobcat-logo signs. After a brief climb, the initial 0.5-mile stretch traverses relatively flat terrain. Proceed through the white pine and mixed hardwood forest while scanning the surrounding habitat for wildlife—real-life examples as well as a handful of exquisite wood carvings inspired by resident species (with one fantastical exception). Past boulders and vernal pools, the path reaches the start of the loop.

Stay left on the Harriskat Trail and begin weaving up the mountain slope. The white-blazed route rises 1.1 miles at a gentle but steady grade. Hike over and parallel a few stone walls that are reminiscent of a time when the present-day forested landscape was dominated by pasture. Today, the maturing trees welcome woodpeckers and nuthatches searching for insects and cavity nest sites. As you approach the 1998-foot summit of Skatutakee Mountain, the terrain becomes rockier and the soils shallower. Emerge atop

Discover elaborate wood carvings along Harriskat Trail.

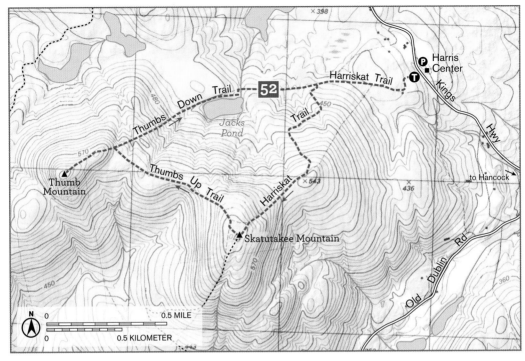

the semi-open summit to enjoy views of Pack Monadnock to the south and Mount Monadnock, its larger neighbor towering to the west.

From the summit's three-way intersection, venture north on the Thumbs Up Trail as it descends the moss-filled evergreen forest. The 0.9-mile hike along the ridge quickly levels off and gently makes its way past mushrooms, ferns, and small boulders to the base of Thumb Mountain. At a junction, turn sharply left to tackle the short scramble up the hillside. The 0.2-mile spur heads over the 1986-foot high point before ending at an open ledge with the day's finest view

of Mount Monadnock, the region's most iconic natural feature.

Retrace your steps and stay left on the Thumbs Down Trail. It drops steadily and in 0.6 mile arrives at Jacks Pond. Tucked away, this quiet locale is the perfect venue to scan for songbirds and waterfowl. The route swings left and then veers right in 0.1 mile. Cross the pond's outlet stream and hike 0.2 mile along an old road. Stay on the yellow-blazed trail as it bears right onto a narrower corridor and climbs gently another 0.2 mile. Retrace your steps along the Harriskat Trail to complete the journey.

53 North Pack Monadnock

Distance: 5.6-mile loop
Difficulty: moderate–challenging
Hiking time: 4 hours
Elevation gain: 1375 feet
High point: 2276 feet

Management: Wapack NWR
Season: year-round
Map: Trail Finder website
GPS coordinates: 42.90781°, −71.85093°

Getting there: From the junction of Routes 101 and 31 in Wilton, follow Route 31 north. Drive 0.4 mile and turn sharply left in downtown Wilton to stay on Route 31. Proceed another 5.9 miles, then turn left onto Gulf Road. In 1.4 miles, stay left on Mountain Road. Continue 0.5 mile to a parking area on the right. ***Note:*** Hike begins on private land.

North Pack Monadnock, the centerpiece of the 1672-acre Wapack National Wildlife Refuge, features sweeping views from many ledges and one exceptional clifftop perch. The refuge was established in 1972 to protect habitat for upland wildlife species as well as a broad diversity of migratory raptors and songbirds. This moderate loop offers opportunities to spot resident fauna while exploring changing habitats, cascading streams, and moss-draped forests.

The trail begins on private land on the road's south side. Follow the yellow-blazed path as it meanders 0.1 mile to a bridge that crosses a quaint brook. Hike 0.4 mile farther to a junction and the start of the loop.

Bear left onto Teds Trail. Rising gently under a canopy of tall pines and mixed hardwoods, the path reaches a sign welcoming you to the wildlife refuge and in 0.5 mile arrives at the edge of a small stream that cascades down exposed rock. Carefully cross the water to a trail junction. Departing right, a connector leads to Carolyns Trail. Turn sharply left and follow the path upstream as it briefly reenters private land before returning to the refuge.

Over the next mile, the hike parallels the running water and encounters numerous stone walls while becoming progressively more challenging. The mostly deciduous forest slowly transitions to conifer as the soils grow thinner. Follow the main route carefully. During the final stretch, pass two connector trails that exit right as the main route winds over a series of semi-open ledges with bucolic views to the east.

At an intersection with the Cliff Trail, turn right and immediately arrive at a short spur that rises atop the hike's most scenic promontory. From this impressive rock face, enjoy breathtaking 180-degree views that include the Boston skyline and Mount Monadnock. Weaving across ledge and through spruce forests, the Cliff Trail continues 0.4 mile to the top of Carolyns Trail

and then proceeds 0.1 mile to the high point. A large cairn and a junction with the Wapack Trail await. There are modest western views visible over the growing evergreen forest, including scenes of Vermont's Green Mountains.

Retrace your steps 0.1 mile east along the Cliff Trail, and turn left onto Carolyns Trail. The hike down is less circuitous than the ascent.

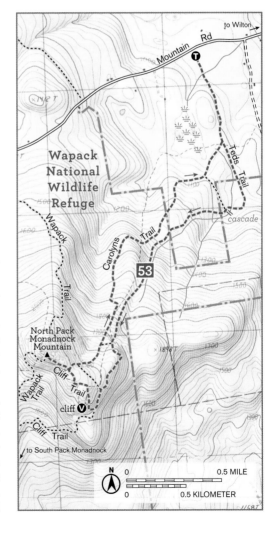

The Cliff Trail's signature natural feature

Initially in the open, there are delightful scenes across rolling hills stretching north toward the state's capital. Watch your step as you reenter the forest. The route wastes little time descending, and the footing is rough in places, but the incline and terrain grow more inviting about halfway down. After exiting the wildlife refuge and passing a marshy wetland on the left, the loop ends. Continue 0.5 mile to reach the trailhead.

Extend Your Trip: A great option for a longer excursion is to follow the Wapack Trail south from the North Pack summit. The well-marked route meanders 2.3 miles across a pleasant ridge to the top of South Pack Monadnock, where views can be found from various ledges and the summit tower. Retrace your steps back to North Pack or use the Cliff Trail to reach the top of Carolyns Trail.

54 *Mount Monadnock*

Distance: 5.8-mile loop
Difficulty: challenging
Hiking time: 4 hours
Elevation gain: 1900 feet
High point: 3165 feet

Management: New Hampshire SP
Season: year-round
Map: NHSP website
GPS coordinates: 42.84485°, −72.08739°

Getting there: From the junction of Routes 202 and 124 in Jaffrey, drive west on Route 124. In 2.1 miles, turn right onto Dublin Road. Continue 1.3 miles and then bear left onto Poole Road. Proceed for 0.7 mile to the parking area entrance. Space is limited; securing advanced reservations through the state park website is recommended. **Note:** Entrance fee required. Dogs prohibited.

Mount Monadnock is the centerpiece of a 3500-acre Society for the Protection of New Hampshire Forests (SPNHF) reservation that began in 1915. Although still owned by SPNHF, the conservation area is managed as a state park through a lease. The mountain's elevation and barren summit, which was torched by over-zealous wolf hunters in the nineteenth century, provide some of the finest views in New England.

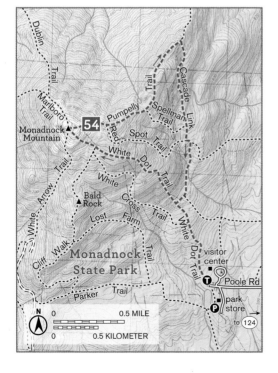

Amid a vast trail network on one of the world's most hiked mountains, this recommended loop combines Monadnock's most popular route with a couple of less-traveled paths.

Look for the park store on the edge of the main parking area. Here, stone steps lead to the trailhead. Follow the well-trodden White Dot Trail, which quickly reaches a visitor center with information on the area's cultural and natural history. Beyond, the wide path rises gradually 0.5 mile to a junction with the White Cross Trail.

Continuing straight, the White Dot Trail ascends 0.2 mile to an intersection with the Cascade Link to the right. Although the footing is uneven in places, the hike to this point is straightforward. That is about to change. Over the next 0.6 mile, take your time scrambling up granite ledges and steep slopes along the White Dot Trail. Gaps in the forest soon appear and then slowly expand. The views grow more impressive as the well-marked route levels off. Meander 0.3 mile across a mostly barren landscape to the upper terminus of the White Cross Trail.

This is a good place to turn around should the weather dictate or if conditions warrant. (Note: Monadnock is prone to icy conditions from late fall to early spring.) Otherwise, after a brief descent, the White Dot Trail scales 0.3 mile up a final steep pitch to the summit. Once on the treeless high point, there are breathtaking views in all directions. Monadnock is an Abenaki word meaning "mountain that stands alone," a trait that provides unobstructed vistas east to

The Pumpelly Trail begins near a small pond below the high point.

Boston's skyline, north to the White Mountains, and west to Vermont's Green Mountains.

When it is time to leave the crowds, look for a *P* painted on the rocks near a couple of small tarns east of the summit. This is the start of the Pumpelly Trail. Follow this scenic route 1.5 miles as it winds northeast along the mostly exposed ridgeline. There are minor ups and an occasional steep descent, but the footing is generally easy to navigate. Be sure to look back at the summit pinnacle as the perspective changes. At the third well-signed trail junction, turn right onto the Cascade Link (continuing beyond this junction leads to a distant trailhead).

Despite its name, the 1.4-mile Cascade Link is mostly dry. Watch your footing early on while navigating ledges that feature scenes east to the Wapack Trail. After a steep descent, the orange-blazed trail encounters three intersections. Stay straight at the first, bear left at the second, and then swing right at the third. The final 0.5 mile is mostly flat but rocky. Upon reaching the White Dot Trail, turn left and hike 0.7 mile back to the trailhead.

Shorter Options: There are many ways to adjust this hike. Most visitors head up the White Dot and descend the White Cross to complete a 3.8-mile loop. For a less-frequented 4.6-mile circuit, scramble up the Spellman Trail from the Cascade Link and follow the Pumpelly Trail to the summit, and then head down the Pumpelly/Red Spot Trails.

Society for the Protection of New Hampshire Forests

Founded in 1901, Society for the Protection of New Hampshire Forests (a.k.a. the Forest Society) has been focused on conserving New Hampshire's most important landscapes for more than a century—iconic places like the White Mountain National Forest, Mount Monadnock, and Mount Major. Today, this membership-based land trust manages nearly two hundred forest reservations in the state, many crisscrossed with hiking trails.

55 *Belknap Range Trail*

Distance: 12.9 miles one-way
Difficulty: challenging–strenuous
Hiking time: 8–9 hours
Elevation gain: 3800 feet
High point: 2382 feet
Management: Belknap Range

Conservation Coalition (BRCC), NH
Division of Forests and Lands
Season: year-round
Map: BRCC website
GPS coordinates: 43.54118°,
−71.36371°; 43.51933°, −71.27316°

Getting there: Shuttle drop-off: From Route 3 in Gilford, take the Route 11A exit and head east. Drive 5.6 miles and turn right onto Panorama Drive. Continue 0.7 mile to Gunstock Ski Area and park near the pond. *Starting point:* Return to Route 11A and turn right. Drive 4.4 miles and then bear right onto Route 11. Proceed 2.4 miles to the Mount Major parking area on the right (overflow parking is prohibited on the road's east side). *Notes:* Mount Major is one of the state's most popular hikes, so visit midweek to avoid the crowds. The route crosses public and private lands.

In 2008, land trusts, municipalities, and sportspeople joined together to accelerate conservation efforts across the Belknap Mountain Range. This coalition partnered with the state to expand the mosaic of public and private lands available for hikers and other outdoor enthusiasts on this prominent ridge of scenic mountains in New Hampshire's Lakes Region. Experience the conservation work firsthand by completing this one-way journey along the Belknap Range Trail, a challenging trek to mountaintop vistas, secluded wetlands, and rock-filled forests.

The Belknap Range Trail (BRT) coincides with numerous paths and encounters many intersections. While the BRT employs uniform arrowhead markers in places, mostly in proximity to trail junctions, the route does not use the

Belknap Mountain's Boulder Trail rises across scenic open ledges.

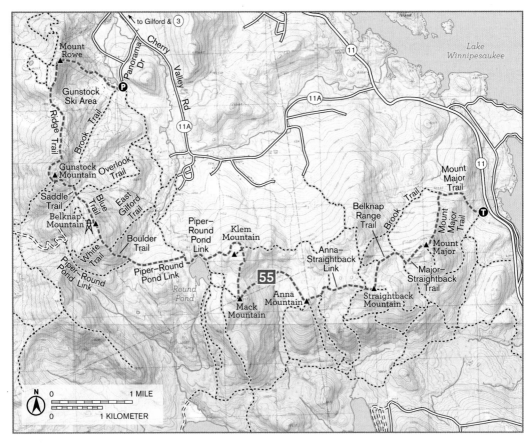

same-colored blaze throughout. Take your time at each junction; it is not difficult to navigate.

Begin on the 1.5-mile Mount Major Trail, which is extremely popular, especially on weekends. Rough in places, stay left as the blue-blazed route intersects the Brook Trail near its halfway point. The incline becomes steeper with elevation. Carefully, scramble up granite ledges to expanding views and reach the wide-open summit, where breathtaking scenery awaits. Panoramic shots of Lake Winnipesaukee's sprawling blue waters, islands, and bays are especially enticing.

The BRT joins the 1.2-mile Major-Straightback Trail. This blue-blazed route descends semi-open terrain before rising to Straightback Mountain's rocky 1890-foot summit. Continue west along the 1.2-mile Anna-Straightback Link. Still blazed in blue, the BRT meanders over scenic ledges,

skirts forested wetlands, scales rocky hillsides, and enters the 3270-acre Hidden Valley Camp, a popular Boy Scouts of America destination that is open to the public with easy-to-follow guidelines outlined on the property's boundary.

At Anna Mountain's forested high point, turn sharply right. Now marked in red, the BRT drops briefly before ascending Mack Mountain's mostly wooded summit in 1.4 miles. At a three-way junction, turn sharply right toward Klem Mountain. The red blazes lead into a saddle and then scale open ledges to a four-way intersection in 0.7 mile. While a short spur leads left to the wooded high point, continue straight to an open meadow with views north to the Ossipee Range and southern White Mountains. The path continues left and makes its way 0.7 mile down to Round Pond, a wildlife-rich water body nestled high atop the range.

Joining the green-blazed Piper–Round Pond Link, the BRT swings right, circles the scenic shoreline 0.4 mile and enters the Belknap Mountain State Forest. A final stop at the water's edge is followed by a short climb. At a three-way intersection, stay left on the Piper–Round Pond Link and proceed 0.8 mile up a hillside, then into a deep notch. Time to tackle another demanding ascent.

Head straight onto the aptly named Boulder Trail. This blue-blazed route scales rocky slopes and ledge. Ever-increasing views continue as you turn left on the yellow-blazed East Gilford Trail in 0.3 mile. Swing right on the White Trail 0.4 mile later. A final 0.2-mile jaunt leads to Belknap Mountain's summit tower, where stairs rise above the forest canopy to 360-degree views from the range's highest peak.

The BRT descends gradually 0.5 mile along Belknap Mountain's Blue Trail. Hike straight on the white-blazed Saddle Trail and, in 0.1 mile, stay left on the Brook Trail. Follow the yellow markers that lead 0.3 mile to the top of Gunstock Mountain. From the open ski slopes, there are views in most directions and plenty of spots to enjoy the scenery.

Retrace your steps a few dozen feet before turning right on the 2.2-mile Ridge Trail. It wraps around Gunstock's summit, offering an occasional glimpse west. The footing improves as the white-blazed trail descends through the beech forest. Hike across a col near the halfway point, and then scale Mount Rowe's open ledges. Near a communications tower, turn right onto a service road. The BRT descends steeply 0.8 mile along this wide corridor to the base of the ski area and the journey's end. As an alternative, follow a narrower path that closely parallels the road on the left.

Shorter Options: Do a much-shorter loop of Mount Major or Gunstock Mountain. There are also a number of alternative trailheads available to explore the many peaks in between. Check out the Belknap Range Conservation Coalition's website for more information on available options.

56 *Mount Roberts*

Distance: 9.4-mile loop
Difficulty: moderate–challenging
Hiking time: 6 hours
Elevation gain: 1825 feet
High point: 2670 feet

Management: Lakes Region Conservation Trust (LRCT)
Season: year-round
Map: LRCT website
GPS coordinates: 43.73199°, −71.32446°

Getting there: From the junction of Routes 171 and 109 in Moultonborough, drive 0.5 mile east on Route 171 and then turn left onto Ossipee Park Road. Drive 1.3 miles and park on the right (before the gate) or just beyond the gate on the left.

Surrounding a longtime tourist destination and offering 30 miles of hiking trails, the 5381-acre Castle in the Clouds Conservation Area encompasses the core of the Ossipee Mountain Range. The Lakes Region Conservation Trust manages this exceptional hiking destination. They are a membership-based land trust dedicated to protecting community character, wildlife habitat, water quality, scenic landscapes, and outdoor recreation. Although long, this recommended loop takes advantage of modestly inclined paths while visiting scenic promontories and dense hardwood forests on the slopes of an ancient volcano.

Hike through the gate and follow the paved road east. Down a short incline, the road forks. Stay left to find the start of the Mount Roberts Trail. It hugs the side of a large field before

Late fall snow blankets the Mount Roberts Trail.

entering the forest to begin a methodical 2.5-mile ascent of its namesake feature. Blazed in red, the wide corridor is easy to follow as it rises steadily.

In 1 mile, a spur departs left to a scenic bluff with views across lakes and rolling hills. The forest becomes sparser beyond the halfway point as open ledges offer a more expansive panorama of Mount Shaw to the east and the Belknap Range across Lake Winnipesaukee to the south. A final stretch through evergreens leads to a short summit loop. Stay right to reach the 2582-foot high point and scenes north to the White Mountains.

From the summit sign, head west to quickly arrive at the start of the High Ridge Trail. Meandering atop the mountain range, the wide corridor features modest elevation changes. In 1.5 miles, reach the Faraway Mountain Overlook—another opportunity to gaze out across the distant landscape of lakes and surrounding mountains. The High Ridge Trail proceeds through a long hairpin turn before arriving at a junction in 0.9 mile.

Turn right onto the Faraway Mountain Trail, which drops gradually along a series of sweeping switchbacks. Take advantage of the gentle terrain to scan the northern hardwood trees for resident songbirds and the forest floor for carpets of wildflowers. In 1.7 miles, stay left at an intersection with the Cold Spring Trail (a slightly shorter route back to the start).

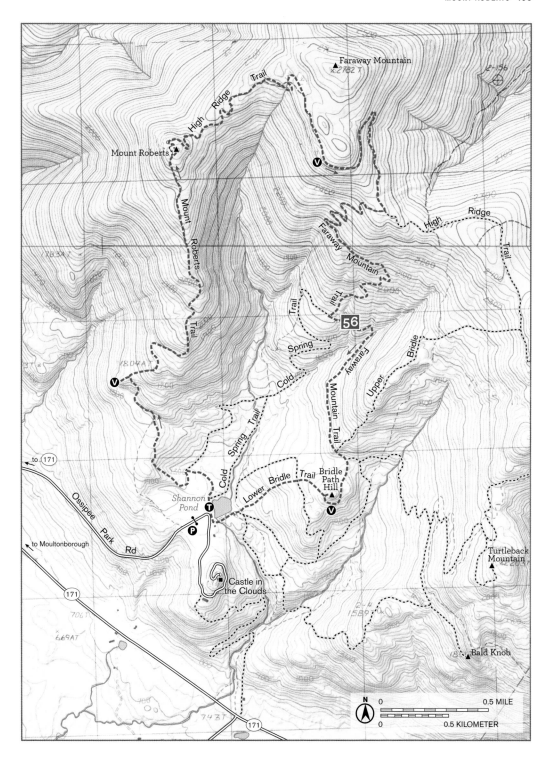

▲ Faraway Mountain
X 2782

High Ridge Trail

Mount Roberts ▲

Mount Roberts Trail

Ⓥ

Faraway Mountain Trail

High Ridge Trail

Ⓥ

Spring

Cold

56

Faraway Mountain Trail

Upper Bridle

Cold Spring Trail

to ⟨171⟩

Shannon Pond

Ⓣ

Ⓟ

Lower Bridle Trail

Bridle Path Hill ▲

Ⓥ

to Moultonborough

Ossipee Park Rd

⟨171⟩

Castle in the Clouds

Turtleback Mountain ▲

X 1589

Bald Knob ▲

⟨171⟩

N
0   0.5 MILE
0   0.5 KILOMETER

Continue another 1.1 miles on the Faraway Mountain Trail, then turn right onto the Lower Bridle Trail. This green-blazed route meanders easily 0.4 mile around Bridle Path Hill, a rocky knoll with a short spur that leads to the top of it. Check out this diversion for one last scenic vista before rejoining the Lower Bridle Trail.

Descend steadily 0.5 mile to the edge of Shannon Pond. The route continues across the earthen dam. Turn right and follow the pavement back to the parking area. If you want to add an extra stop to your adventure, consider exploring south of Shannon Pond, where Shannon Brook forms a series of picturesque cascades in a deep ravine.

Shorter Options: Limit the day's journey by hiking out and back along the Mount Roberts Trail to complete a rewarding 5.4-mile excursion to the summit.

57 *Mount Cardigan*

Distance: 5.4-mile loop
Difficulty: challenging
Hiking time: 4 hours
Elevation gain: 1900 feet
High point: 3121 feet

Management: New Hampshire SP, Appalachian Mountain Club
Season: year-round
Map: No official online map
GPS coordinates: 43.64931°, −71.87788°

Getting there: From the town offices in Alexandria, head northwest on Washburn Road. In 0.1 mile, veer right on Cardigan Mountain Road and continue 3.1 miles. Stay right at a junction with Hutchins Hills Road. In 0.5 mile, at a three-way intersection with Brook Road, continue straight on Shem Valley Road. After crossing a brook, follow Shem Valley Road right. This dirt road leads 1.4 miles to the Appalachian Mountain Club's (AMC) Cardigan Lodge. *Note:* The lodge, nearby campsites, and a backcountry cabin on the mountain are available for overnight stays. Contact AMC to make reservations.

Mount Cardigan's bald granite summit overlooks 6000 acres of conservation land on the western side of Newfound Lake. Although Mount Cardigan is not one of the state's highest points, the trails ascending the scenic peak are as steep and challenging as many that scale New Hampshire's more-noteworthy 4000-foot mountains. Many visitors choose the shorter state park hikes beginning in the west, but Cardigan's more interesting trails begin at the AMC lodge in the east, where multiple loop hikes like this one are possible.

Begin on the Holt Trail and hike 0.3 mile to the start of the loop. Stay straight and continue paralleling Bailey Brook. In 0.5 mile, the Holt Trail crosses a bridge to the other side and soon ascends to Grand Junction.

You can tackle the steep scramble straight up the Holt Trail, but for a more straightforward climb, stay left on the Cathedral Forest Trail. Climbing steadily up the slope, the path rises 0.5 mile to a junction. Turn right onto the Clark Trail and continue ascending. In 0.3 mile, the terrain becomes rockier as the path skirts under Cardigan's South Peak and reaches a scenic viewpoint. Another 0.3-mile push in and out of the thinning forest leads to an old cabin beneath polished granite ledges.

Carefully scale 0.1 mile up the steep pitch that ends atop the barren summit. From the base of the fire tower, there are 360-degree views of the surrounding terrain, with Vermont's Green Mountains dominating the western horizon, the Monadnock Region rising in the south, and the White Mountains towering to the north.

Cardigan's summit from Manning Trail

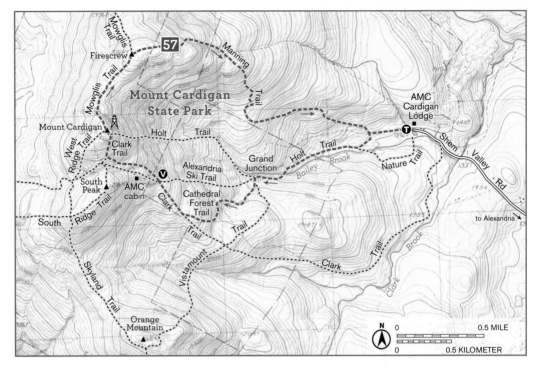

In addition to displaying abundant beauty, the oft-breezy summit can be crowded. Head north along the Mowglis Trail when you are ready to begin the descent. After an initial steep drop, explore the mostly open ridgeline trail 0.6 mile through a saddle and up to a junction near the top of the Firescrew, a name that describes the shape of smoke that emanated from the 1855 fire that burned much of the mountain. Stay right on the Manning Trail and head across a flat, barren ridge offering continual vistas over inviting terrain. Following a few short descents, pass a final open ledge and cross a small stream. Steeply dropping along a narrow pine-covered spine, the route eventually becomes more gradual, meandering to its conclusion. Turn left on the Holt Trail and return 0.3 mile to the start.

Extend Your Trip: For a longer start to the trek, pick up the Vistamont Trail just south of Grand Junction. Follow this path to Orange Mountain and then turn right. Follow the Skyland and South Ridge Trails before joining the Clark Trail at the base of the summit. There are many scenic spots along this less-traveled ridgeline hike; it adds a little more than a mile to the described hike.

Appalachian Mountain Club (AMC)

Since 1876, this membership-based organization has protected mountains, forests, waters, and trails throughout the Northeast, but AMC has always had a strong focus on New Hampshire and the White Mountains. Signs of their work are scattered around the state: well-maintained trails, overnight huts and lodges, backcountry campsites, and volunteer-led trips.

58 *Smarts Mountain*

Distance: 7.2-mile loop
Difficulty: challenging
Hiking time: 5 hours
Elevation gain: 2400 feet
High point: 3238 feet

Management: White Mountain NF
Season: year-round
Map: WMNF website
GPS coordinates: 43.79697°, −72.07157°

Getting there: Near the Congregational Church on Route 10 in the center of Lyme, drive east on Dorchester Road. Drive 3 miles and then stay left on Dorchester Road. Continue another 1.7 miles to the parking area on the left. **Note:** Backcountry campsite available.

Rising above the upper valley of the Connecticut River, Smarts Mountain is the first significant peak that northbound Appalachian Trail (AT) thru hikers encounter after entering New Hampshire. From the southern edge of the White Mountain National Forest, the summit observation tower showcases sweeping views of Vermont, southwestern New Hampshire, and the Granite State's highest peaks. This 7.2-mile loop combines a journey up the scenic ledge-covered slopes of Lambert Ridge with a pleasant jaunt near the banks of Grant Brook.

Pick up the AT as it departs near the parking lot entrance. The white-blazed path wastes little time gaining elevation; ascend switchbacks 0.5 mile to the first of many openings in the forest canopy. With an occasional view south toward the Dartmouth Skiway, climb 0.3 mile to a more impressive ledge with breathtaking scenes south and east. Rising less steeply over the next 0.6

The Appalachian Trail stops at numerous vistas along Lambert Ridge.

mile, the trail traverses Lambert Ridge. Watch your footing while meandering over small knobs and open ledges, many showcasing views of Smarts Mountain rising to the northeast.

After descending the ridge, the trail heads across a wide, flat expanse of beech and birch. The incline is modest for a mile. As the forest transitions to evergreens, the surface becomes rougher and the slope steeper. Rise 0.2 mile to a junction with the Smarts Ranger Trail. Stay left on the AT to tackle the final 0.5-mile stretch to the summit.

Rock, wood, and iron steps ease the way up the rugged terrain. Take your time; although challenging, the climb is short. After leveling off, pass a spur right that leads to an attractive tent site—an ideal spot to spend the night after watching the setting sun. Just beyond, arrive at the summit tower, where stairs lead above the treetops to breathtaking 360-degree views, including Mount Moosilauke's impressive profile to the north and the rest of the White Mountains beyond. Much of Vermont's Green Mountains are visible to the west. Nearby, the former fire tower warden's cabin provides another overnight camping spot.

Retrace your steps 0.5 mile to the Smarts Ranger Trail and stay left on the 3-mile-long, blue-blazed route. The first 0.5 mile is rough and rocky; use caution, especially when wet. Before long, the surface becomes more inviting, especially after crossing Grant Brook, which it follows for much of the remaining 2 miles. The

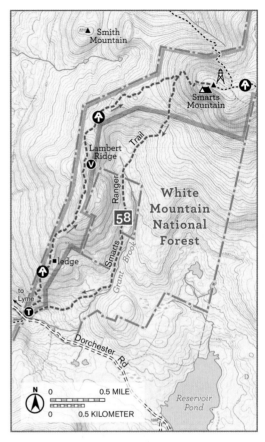

relaxing conclusion to the loop affords many opportunities to scan the surrounding forest for resident songbirds warbling above and splashes of color from the abundant wildflowers thriving below.

59 *Welch and Dickey*

Distance: 4.4-mile loop
Difficulty: moderate–challenging
Hiking time: 3 hours
Elevation gain: 1775 feet
High point: 2734 feet

Management: White Mountain NF
Season: year-round
Map: WMNF website
GPS coordinates: 43.90429°, −71.58842°

Getting there: From Interstate 93 in Campton, take exit 28. Drive 5.6 miles northeast on Route 49 and turn left onto Upper Mad River Road. Cross the bridge, continue 0.6 mile, and turn right onto Orris Road. Follow Orris Road 0.6 mile to the parking area on the right.

Ravaged by fires in the 1880s, Welch and Dickey's smooth granite domes now provide some of the finest views in the White Mountains. This popular loop scales both summits and offers great dividends for the effort, but do not underestimate the challenge. Steep in sections, the trail scrambles up exposed rocks from one dramatic perch to another. While accessible year-round, the mountains' many ledges can be very icy from late fall through early spring.

Do the loop in a counterclockwise direction by heading northeast toward Welch Mountain. Across a small stream, the route gently meanders 0.7 mile through the shady valley. Abruptly swing right near a large boulder and begin a steadier climb up the ridgeline. The forest thins as the landscape hardens. Pass a sign explaining the fragility of the summit's plant life, and heed the advice to remain on the marked trail. Ahead lies the first of many panoramas.

The Welch-Dickey Loop descends over Dickey Mountain's extensive open ledges.

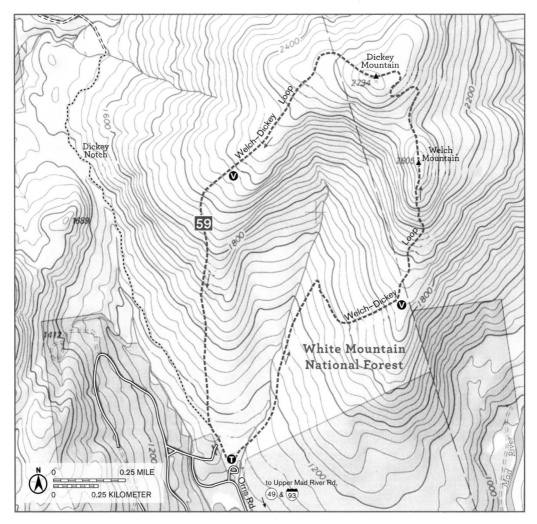

With the mountaintop in view, veer left and carefully make your way up the increasingly steep slope. Each step brings broader vistas as the path winds methodically up rock, around ledges, and through patches of forest, including dwindling groves of jack pine—a fire-dependent species uncommon in the region. Take your time, enjoy the scenery, and you will soon reach Welch Mountain's barren top. Of the incredible views in all directions, the scenes of Mount Tripyramid's distinctive three-peaked ridge and the south slide that scars its slopes are particularly noteworthy.

The loop drops 0.2 mile into a saddle buried under a large cairn. Scale the rocky path to open ledges on Dickey Mountain's east side. Continue just beyond the high point to enjoy views north toward Franconia Notch and west to Mount Moosilauke. The loop soon descends into the evergreen forest but soon reemerges onto an exceptional open ridge that offers stunning near and distant views. Bearing right, reenter the forest for good, pass a small cliff face, and then steadily head down the slope. Continue along relaxing grades to a signed junction. Turn left and follow the old road a few hundred feet to the parking area.

60 *Cannon Mountain and Lonesome Lake*

Distance: 8-mile loop
Difficulty: challenging–strenuous
Hiking time: 7 hours
Elevation gain: 2500 feet
High point: 4100 feet

Management: New Hampshire SP
Season: year-round
Map: NHSP website
GPS coordinates: 44.16920°, −71.68660°

Getting there: From Lincoln, follow Interstate 93 north to Franconia Notch. In 9.5 miles, take exit 34B and drive 0.1 mile into Tramway parking area. Follow the pavement as it loops around and past the ski lift building, then exit right on road that leads to a well-marked hiker's parking area just south of the main lot. *Note:* Backcountry hut available.

Spectacular views from multiple angles and diverse perspectives highlight this challenging but extremely rewarding loop in New Hampshire's Franconia Notch. The circuit scales Cannon Mountain's dome-shaped summit and rises to the top of the immense cliffs that the majestic Old Man of the Mountain once called home. Descend ladders and wander over scenic ledges as this route drops to the placid waters of Lonesome Lake and its famous mountain backdrops. Concluding along the banks of the Pemigewasset River, the full-day journey has much to offer to the hardiest of travelers.

The Kinsman Ridge Trail begins in the southwest corner of the parking lot and wastes little time scaling the steep and partially eroded mountainside. Climb to an occasional glimpse of tramway towers to the right and Echo Lake far below. The route methodically ascends to, and then briefly parallels, a narrow alpine ski trail. After veering sharply east, the 1.2-mile start of the day's journey slowly eases. Reach a 0.1-mile spur that departs left. It ends at the top of Cannon Mountain's cliffs, where mesmerizing views of Mount Lincoln and Mount Lafayette towering above Franconia Notch await.

The main trail continues west 0.5 mile along the ridge. After a brief descent, scramble up and over rocks to reach a more manicured surface. Turn left on the gravel path and enjoy the many views, signs, and benches scattered along this 0.2-mile stretch of the Kinsman Ridge Trail. At a well-signed junction, a short path exits right

to the summit tower and extensive 360-degree views. During the summer and fall, especially on weekends, this can be a popular destination for visitors arriving at the nearby tramway station.

Return to the Kinsman Ridge Trail and continue 0.3 mile south over mostly level terrain to an intersection. To the right, a more straightforward, but less scenic option, leads to the Lonesome Lake Trail—a good choice, especially if hiking with a dog. Otherwise, follow the more rugged Hi-Cannon Trail to the left. Carefully make your way 0.5 mile down to the first of many impressive yet precarious ledge outcrops. Each offers aerial views of Lonesome Lake and Kinsman Mountain. Beyond the final perch, descend a steep, wooden ladder, and then wind through the boulder-filled landscape. The path levels off near a junction with the Dodge Cutoff. Turn right and follow this 0.3-mile trail over rolling terrain to the shores of scenic Lonesome Lake.

To fully appreciate the area's beauty, embark on the 0.8-mile boardwalk-laden loop that circles the reflective blue waters. In a clockwise direction, head left through dense forests and across the pond's outlet to the Appalachian Mountain Club's Lonesome Lake Hut, which is open for overnight stays by reservation only (limited service in the winter). The popular hut's idyllic setting includes a million-dollar view of the Franconia Range and Cannon Mountain. The loop continues through marshes and past one vista after another as it winds around the pond's north shore. Turn right onto the Lonesome Lake Trail to complete the circuit.

Remain on the Lonesome Lake Trail. This gradual, well-used pathway winds 1.2 miles before reaching the Lafayette Place Campground. Descend past campsites to a junction with the Pemi Trail and turn left on the paved road. Hike 0.1 mile to the campground entrance and then exit north on the Pemi Trail, near the banks of its namesake river.

Franconia Range from the shores of Lonesome Lake

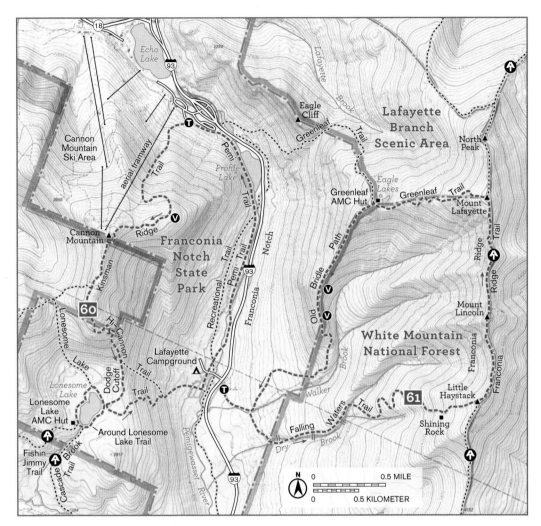

The hike's final 2.2-mile stretch rises gradually throughout. After crossing a paved recreational trail and the river, parallel the water upstream. The undulating trail recrosses the river, briefly follows the bike trail right, and then swings left to Profile Lake. Enjoy excellent views of Eagle Cliff while hiking along the lake's west shore and then ascend to the trail's end. Head straight through the large parking area and follow the driveway north until it bends right. Here, a short, unmarked path cuts through the forest to the Kinsman Ridge trailhead.

Shorter Options: Begin at the Lafayette Place Campground (day-use parking fills quickly, especially on weekends) and follow the Lonesome Lake Trail 1.2 miles to its namesake feature. Loop around the water body before heading back the same way to complete a moderate 3.2-mile hike with many pleasant rewards. Many also opt for a 4.2-mile roundtrip hike to Cannon Mountain by retracing their steps along the Kinsman Ridge Trail.

61 *Franconia Ridge*

Distance: 8.8-mile loop
Difficulty: strenuous
Hiking time: 7 hours
Elevation gain: 3800 feet
High point: 5260 feet

Management: New Hampshire SP
Season: year-round
Map: NHSP website
GPS coordinates: 44.14181°, −71.68128°

View of Mount Lafayette from Greenleaf Hut

Getting there: From Lincoln, follow Interstate 93 north. Drive 2.3 miles past exit 34A and turn right into the parking area. If you are staying at Lafayette Place Campground, take the tunnel under the highway to reach the trailhead. *Notes:* Parking is limited and not allowed on the side of the road. If the parking area is full, park near the Cannon Mountain Tramway, 2.5 miles north (see Other Options). Backcountry hut available.

Being perhaps the most popular high-eleva-tion route in New England, Franconia Ridge is not a place of solitude. While this loop's alpine portion is as spectacular as any other Granite State trail, its difficulty should not be underes-timated. Come ready for a strenuous daylong adventure and the potential for challenging weather conditions. With ample preparation, you will go home with fond memories of cascading rivers, panoramic scenery, and incredible vistas that honor the legacy of two men who left a last-ing mark on the country.

Near the center of the parking area, the Old Bridle Path leads into the forest. Hike 0.2 mile to a junction and the start of the day's loop. Bear right onto the Falling Waters Trail and immedi-ately cross Walker Brook. In 0.4 mile, the path approaches Dry Brook before swinging left. Begin a steady ascent while visiting three cascades and occasionally crossing the rushing water. Each set of waterfalls is more impressive than the last.

Eventually, the well-used path crosses Dry Brook one last time, only to begin a challenging climb. Small switchbacks moderate the relent-less ascent. Just before reaching the alpine zone, arrive at a short spur leading to the base of Shining Rock—an impressive ledge that is a worthwhile diversion. The final 0.3-mile pitch to Little Haystack Mountain is difficult, but it offers expanding views of the notch with each step.

At the junction with the Franconia Ridge Trail (Appalachian Trail), catch your breath and prepare for the exposure that awaits. The next 1.6-mile trek to the summit of Mount Lafayette is a glorious stretch of high-elevation hiking. How-ever, with no safe means of escape, it should be avoided during inclement weather. With views in all directions, the white-blazed trail winds north along the ridge. While abundant beauty distracts, do your best to stay on rocky surfaces and avoid damaging fragile alpine plants. A short pitch ends atop the five-thousand, four-score, and nine-foot-high pinnacle of Mount Lincoln. Named in honor of the nation's sixteenth president, the scenic mountain is a fitting tribute to the Great Emanci-pator and author of the Gettysburg Address.

A brief drop into a grove of stunted trees is followed by the final push to the seventh-highest peak in New England. Named for a French national who aided America's battle for independence, Mount Lafayette stands nearly a mile high. Take your time and savor the 360-degree views and surrounding beauty; it is 4 miles and all downhill from here.

Follow the Greenleaf Trail west from the summit. The path meanders down the barren landscape, eventually reaching a thin forest and Eagle Lakes, a collection of small ponds. Climb up to the AMC's Greenleaf Hut (available by reservation only) before turning left onto the Old Bridle Path. Traversing Agony Ridge, the steep trail punishes the knees while thrilling the eyes. There are many exceptional vistas into Walker Ravine and the towering peaks above. After the last viewpoint, the trail drops quickly. Enter the shady forest as the route moderates over the remaining 1.5 miles—a quiet end to a classic trek in the White Mountains.

Other Options: If you are unable to secure a parking spot, consider completing a slightly longer loop by ascending the Greenleaf Trail, which begins near the bottom of the exit 34B ramp (exit for the Cannon Mountain Tramway parking lot). Complete the loop in reverse: upon descending the Falling Waters Trail, follow the path under the highway to reach Lafayette Place Campground. Pick up the Pemi Trail here and hike north 2 miles back to the tramway parking area. Visit the state park website for the latest information on where to park in Franconia Notch, including the availability of shuttle service during peak weekends.

62 *Pemigewasset Wilderness*

Distance: 26.4-mile loop
Difficulty: strenuous
Hiking time: 2–3 days
Elevation gain: 5300 feet
High point: 4902 feet

Management: White Mountain NF
Season: year-round
Map: WMNF website
GPS coordinates: 44.06357°, −71.58822°

Getting there: From Interstate 93 in Lincoln, take exit 32. Travel 5.4 miles east on Route 112 (Kancamagus Highway) and turn left into the large parking area for the Lincoln Woods Trail. *Notes:* Parking fee required. Backcountry hut and campsites available.

The 45,000-acre Pemigewasset Wilderness is a place to escape the hustle and bustle of the real world, which makes it hard to believe that prior to the 1940s, much of the region was heavily logged and burned. Thanks to the foresight of many conservationists, today the land is noteworthy for its roaring rivers, wildlife-rich forests, rugged landscapes, and remote summits. This loop that cuts through the heart of the wilderness is a classic New England backpacking adventure that traverses easy-to-moderate terrain, with a few notable exceptions.

An iconic shot near the summit of Bondcliff

After crossing the large suspension bridge spanning the Pemigewasset River's east branch, turn right onto the Lincoln Woods Trail. Follow the abandoned railbed once used to haul lumber out of the forest. It parallels the rushing water 2.9 miles, with little elevation change, to a bridge that spans Franconia Brook. Cross the rushing water to a three-way intersection on the Pemigewasset Wilderness boundary.

Head left on the Franconia Brook Trail. The route ascends modestly while passing wetlands that occasionally flood portions of the trail. While beavers and a growing forest continue to erase signs of the area's history, abandoned logging camps remain, with all artifacts protected by federal law. At 8.1 miles from the start, reach the Appalachian Mountain Club's (AMC) Thirteen Falls tent site (the first of two AMC campsites available for a small fee on a first-come, first-served basis). Located near a series of scenic cascades, Thirteen Falls is a serene spot far removed from modern civilization.

From the campsite, join the Twin Brook Trail. It climbs steadily northeast through dense forest surroundings and ends in 2.7 miles at a junction with the Frost Trail. To the left, the mostly wooded summit of 4024-foot Galehead Mountain can be scaled in 0.4 mile. Stay right to quickly make your way to AMC's Galehead Hut. Open from late spring to early fall, this inviting facility provides bunks and meals—advanced reservations required.

Just beyond the hut, reach the Twinway (Appalachian Trail). Turn right and tackle the hike's most difficult section. The 0.8-mile climb rises 1100 feet up boulders and over roots but eventually pays dividends atop 4902-foot South Twin Mountain. The highest peak between the Franconia Ridge and the Presidential Range, South Twin provides a dazzling 360-degree panorama that includes views of both, as well as countless peaks and valleys in all directions.

Remain on the Twinway as it proceeds south through an inviting high-elevation boreal forest. The path leads pleasantly 2 miles before entering a barren landscape at a junction. Stay right on the Bondcliff Trail and hike 0.3 mile to Mount

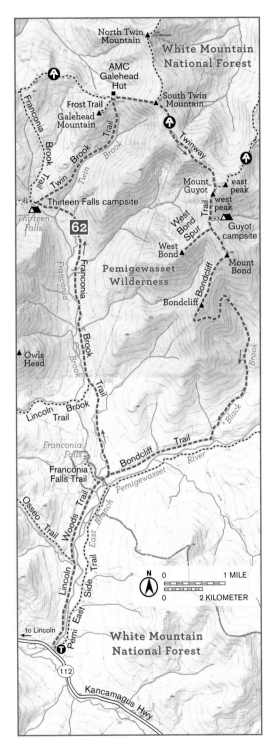

Guyot's scenic west peak. The route drops 0.5 mile into a forested saddle, where a 0.2-mile trail leads left to the AMC's Guyot campsite. Only 6.3 miles from Thirteen Falls, this popular spot includes a shelter and tent sites.

Rising steadily from the col, quickly arrive at an intersection with the 0.5-mile West Bond Spur. Check out this spectacular diversion that begins with a brief descent, followed by a short scramble to the top of New England's most isolated 4000-footer and its jaw-dropping panorama. Back on the main route, the Bondcliff Trail ascends 0.7 mile to the summit of 4698-foot Mount Bond and sweeping views that encompass most of the White Mountains.

Descend rapidly to the southwest through the forest, but not for long. The route enters a tree-stunted, windswept landscape surrounded by rugged beauty unlike anywhere else in the region. For nearly a mile, enjoy the wide-open expanse while scaling the dramatic edge of Bondcliff (not an ideal place to be in bad weather). There are few backdrops in the White Mountains more amazing and photogenic.

After cresting the high point, take time to savor the wild, remote landscape. The trail down is tricky at first, but back in the trees, a more straightforward 4.4-mile stretch ensues. During the second half, parallel and cross Black Brook on four occasions. The incline levels off while approaching the Pemigewasset River. Swing sharply right onto a wide corridor and follow the mostly level former railbed 1.8 miles to end the loop. Retrace your steps 2.9 miles along the Lincoln Woods Trail to reach the parking area.

63 Hedgehog Mountain

Distance: 4.8-mile loop
Difficulty: moderate–challenging
Hiking time: 3 hours
Elevation gain: 1425 feet
High point: 2535 feet

Management: White Mountain NF
Season: year-round
Map: WMNF website
GPS coordinates: 43.99417°, −71.36938°

Getting there: From Interstate 93 in Lincoln, take exit 32 and travel 21.2 miles east on Route 112 (the Kancamagus Highway). Alternatively, from Route 16 in Conway, travel 14.2 miles west on Route 112. Across from the USFS Passaconaway Campground, turn south on the driveway and quickly arrive at the UNH Trailhead.

Hedgehog Mountain is a rewarding half-day circuit to numerous open ledges surrounded by larger peaks in all directions. The trail is within walking distance of one US Forest Service campground and near two others and is the perfect mountain trek on the region's most famous scenic highway. A fun hike for people of all ages, Hedgehog Mountain is also a great introduction to the White Mountain National Forest's geology, forest habitats, and rugged beauty.

Just beyond the information kiosk and gate, find the start of the yellow-blazed UNH Trail on the left. Up the sandy hillside, quickly level off and proceed 0.2 mile under a shady canopy of pine trees. Turn sharply right at a trail sign, where a cross-country ski route continues straight. The easy start to the hike continues past another ski trail intersection before beginning a moderate ascent to the start of the loop, 0.8 mile from the parking lot.

Stay right and tackle the increasingly steep slope. Winding through the spruce forest, reach a spur trail in 0.2 mile. This short diversion left scales a granite face to the top of Allens Ledge, the day's first scenic promontory. Enjoy pleasant views across the Swift River valley and scan the

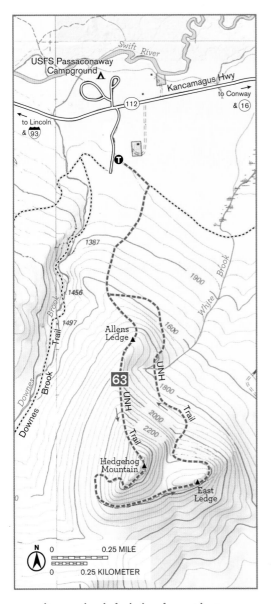

Falls colors add texture to Hedgehog Mountain's East Ledge.

Watch your footing as the loop drops down the ledge-covered slopes to the south. In and out of the forest, the route descends switchbacks before leveling off in 0.4 mile. Weaving under the steep summit cliffs and through a boreal forest accented with boulders, the path leads 0.4 mile to the mountain's east ledge. There is plenty of space a safe distance from its precipitous edge. Enjoy the loop's most-impressive views, dominated by Mount Passaconaway towering high above. The trail briefly returns to the forest before arriving at one last vista, featuring scenes east toward Mount Chocorua.

Follow the route into the forest. Over the next 1.2 miles, the footing is rough to start, but improves as the trees transition to northern hardwoods. Cross White Brook and weave past a scattering of large boulders. This is followed by a brief ascent to complete the circuit. Turn right and retrace your steps 0.8 mile back to the start.

sprawling wetlands far below for resident moose. Above the spur, the hike's steepest section awaits. The well-marked route rises 0.8 mile up the narrowing ridgeline before emerging atop summit ledges, where rocky perches feature exceptional views through the stunted forest.

Nearby Options: A great way to complement this scenic hike on the Kancamagus Highway is to explore two nearby excursions that are much shorter: Sabbaday Falls to the west and Rocky Gorge to the east.

64 *Mount Chocorua*

Distance: 8.5-mile loop
Difficulty: challenging
Hiking time: 6 hours
Elevation gain: 2800 feet
High point: 3500 feet

Management: White Mountain NF
Season: year-round
Map: WMNF website
GPS coordinates: 43.94043°, −71.22883°

Getting there: From the junction of Routes 16 and 113 in Tamworth, follow Route 16 north. Drive north 4.9 miles and then turn left onto Piper Trail Road. Follow the dirt road 0.2 mile to the Piper Trail parking lot. **Note:** Backcountry campsites available.

Believed to be the site of the final chapter in an all-too-common struggle between European settlers and Indigenous Americans, the mountain may hold the remains of a courageous young Chocorua, who plunged to his untimely death hundreds of years ago. Today, the prominent pinnacle that bears his name is one of the region's most popular and frequently photographed peaks. Although there are many options to its rocky summit, this well-traveled loop is arguably the most scenic.

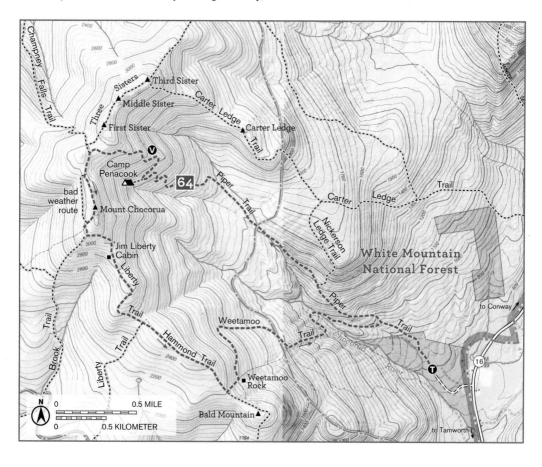

The Piper Trail meanders up the exposed granite toward the summit pinnacle.

Built by Joshua Piper, the historical trail winds through the site of his former farmstead turned tourist destination. Today, any signs from these earlier eras are hidden beneath a maturing forest. Follow the yellow-blazed route on gentle grades 0.6 mile to a junction. Continue climbing moderately up the Piper Trail and then head straight through another junction in 0.6 mile. The path reaches a series of switchbacks 2.3 miles from the start.

Climbing more steadily, the route is rougher over the next 0.6 mile, but rock steps ease the way. Wind between boulders and ledge while noticing the forest transition from hardwoods to evergreens. At the fifth switchback, a spur departs left to Camp Penacook, which has a small shelter and a pair of tent platforms available on a first-come, first-served basis. Continue climbing to the ridgeline, where the trail emerges atop an open bluff with impressive views of the distinctively shaped summit looming high above. Over the next 0.4 mile, scramble up the exposed granite to more expansive scenery and more-intimate shots of the high point. The trail reenters the

forest and moderates before reaching a junction with the Champney Falls Trail in 0.2 mile.

Remain on the Piper Trail. It carves through the boreal forest and passes a bad-weather route before entering a wide-open landscape in 0.2 mile. Take your time and carefully follow the cairns and yellow marks that meander 0.4 mile over the mostly treeless landscape. The rocks can be slick if wet or icy; otherwise, the footing is good. Just below the summit, the Piper and Liberty Trails meet. Turn left to steeply ascend the final pitch and enjoy panoramic views in all directions. The scenes of Mount Washington to the north and the views west into the Swift River valley, paralleling the Kancamagus Highway, are especially impressive.

Use caution descending south along the Liberty Trail. Pass the intersection where the bad-weather route enters from the right and then arrive at a large cairn that marks a junction with the Brook Trail—0.2 mile from the summit. Stay left on the Liberty Trail. Skirting along the mountain's steep slopes, the next 0.3-mile section demands extra attention until arriving at the Jim Liberty Cabin. Located high on the ridge, this historical building is available for overnight camping on a first-come, first-served basis. The Liberty Trail drops steadily another 0.6 mile to a junction as the terrain becomes easier to navigate.

Hike straight on the more-lightly used Hammond Trail. This mostly forested route occasionally traverses open ledges with limited views. In 0.8 mile, be sure to turn sharply left on the Weetamoo Trail, as the Hammond Trail continues to a distant trailhead. The 1.9-mile Weetamoo Trail descends steadily. Near the beginning, pass its namesake rock, an immense boulder that is difficult to miss. The footing improves at lower elevations. Reach the banks of the Chocorua River and cross its narrow streambed. The path proceeds 0.5 mile farther. Turn right on the Piper Trail and re-hike the final 0.6 mile to complete the adventure.

65   *South and Middle Moat*

Distance: 6.6 miles roundtrip
Difficulty: moderate–challenging
Hiking time: 5 hours
Elevation gain: 2450 feet
High point: 2805 feet

Management: White Mountain NF
Season: year-round
Map: WMNF website
GPS coordinates: 43.99357°, −71.18345°

Getting there: At the junction of Routes 16 and 153 in Conway, drive north on Washington Street. In 0.2 mile, stay left at a fork in the road and continue 0.7 mile (becomes West Side Road). Turn left onto Passaconaway Road and drive 3.2 miles to the parking area on the right.

Rising above the Mount Washington valley, Moat Mountain's sweeping ridgeline features exceptional views of the White Mountains' highest summits. The 3.3-mile excursion to the ridge's two most-southern peaks begins gradually, becomes more challenging, and eventually

Enjoy numerous vistas before reaching the top of South Moat.

traverses an open expanse featuring scenic promontories. This is an excellent hike throughout the year, and the mountain's southern exposure often allows exploration on snow-free spring terrain weeks before neighboring trails.

The Moat Mountain Trail rises gradually 1.3 miles to start, taking advantage of old woods roads. After descending to and then crossing a pair of small streams, the final one over a wooden bridge, reach the base of the hike's major climb. Here, the terrain becomes more demanding, but also more intriguing. A handful of switchbacks leads up the rocky slope. Make your way through the increasingly open landscape. In the thin soils below, carpets of wildflowers blossom profusely, including the fragile pink lady's slipper.

The route leads to another maze of switchbacks, this time through a rocky landscape. Arrive at the base of a large granite ledge and carefully navigate your ascent. The thinning forest offers an occasional glimpse of distant peaks before you emerge at a wide-open vista showcasing a snapshot view of Mount Chocorua's pinnacle-shaped summit. Over the next 0.6 mile, scale numerous open rock faces that can be tricky if wet or icy. The route occasionally weaves in and out of a pine-and-oak forest that attracts numerous songbirds, including the indigo bunting. Before long, the effort pays off with rewarding 360-degree views atop South Moat. Towering to the north is Mount Washington; to the west, the Kancamagus Highway winds into the heart of the White Mountains; and looking east, the Green Hills sit near the Maine border.

South Moat is a popular turnaround point for many hikers, but to find quieter viewing areas, plod 0.6 mile north to the slightly higher, equally exposed Middle Moat summit. The scenic route to get there is relatively flat, with one

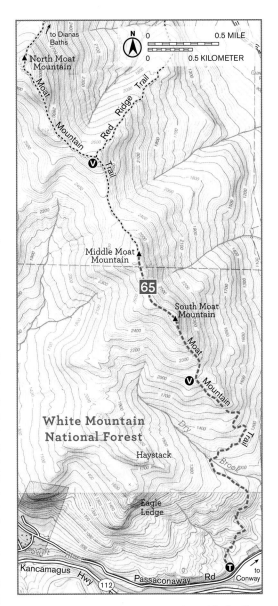

minor descent, and well worth the added effort. Retrace your steps on the same trail to complete the journey.

Extend Your Trip: If you are looking for a longer adventure, consider extending the hike another 3.8 miles roundtrip by taking the Moat Mountain Trail all the way to North Moat's treeless summit, the ridge's highest point. Or, if you can spot cars or arrange to be picked up, consider a traverse of the entire 9.7-mile Moat Mountain Trail by continuing to its northern terminus on West Side Road in Conway, near Dianas Baths.

66 Davis Path

Distance: 9.8 miles roundtrip
Difficulty: challenging
Hiking time: 6–7 hours
Elevation gain: 3750 feet
High point: 3463 feet

Management: White Mountain NF
Season: year-round
Map: WMNF website
GPS coordinates: 44.11850°, −71.35374°

Getting there: From Bartlett, follow Route 302 northwest 6.2 miles and turn right into the large parking area near the Saco River.

In 1845, Nathaniel Davis constructed a 15-mile bridle trail to Mount Washington, a venture that quickly became too difficult to maintain. Fortunately, the route was resurrected in 1910 for hiking, and for more than a century, the Davis Path has led many an adventurer on an enjoyable excursion on a southern ridge of New

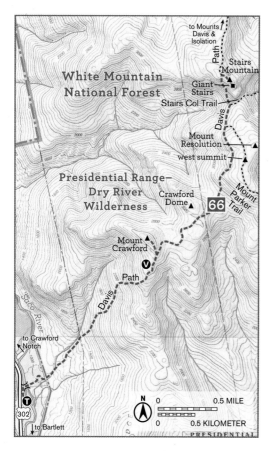

Hampshire's Presidential Range. Combining pleasant high-elevation hiking with classic White Mountain scenery, this recommended daylong trek ventures along the path's first 4.4 miles, providing access to three distinct peaks.

From the parking area, follow the dirt road that leads a few hundred feet upstream beside the Saco River. Cross the large suspension bridge to a trail sign and plaque commemorating the conservation of the trailhead area. Proceed straight around a small marshy wetland and then swing right into a pleasant hardwood forest. After crossing a small brook, the path enters the Presidential Range–Dry River Wilderness, a 29,000-acre expanse that dominates the southern slopes and ridges emanating from New Hampshire's highest mountain.

Over the next 1.6 miles, plod up an aggressive but straightforward ascent. It provides an excellent workout and before long reaches a rock outcrop with splendid views of Mount Carrigain and Crawford Notch. Continue another 0.3 mile to the base of a large ledge, where a spur leads left. Scramble up the exposed granite 0.3 mile to the barren top of Mount Crawford, where an incredible panorama awaits, highlighted by Mount Washington, Oakes Gulf, and the Southern Presidential Range.

Upon returning to the Davis Path, turn left and enter a dark evergreen tunnel. For the next 1.5 miles, the trail enjoys mostly moderate grades and traverses many scenic ledges before skirting beneath Mount Resolution's scree-sloped west side. The oft-damp footway soon leads to a junction. To the right, the Mount Parker Trail climbs 0.4 mile to Mount Resolution's west summit and

Mount Crawford features splendid views of Crawford Notch to the west.

expansive scenery in most directions—a worthwhile extension to the journey.

Continuing straight on the Davis Path, proceed 0.3 mile into a narrow gap on the ridge. At an intersection with the Stairs Col Trail, stay left and begin a challenging 0.4-mile ascent. While it is difficult to imagine this location as a bridle path, it is easy to see why it was short-lived. After leveling off, bear right on a spur. This easy 0.2-mile path heads over Stairs Mountain's forested high point to reach the top of Giant Stairs, the summit's signature ledge. Aptly named for its appearance as seen from the east and west, Stairs Mountain showcases spectacular views from the edge of a precipitous cliff. From here, retrace your steps to the trailhead.

Other Options: This challenging excursion can be shortened to 5 miles roundtrip by limiting the day's hike to Mount Crawford. Or consider a longer overnight adventure by continuing north 3.7 miles to Mount Davis and 1.1 miles farther to Mount Isolation. While not frequently climbed, the former peak offers some of the finest scenery in the White Mountains. Primitive backcountry campsites are available a mile beyond Mount Isolation's equally scenic summit.

Arethusa Falls are New Hampshire's highest.

67 *Arethusa Falls and Frankenstein Cliff*

Distance: 5-mile loop
Difficulty: moderate–challenging
Hiking time: 3 hours
Elevation gain: 1500 feet
High point: 2530 feet

Management: New Hampshire SP
Season: year-round
Map: NHSP website
GPS coordinates: 44.14829°, −71.36651°

Getting there: From Bartlett, head northwest on Route 302 toward Crawford Notch. Travel 8.2 miles and turn left onto Arethusa Falls Road. There are two parking areas: a large area at the base of the hill and a second smaller spot 0.1 mile up the road. **Note:** Parking fee required.

This half-day adventure combines a stop at New Hampshire's highest waterfalls with a trek to the precarious edge of a 600-foot cliff featuring exceptional views. The route generally follows easy-to-moderate terrain, and the hike's one steep section becomes a faded memory as wildflowers, balsam-scented forests, warbling songbirds, and cascading rivers quickly form more-lasting memories. Choose this popular hike during midweek if you are looking for a bit of solitude.

Leaving from the lower lot's northern end, the trail climbs quickly to a junction. Turn right on the Frankenstein Cliff Trail and hike along the mostly flat terrain for a half mile to the Frankenstein Trestle. This impressive bridge spans a small stream along the historical Conway Scenic Railroad line that leads from North Conway to Crawford Depot. Swing under the tracks and begin an aggressive climb up the loose, rocky soil. Gaining more than 800 feet in less than 0.75 mile, the trail passes beneath sheer rock faces

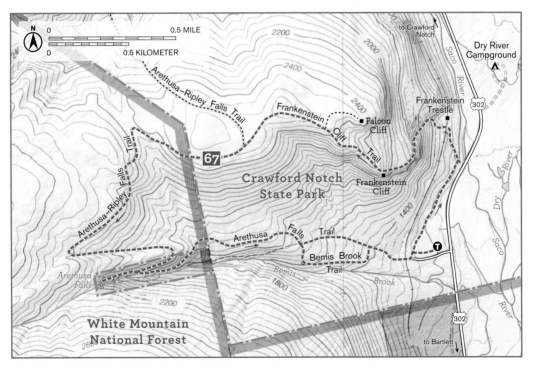

and ascends a small ledge before emerging onto the precipitous cliff. Named for a German-born artist and not the infamous monster, Frankenstein Cliff is an excellent perch to check out Arethusa Falls plummeting in the distance and more mesmerizing scenes of the Saco River far below.

Returning to the forest (the site of a significant fire in 2022 that burned more than 100 acres on and around the cliff), the trail continues near the rim and eventually heads to less-tenuous locales. In 0.3 mile, pass a lightly used path that leads 0.3 mile to Falcon Cliff. The main route continues rising steadily, eventually reaching a view of Mount Washington near the highest point of the hike. Past this rocky outcrop, the path becomes much easier.

At a junction, stay left on the Arethusa–Ripley Falls Trail and begin a moderate 1-mile descent. Past a small cascade, the path winds through a dark evergreen forest, ending at a junction with the Arethusa Falls Trail. Turn right and drop 0.2 mile to Bemis Brook. The official trail ends at the base of the impressive falls, where water crashes over a short ledge before taking a final plunge to the pool below. Although this is an idyllic location to stay cool during the summer, be sure to watch the falls safely from below and resist the temptation to scale the treacherous adjacent slopes.

Begin the 1.5-mile conclusion by retracing your steps east. Stay right and remain on the Arethusa Falls Trail as it meanders across mostly level terrain before moderately losing elevation. One mile from the falls, arrive at a junction with the Bemis Brook Trail. This more interesting but difficult route initially drops very rapidly 0.1 mile before paralleling the cascading water. To the left, the Arethusa Falls Trail descends fairly uniformly. They reconnect near the trail's end.

Upon reaching the trailhead, carefully cross the active railroad tracks. Walk through the upper parking area and pick up the trail which points toward Frankenstein Cliff. Once in the woods, quickly arrive at a junction. Turn right to return to the lower parking area.

Shorter Options: If you are looking for a shorter and less rigorous adventure, skip the cliffs and opt for the more popular 3-mile out-and-back hike to Arethusa Falls.

68 *Mounts Webster and Jackson*

Distance: 6.5-mile loop
Difficulty: challenging
Hiking time: 5 hours
Elevation gain: 2600 feet
High point: 4052 feet

Management: White Mountain NF
Season: year-round
Map: WMNF website
GPS coordinates: 44.21488°, −71.40834°

Getting there: From the junction of Routes 302 and 3 in Twin Mountain, follow Route 302 east and drive 8.7 miles to the trailhead (on the left). Park in the lot on the opposite side of the road. Overflow parking is available along both sides of the road between the trailhead and Crawford Depot.

These two summits on the Presidential Range's most prominent southern ridgeline are a great introduction to New Hampshire's 4000-foot mountains, especially for those looking for winter adventures in the heart of the White Mountains. Although shorter than many nearby treks to higher peaks, this loop features challenging terrain that should not be underestimated. Fortunately, the rewards for completing the circuit are dramatic mountaintop vistas of

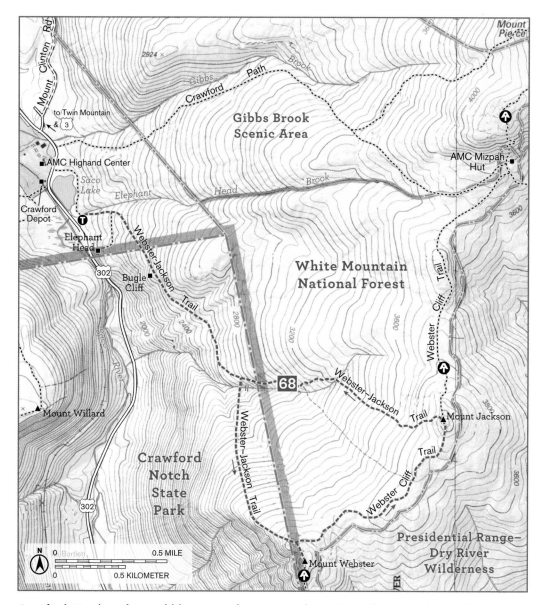

Crawford Notch and incredible views of surrounding summits in all directions.

Safely make your way across the busy road and pick up the Webster-Jackson Trail just south of Saco Lake. The blue-blazed path meanders easily 0.1 mile to a junction. Here, a spur leads right 0.2 mile to the top of Elephant Head. This rocky bluff at the top of Crawford Notch is a worthwhile addition to the day's travels. Remain on the main trail as it rises steadily above a mountain stream before swinging right.

The climb continues over the next mile across a rugged landscape with steep pitches occasionally interrupted with more-moderate terrain, brook crossings, and occasional descents. Near the halfway point, a spur departs right and immediately leads to Bugle Cliff, a scenic perch high above the notch.

A blanket of winter snow and ice covers Mount Jackson's summit.

Arrive at a three-way junction 1.3 miles from the start. Stay right on the Webster branch of the Webster-Jackson Trail. It descends steeply less than 0.1 mile to the base of a cascade. This is a good place to catch your breath and prepare for the challenging 1-mile ascent that follows. While the terrain is easy to navigate, the steady incline gets the blood pumping. Before long, arrive at an intersection with the Webster Cliff Trail (Appalachian Trail).

Follow the white blazes to the right. They cut through the ledge-covered landscape and quickly lead to Mount Webster's rocky high point, atop its slide-scarred slopes. There is incredible scenery in most directions, but especially of the glacier-carved Crawford Notch far below, the Willey Range across the way, and countless peaks beyond.

Retrace your steps north and remain on the Webster Cliff Trail (AT) as it meanders pleasantly another 1.3 miles through the high-elevation boreal forest. In places, extra care is needed on steeper pitches. This is especially true toward the end, as you scramble up rock and exposed ledge to the 4052-foot summit of Mount Jackson. Just before the high point, a sign marks the start of the Jackson branch of the Webster-Jackson Trail, exiting left. Turn right here and walk a few dozen steps through the stunted trees to reach an open landscape with breathtaking views of Mount Washington and the Dry River valley. Most hikers are greeted by resident gray jays who frequent this summit.

Return to the Webster-Jackson Trail junction and swing right. Watch your step and enjoy some final views as you descend back into the trees. The 1.2-mile blue-blazed route levels off at first but soon drops moderately through the spruce-and-fir forest. Approach a mountain stream and parallel it to a junction. Stay right and retrace your steps back to the start.

Nearby Options: Leaving south from the nearby Crawford Depot, pick up the Mount Willard Trail. This moderate 3.2-mile-roundtrip hike is a popular journey to a breathtaking clifftop in the heart of Crawford Notch. There are few hikes in the White Mountains that offer more significant rewards for the relatively modest effort required.

69 *Pondicherry Wildlife Refuge*

Distance: 5.1 miles roundtrip
Difficulty: easy
Hiking time: 2.5 hours
Elevation gain: 100 feet
High point: 1130 feet

Management: USFWS, NH Audubon
Season: year-round
Map: Trail Finder website
GPS coordinates: 44.35822°, −71.53979°

Getting there: From the junction of Routes 115 and 3 north of Twin Mountain, follow Route 115 north. Drive 4.4 miles and then turn left onto Hazen Road. Continue 1.4 miles (becomes Airport Road) to the parking area on the right. **Note:** Multiuse trail frequently used by bicyclists.

New Hampshire Audubon and the state's Fish and Game Department acquired 312 acres near the shores of Cherry and Little Cherry Ponds in 1963. With support from the Silvio O. Conte National Fish and Wildlife Refuge, this ecologically rich conservation area has grown to more than 6500 acres. Today it is home to an extensive trail network that showcases exceptional bird-watching opportunities, excellent fall-foliage viewing, and spectacular scenes of the Presidential Range throughout the year.

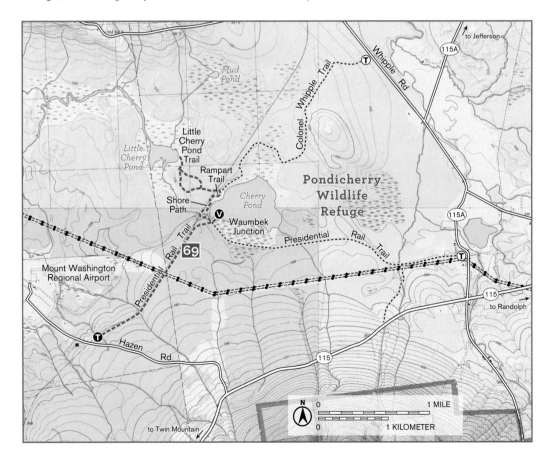

The heart of the refuge lies near the site of the former Waumbek Junction, which was located near two interconnected railroads. One rail line remains active, while the other has been transformed into a multiuse trail corridor. From Waumbek Junction, visitors can access a network of short loops and scenic shorefront paths. Hikers can reach this site on Cherry Pond from three different trailheads. The shortest and most direct route is this one, beginning near the Mount Washington Regional Airport.

Pick up the Presidential Rail Trail as it heads north at a large gate. The wide, mostly level corridor is also popular with bicyclists. Traversing the crushed-stoned surface, hike 1.4 miles through changing forest habitats and occasional openings. There are ample opportunities to survey the surrounding vegetation for colorful warblers, boisterous sparrows, and other songbirds. The trail swings right before arriving at Waumbek Junction.

Straight ahead, the Presidential Rail Trail leads 2.6 miles to a parking lot on Route 115A. This alternative access route crosses a wide-open bog before winding through a thicker forest with an occasional wetland. To the left, check out the wooden decking that leads to the Tudor Richards Viewing Platform. This is a great spot to view Cherry Pond, with Mount Starr King and Mount Waumbek rising to the north. Look for waterfowl and wading birds feeding in the marshy wetland.

At the entrance to the platform, turn sharply left onto the Waumbek Link. This more rustic trail leads to active railroad tracks. Follow them briefly, before swinging right onto a narrower Shore Path. Hike back to the pond and excellent views of Mount Washington. A short spur exits right to visit a small cove, while the main route bends left, hugging the shore until reaching the tracks once again.

Follow the rail line to the right. A brief walk leads to the start of the Rampart Trail. Follow this route back to the water's edge to a junction with the Little Cherry Pond Trail. Ahead, the Rampart Trail passes numerous scenic spots over the next 0.2 mile before ending at a junction with the 2-mile Colonel Whipple Trail—the quietest option for hikers accessing Cherry Pond.

Turn left on the Little Cherry Pond Trail. After crossing the rail tracks, pass a sign welcoming you to a New Hampshire Audubon preserve. Weave through the evergreen forest 0.3 mile to the start of a 0.7-mile loop. Near the circuit's halfway point, explore the 0.2-mile spur that leads to Little Cherry Pond. With a little luck, you might spot a moose or other wildlife browsing near this remote water body. After completing the loop, retrace your steps back to the start and catch a few more glimpses of Cherry Pond's scenic waterfront along the way.

Fall foliage reflecting on Cherry Pond

70 *Presidential Traverse*

Distance: 19.5 miles one-way
Difficulty: strenuous
Hiking time: 14 hours / 2–3 days
Elevation gain: 8700 feet
High point: 6288 feet

Management: White Mountain NF
Season: May–Oct
Map: WMNF website
GPS coordinates: 44.37155°,
−71.28895°; 44.21987°, −71.41020°

Getting there: Starting point: To reach the northern trailhead, drive 7.1 miles east on Route 2 from the junction of Routes 2 and 115 in Jefferson. Alternatively, drive 5.3 miles west on Route 2 from the junction of Routes 2 and 16 in Gorham. The trailhead is located at Appalachia on Route 2 in Randolph. *Shuttle drop-off:* To reach the southern trailhead near the Crawford Depot, drive 8.5 miles east on Route 302 from its junction with Route 3 in Twin Mountain. Parking is available near the depot, along the side of Route 302, in a lot on Mount Clinton Road, and at the Appalachian Mountain Club's Highland Center (for guests). *Notes:* Backcountry huts and campsites available. The best overnight options are the AMC huts located along the route (tent camping sites are limited and not as convenient). Both huts require reservations, which fill quickly. You can also carve the traverse into shorter excursions from either trailhead (see Shorter Options).

The ultimate adventure for experiencing New England's highest peaks, the rugged Presidential Traverse can be done in a single day but is more often tackled on a multiday journey. Regardless of your desired itinerary, be sure to keep the weather in mind, as the bulk of the excursion occurs well above tree line, with full exposure to the elements and little margin for error. If you come prepared and the weather gods are kind, you will exit the trail near Crawford Depot with memories to last a lifetime.

The hike begins from the northern trailhead, on the popular Valley Way. Those tackling the trek in a single day should begin before sunrise. However, this well-trodden path is not difficult to navigate with a headlamp. Be sure to pay attention at the many signed junctions. The 3.6-mile Valley Way is well protected for much of the way and parallels Snyder Brook throughout, but mostly from afar. Enjoy the gradual incline over the first mile. The trail rises more steadily in the middle, until a final challenging stretch leads above tree line near the AMC's Madison Spring Hut. Catch your breath and be prepared; you will not encounter many trees over the next 11 miles.

Before embarking south from the hut, scramble 0.5 mile up the Osgood Trail/Appalachian Trail (AT). It leads steeply to the summit of Mount Madison, the first of nine peaks along the traverse. From atop the narrow high point, there are exquisite views of the terrain that lies ahead, including Mount Washington looming in the distance. Use caution descending back to the hut as you acclimate to the ubiquitous rocks and rugged landscape that typify much of the traverse.

The hike's next segment takes advantage of the 6.5-mile Gulfside Trail (AT). With few exceptions, this route traverses a treeless expanse bordered with fragile alpine plants and incredible natural beauty. There are steep approaches to all four mountains along its course, but also a few level sections in between. To set foot on the next three peaks, you will need to take slightly longer, parallel diversions. Follow the Air Line up Mount Adams and the Lowe's Path down it. Beyond Edmands Col, use the Loop Trail to climb up and over Mount Jefferson. Exit Sphinx Col along the aptly named Mount Clay Trail to scale its barren ridgetop. Affording breathtaking scenes north across the Great Gulf, the Gulfside Trail's final mile is a methodical ascent to New England's highest point.

While Mount Washington is near the midway point, the bulk of the route's elevation climb is

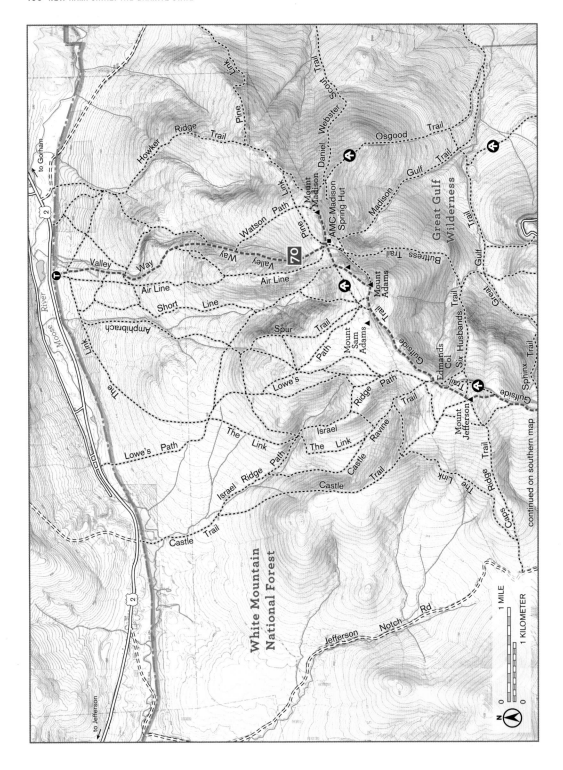

continued on southern map

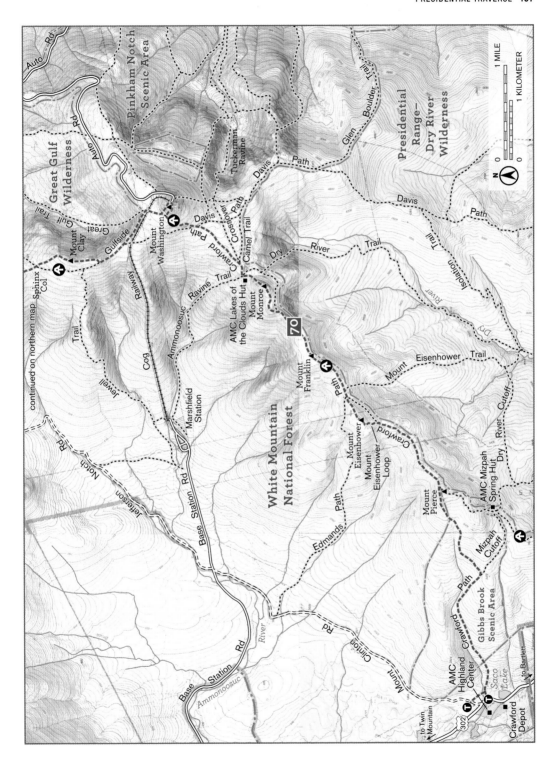

A hiker traverses Crawford Path with Mount Washington in the distance.

now in the rearview mirror. In the summer, you can find restrooms and other services here, but the summit can also be quite crowded with fellow travelers arriving by car and via the cog railway. On a clear day, the views appear limitless, with lower mountains and deep valleys visible in all directions.

Pick up the Crawford Path (AT) as it departs west from the summit. The oldest continuously used hiking corridor in New England, this 8.5-mile historical route dominates the second half of the traverse. Pay attention to the trail signs as you make your way 1.4 miles down the rocky slopes to AMC's aptly named Lakes of the Clouds Hut. Just beyond, explore the first of three parallel side trails to scale the picturesque peaks along the ridge. The Mount Monroe Loop is a short steep climb followed by a more modest descent. Next, an unmarked path loops easily over Mount Franklin's flat high point. Lastly,

after a rapid descent to the edge of the boreal forest, head up the Mount Eisenhower Loop to scale the peak's scenic rounded summit.

South of Mount Eisenhower, the Crawford Path remains atop the ridge another 1.2 miles while weaving in and out of the forest to a junction. Before staying straight on the Crawford Path, scramble 0.2 mile up the Webster Cliff Trail (AT) to the top of Mount Pierce (formerly Mount Clinton). This is a great spot for a final dramatic view of Mount Washington.

Return to the Crawford Path and turn left. The final 3 miles of the journey are mostly straightforward. The route descends steadily, but the footing is uneven in places. After approaching Gibbs Brook, the end of the trail is near. The blue blazes lead to Route 302 and the top of Crawford Notch (or follow the short spur right to Mount Clinton Road if ending here). Take a deep breath; you have completed the Presidential Traverse!

Shorter Options: There are many options from either trailhead. From the north, consider a loop to the summit of Mount Adams and/or Mount Madison that combines the Air Line, Gulfside, and Valley Way trails. From the south trailhead, hiking out and back along the Crawford Path to Mount Eisenhower and/or Mount Pierce is a great choice. Although very challenging, both hikes are popular throughout the year.

71 *Mount Madison*

Distance: 10.6-mile loop
Difficulty: strenuous
Hiking time: 8 hours
Elevation gain: 4300 feet
High point: 5366 feet

Management: White Mountain NF
Season: May–Oct
Map: WMNF website
GPS coordinates: 44.3104°, −71.22019°

Getting there: From the junction of Routes 302 and 16 in Glen, drive north on Route 16. In 16.2 miles, turn left into the Great Gulf Trail parking area. Alternatively, beginning at the junction of Routes 16 and 2 in Gorham, follow Route 16 south 6.3 miles to the parking area on the right. **Note:** Backcountry campsites available.

Named for the nation's fourth president, Mount Madison is a fitting tribute to the Founding Father most instrumental in the drafting of the United States Constitution. Its impressive pinnacle-shaped summit and glorious exposed ridgeline feature mesmerizing views of the Great Gulf Wilderness and Mount Washington. There are many challenging options to scale the peak's steep slopes, including this delightful all-day loop that begins near the banks of the Peabody River.

Pick up the Great Gulf Trail as it departs from the cul-de-sac at the northern end of the parking area. Briefly parallel the rushing river to the large suspension bridge that leads to the other side. Continue another 0.2 mile to a junction and the start of the loop.

Turn right onto the Great Gulf Link. This wide corridor proceeds 0.9 mile north, not far from the rushing water. Arrive at the southern tip of the White Mountain National Forest's Dolly Copp Campground and follow the pavement left 0.1

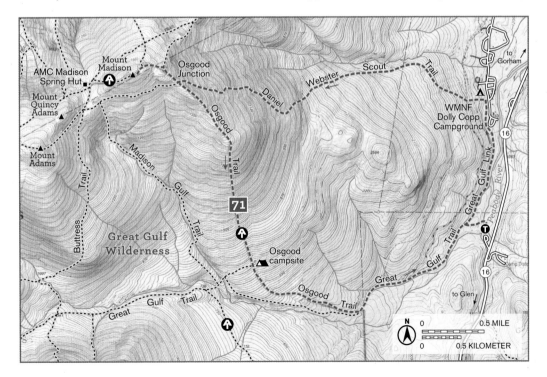

mile to the start of the Daniel Webster Scout Trail on the left.

Catch your breath before embarking on the relentless climb that awaits. Bearing the name of a famous nineteenth-century New Hampshire–born orator and secretary of state under three US presidents, the Daniel Webster Scout Trail is a steady climb at first. Beyond the halfway point of the 3.5-mile blue-blazed route, the forest transitions to evergreens and the incline becomes more pronounced. Plod up the increasingly steep terrain as the surrounding forest thins. Much of the final 0.5-mile stretch is across a mostly open rocky landscape. Follow the blazes and cairns closely while marveling at the incredible scenes across Pinkham Notch to the Carter Range.

Crest the ridgeline at Osgood Junction to behold breathtaking views of the northern Presidential Range looming high above the 5552-acre Great Gulf Wilderness that lies just north of the trail. The final 0.6-mile hike to the summit features views in all directions. Follow the Osgood Trail/Appalachian Trail (AT) right and scale the rugged corridor. Two abrupt climbs are interrupted by a brief reprieve near a trail intersection. The final scramble leads to the pointy 5366-foot peak. Enjoy scenes of mountains and valleys in all directions before retracing your steps east along the Osgood Trail (AT).

On the descent, continue southeast beyond the Osgood Junction. Blazed in white, the Osgood Trail (AT) traverses a spectacular high-elevation ridge that remains above tree line for nearly a mile. Take your time and watch your footing on the uneven rocky surface. Eventually dropping back into the shady boreal forest, the trail soon grows steeper. Slowly, the degree of difficulty moderates. At 2.6 miles from the summit, pass the Osgood tent site near a junction with the Osgood Cutoff Trail (AT).

Rocks and scenery abound along the Osgood Trail.

Stay straight on the now blue-blazed Osgood Trail. Descending through the northern hardwood forest, this path drops 0.8 mile to an intersection. Bear left on the Great Gulf Trail. Only 1.8 miles from the trailhead, this final stretch is a relaxing conclusion to the day's travels. Remain on the Great Gulf Trail as it approaches the Peabody River. Then recross the suspension bridge to reach the trail's end.

Other Options: Consider exploring deeper into the Great Gulf Wilderness on more-remote and rugged paths, such as the Madison Gulf and Buttress Trails. Both lead to the Appalachian Mountain Club's Madison Spring Hut and can be combined with each other or with either the Osgood or Daniel Webster Scout Trails to form loops. The AMC Hut provides overnight accommodations; reservations required.

72 *Carter Dome and Mount Hight*

Distance: 10.2-mile loop
Difficulty: challenging–strenuous
Hiking time: 8 hours
Elevation gain: 3500 feet
High point: 4832 feet

Management: White Mountain NF
Season: year-round
Map: WMNF website
GPS coordinates: 44.30217°, −71.22093°

Getting there: From the eastern junction of Routes 2 and 16 in Gorham, follow Route 16 south 6.9 miles to the parking area on the left. Alternatively, from the height of land in Pinkham Notch, follow Route 16 north 3.7 miles to the parking area on the right. *Note:* Backcountry campsites available.

The Carter Range is one of the finest vantage points from which to gaze onto the rocky summits and deep ravines of New Hampshire's Presidential Range towering to the west. This challenging all-day hike parallels soothing mountain streams, explores a rugged boulder-filled notch, and visits the ridge's most scenic summit. Accessible in all four seasons, this is a popular loop; visit midweek to find greater solitude.

One of the shorter and less-exposed paths to an Appalachian Mountain Club hut, the Nineteen Mile Brook Trail is well trodden throughout the year (the hut remains open all year, with limited service during the winter). The first 1.9 miles closely follow its namesake mountain stream while rising gradually to an intersection with the Carter Dome Trail. Near the section's halfway point, pass a dam that briefly blocks the rushing water.

Beyond the intersection, continue ascending moderately on the Nineteen Mile Brook Trail. Passing through pleasant forests, the route reaches the Appalachian Trail (AT) at mile 3.6. To the right, the white-blazed path rises very

Mid-winter adventure near the summit of Mount Hight

steeply to the top of Wildcat Mountain. Stay left and descend 0.1 mile to the lily-pad waters of Carter Lake and the start of the Carter-Moriah Trail (AT). Located in the heart of Carter Notch, this junction lies 0.2 mile north of the Carter Notch Hut complex. Before heading up the mountain, hike to the hut and just beyond to a short spur left that leads to the Rampart. The base of this

sprawling boulder field is a great place to imagine the power of the glaciers that ripped through this landscape thousands of years ago.

From Carter Lake, begin the day's toughest stint—a 1.2-mile, 1500-foot climb to the top of Carter Dome. While not technically difficult, the incline is incredibly demanding, particularly in the beginning. However, the views across

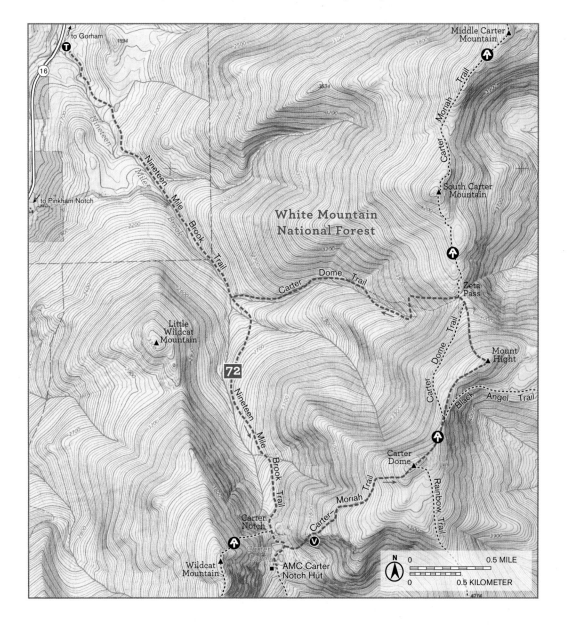

the notch to Wildcat Mountain are breathtaking. After passing a short spur that rises to a precarious scenic perch, the route moderates slightly before reaching the large summit cairn. Continue a few dozen feet beyond the high point to a northern view, where the growing trees are slowly obscuring the scenery except in winter.

For a more spectacular vista, proceed gently 0.8 mile north to Mount Hight by staying straight on the Carter-Moriah Trail at its junction with the Carter Dome and Black Angel trails. Although less prestigious than its taller neighbor, Mount Hight's barren summit is the most inviting spot in the Carter Range. It offers 360-degree scenery that includes the Wild River Wilderness area

to the east, the Presidential Range to the west, and the Mahoosuc Mountains rising north into Maine.

The 4.4-mile descent continues along the Carter-Moriah Trail (AT). Watch your footing while dropping steeply into the evergreen forest. In 0.5 mile, bear right on the Carter Dome Trail (AT) and arrive at Zeta Pass in 0.2 mile. Leaving the AT behind, stay left on the Carter Dome Trail. The first half of its 1.9-mile course is a steady decline moderated with numerous switchbacks. Near the midpoint, cross a stream twice and then descend more modestly, following its course. Swing right onto the Nineteen Mile Brook Trail for the final 1.9-mile stretch to Route 16.

73 Baldfaces

Distance: 9.8-mile loop
Difficulty: challenging–strenuous
Hiking time: 8 hours
Elevation gain: 3550 feet
High point: 3610 feet

Management: White Mountain NF
Season: year-round
Map: WMNF website
GPS coordinates: 44.23761°, −71.01139°

Getting there: From Route 302 in Fryeburg, Maine, follow Route 113 north 17.4 miles to North Chatham. Alternatively, from Route 2 in Gilead, Maine, drive south 12.7 miles on Route 113. The parking lot is on the east side of the road. **Notes:** Access in the winter is from the south only. Backcountry campsite available.

At just over 3600 feet, North and South Baldface Mountains lie more than 1000 feet below many of their neighbors to the west, but they tower over the foothills and bucolic countryside to the east. Left significantly bare in the wake of a 1903 fire, their exposed granite ridges provide innumerable scenic vistas, while their lower slopes enjoy cascading streams in wildlife-rich forests. This popular hike is a workout that is exceeded only by its many rewards.

The Baldface Circle Trail begins easily on the west side of Route 113 (just north and across the street from the parking area) and in 0.7 mile reaches the start of the loop. To the right a 0.1-mile spur leads to Emerald Pool, a popular swimming hole beneath a small cascade. Turn left on

the Baldface Circle Trail. In 0.2 mile, stay right at a junction with the Slippery Brook Trail. Ahead, a side path leads to intriguing Chandler Gorge before returning to the main route (choosing this option adds 0.4 mile to the hike). Beyond the gorge, the Baldface Circle Trail ascends gradually 1.2 miles to a lean-to, available on a first-come, first-served basis. Catch your breath, as the degree of difficulty is about to greatly intensify.

Over the next 0.7 mile, the trail scrambles up very steep ledges and increasingly open terrain. Watch your footing, especially over the first half of the climb, and carefully navigate the polished slope. The views become more and more breathtaking as you approach a three-way intersection.

Stay right for the final 0.5-mile climb. It continues in the open, briefly returns to the forest, and ends atop South Baldface, where 360-degree views include Mount Washington and the Carter Range to the west as well as the blue waters of Kezar Lake sprawling in the east.

The Baldface Circle Trail proceeds 1.2 miles to the summit of North Baldface. Meandering in and out of thin forests, the trail provides a scattering of incredible vistas. The final push to wide-open North Baldface leads once again to impressive views in all directions.

In the trees and out onto open ledges, the path continues north and tumbles 0.9 mile down and occasionally up small inclines until reaching a small open bump on the ridge. Breathe in the spectacular scenes of the Wild River Wilderness and north to peaks on both sides of the

Maine–New Hampshire border. Then pick up the Bicknell Ridge Trail on the right. It drops down semi-exposed granite slabs, where views of the large glacially cut basin are stunning. Follow this path 1 mile to a final open spot on the ridge. Here, the Eagle Cascade Link Trail diverges left, a good option early in the season when the water is flowing.

The Bicknell Ridge Trail continues straight 1.3 miles, descending steadily into the forest before moderating near the banks of a rushing stream. Carefully make your way across and then rejoin the Baldface Circle Trail to the right. Here, portions of the trail traverse private lands that are managed for forest products. In 0.7 mile, head across Charles Brook (can be difficult with high water) and enjoy the final 0.7-mile stretch to the parking area.

A final view of the two Baldface summits before heading down Bicknell Ridge

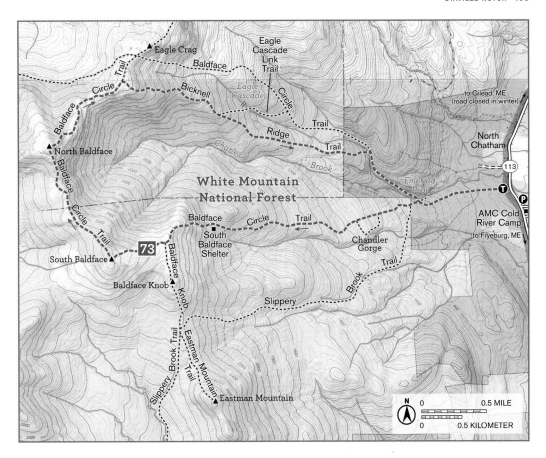

Other Options: To avoid the very steep pitch up South Baldface, consider exploring the much-quieter Slippery Brook Trail and the scenic Baldface Knob Trail. This 1-mile-longer route also provides access to nearby Eastman Mountain's open summit ledges at the end of a 0.8-mile spur. For a similar but less-exposed alternative on the descent, skip Bicknell Ridge and remain on the Baldface Circle Trail.

74 Dixville Notch

Distance: 5.2-mile loop
Difficulty: challenging
Hiking time: 4 hours
Elevation gain: 1900 feet
High point: 2600 feet

Management: New Hampshire SP
Season: year-round
Map: Trail Finder website
GPS coordinates: 44.86535°, −71.31317°

Getting there: From the junction of Routes 3 and 26 in Colebrook, drive 10 miles east on Route 26 to the trailhead on the right. Park on the south side of the road. **Note:** Portions of this route traverse private land.

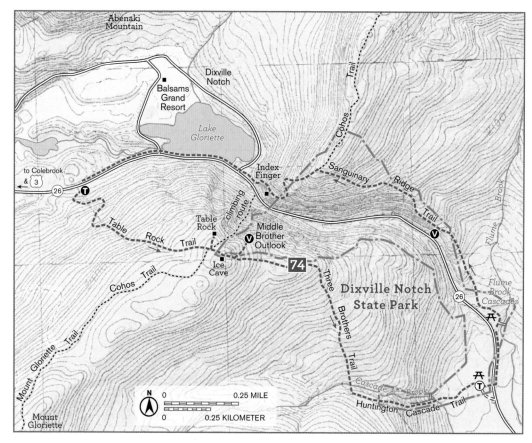

This challenging loop features precarious clifftop vistas, cascading brooks, and rugged natural beauty. Dixville Notch is traditionally one of the first places in the nation to cast ballots in presidential elections, and its remoteness makes this hike even more alluring. It is the perfect introduction to the state's 162-mile Cohos Trail (CT), a long-distance route that dissects New Hampshire's northernmost and least-populated county.

The western half of the day's loop crosses land owned by the Balsams Grand Resort, a turn-of-the-century facility in transition. Begin on the Table Rock Trail. It uses switchbacks and rock steps to rise steadily 0.7 mile to an intersection. Exiting right, the Mount Gloriette Trail (CT) ascends a nearby ski area.

Stay left on the Table Rock Trail (CT) and descend quickly to an intersection with the Three Brothers Trail (CT). Follow the spur left into a narrow saddle where the Table Rock Climbing Trail enters from the right. Straight ahead, the path rises immediately to the top of Table Rock. Like a peninsula, this prominent protrusion juts out, narrowing at the tip. Proceed with caution, as both sides fall precipitously. The eagle-eye views are amazing.

Return to the Three Brothers Trail (CT) and turn left. Hike past the Ice Cave, a narrow gap in the ledge. After a brief climb, the route descends moderately 0.4 mile to a spur that exits left to Middle Brother Outlook. This lightly used 0.1-mile path drops rapidly before climbing to a scenic perch above the notch. The Three Brothers Trail (CT) continues another 0.7 mile and ends at a stream crossing, shortly after entering Dixville Notch State Park.

Cross the water and pick up the 0.4-mile Huntington Cascade Trail (CT). This steep path

Lake Gloriette lies far below Table Rock in Dixville Notch.

parallels the rushing water as it cuts through a narrow ravine. There are numerous waterfalls along the way. The most scenic are toward the bottom. Leveling off significantly, the trail swings left and crosses the brook. Continue straight through a picnic area to reach a parking lot.

Stay right and follow the entranceway toward a small cemetery that serves as the final resting place for some of this area's earliest settlers. Follow the corridor left and hike a few hundred feet to Route 26. Safely cross the highway and rejoin the trail. The yellow blazes wind 0.4 mile toward the Flume Brook Cascades.

At the picnic area, join the Sanguinary Ridge Trail (CT) and rise 0.1 mile past the scenic flume where the route turns sharply left. For the next 0.6 mile, parallel a property boundary that, like the trail, is marked in yellow. While it can be confusing, the hiking path soon becomes more obvious. In 0.4 mile, reach the first of many vistas that offer views of Dixville Notch and distant peaks. Beyond the final promontory, swing right and climb aggressively to a junction, 1.2 miles from the flume. The CT departs right and leads 3 miles to Sanguinary Mountain.

Continue left on the Sanguinary Ridge Trail, which drops steadily 0.3 mile through a dense evergreen forest to an opening with picturesque views of Lake Gloriette. Watch your footing as you meander 0.3 mile down the barren landscape of loose rock and ledge. Beyond the aptly named Index Finger, a final stretch through the forest leads to the road. Follow Route 26 west and take advantage of the wide shoulder to complete the loop in 0.6 mile.

Shorter Options: Head out and back to Dixville Notch's most alluring feature by hiking 2 miles roundtrip to Table Rock. Conversely, park at the eastern trailhead and limit your exploration to Huntington and Flume Brook Cascades.

Opposite, top: Jordan Pond offers many shots of North and South Bubble.

Opposite, bottom: Horn Pond lies high atop Bigelow Mountain Range.

Maine: The Pine Tree State

Nearly as big as the other five New England states combined, Maine is a land of endless forests, bountiful lakes, rushing rivers, rolling mountains, and rugged coastline. While hikers will discover a vast network of trails scattered across public lands and land trust preserves, the state's crown jewels are Baxter State Park, Acadia National Park, and the Appalachian Trail corridor.

Coastal locales are ideal from late spring through fall, but be prepared for much company during the dog days of summer. Head to more-northern destinations between Memorial Day and mid-October to ensure optimum trail conditions. Throughout the year, with proper planning and preparation, Maine is a hiker's paradise, where one is as likely to encounter other fellow hikers as well as wildlife, such as moose or black bear.

75 Mount Agamenticus

Distance: 8.2-mile loop	**Management:** Mount Agamenticus
Difficulty: moderate–challenging	Conservation Program (MACP)
Hiking time: 5 hours	**Season:** year-round
Elevation gain: 1400 feet	**Map:** MACP website
High point: 691 feet	**GPS coordinates:** 43.21682°, −70.69206°

Getting there: From Interstate 95 in York, take exit 7 and head west. Turn right onto Chases Pond Road. In 3.7 miles, stay left on Mountain Road. Drive 2.6 miles to the parking area on the right, at the base of the summit road. **Notes:** Multiuse trails: white-blazed paths are open to mountain bikers; short stretches along fluorescent-blazed routes are available for motorized recreation; a few red-blazed trails are limited to foot traffic.

For decades, the Mount Agamenticus to the Sea coalition, a collection of land trusts, municipalities, and government agencies, has been busy conserving and piecing together this extraordinary 13,000-acre ecologically rich corner of Maine that welcomes outdoor enthusiasts throughout the year. This excursion combines multiple loops into a rewarding adventure to vernal pools, rocky hillsides, shady forests, and pleasant summits.

Begin on the white-blazed Ring Trail, which rises 0.1 mile to a junction. Stay right and follow the circuit's eastern branch 0.5 mile, ascending modestly to a junction with the Rocky Road Trail. Bear right here, leaving the main summit area for later in the excursion. The path heads down the slope and passes an extensive vernal pool before arriving at an intersection in 0.2 mile.

Hike left along the Porcupine Trail. It winds gently into a saddle and across a stream to an unmarked trail in 0.4 mile. Turn right to tackle this 0.3 mile climb up the ledge-covered slopes of Second Hill. There are limited views through the pines and across the lichen-draped rocks that lead to the peak's high point.

Pick up the Ridge Trail and descend north 0.3 mile to a wetland depression before ascending gently once again. Remain atop the ridge, staying straight past two intersections. Once over a low summit, the trail winds down the rocky slopes, wraps around a boulder-filled basin, and comes to an end at a three-way intersection.

Over the next half mile, follow the fluorescent-green-blazed Notch Trail right; turn left onto the fluorescent-orange-blazed Wheel Trail; turn left again on the fluorescent-purple-blazed Great Marsh Trail, and immediately arrive at the start of the Third Hill Trail exiting right. This 1.5-mile path rises up and over a diminutive, forested summit tucked away in a quiet corner of the sprawling conservation area.

After exploring Third Hill, proceed left along the Great Marsh Trail to quickly reach the 0.3-mile Darter Trail on the right. This white-blazed route wraps under an impressive ledge and crosses a small brook before concluding. Swing right onto the wider Notch Trail and hike 0.2 mile to the base of the Incline Trail. Scale this rustic path back to the Ridge Trail. At the

junction, stay left and then immediately veer right onto an unmarked path that ends at the Porcupine Trail.

Head south along the well-used route. It stays far below Second Hill, passing trails that lead to its high point. Make your way to the Chestnut Oak Trail to begin the day's final climb. Rise steadily 0.3 mile to an intersection with the Ring Trail. Continue left and in 0.1 mile, turn right onto the 0.2-mile Witch Hazel Trail.

Upon intersecting the universally accessible Big A Trail, explore this inviting path left. The relaxing grade meanders 1 mile across the summit area, across crushed stones and wooden boardwalks. Enjoy views of the ocean, the White Mountains, and the hills of southern New Hampshire. After a final Mount

Route up the pine-covered ledges of Second Hill

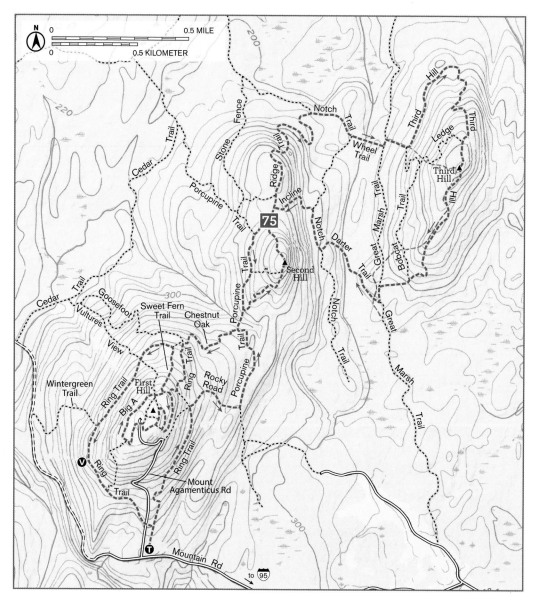

Washington vista, descend the 0.2-mile Sweet Fern Trail.

Back to the Ring Trail one last time, turn left to complete the circuit around the mountain.

Over mostly easy terrain, the wide path meanders past a western viewpoint and arrives at the summit road in 0.9 mile. Cross the pavement and hike 0.1 mile back to the parking area.

Other Options: There are many ways to adjust this recommendation along the well-marked, multiple-use trail network. For a shorter route, consider a loop limited to the main peak by using the Ring, Witch Hazel, Big A, and Sweet Fern Trails. This 3-mile trek showcases the area's most scenic viewpoints.

76 Monhegan Island

Distance: 5.1-mile loop
Difficulty: moderate–challenging
Hiking time: 4 hours
Elevation gain: 675 feet
High point: 150 feet

Management: Monhegan Associates
Season: May–Oct
Map: Monhegan Associates website
GPS coordinates: 43.76504°, −69.32126°

Getting there: There are three boat services that provide passenger-only transportation to the island. These services originate in Boothbay Harbor, New Harbor, and Port Clyde. Visit monheganwelcome.com for more information. The hike begins at the island's dock.
Notes: Smoking prohibited. Keep in mind, the White Head Trail is the best route to get back to the dock in a hurry.

Waves pound the rugged shoreline below Black Head.

Monhegan has lured tourists, artists, and bird-watchers for more than a century. This small island, located 10 miles from the mainland, boasts more than 9 miles of hiking trails and features some of Maine's most spectacular oceanside scenery, including precipitous ledges that drop 150 feet to the crashing surf below. To complete this 5.1-mile circuit that focuses on Monhegan's picturesque Cliff Trail, either spend an overnight on the island or catch an early-morning boat.

Monhegan Associates, a nonprofit land trust, manages more than 350 acres and nineteen trails on the island. When hiking, pay close attention at junctions for numbered markers—they coincide with the various trails. For a nominal fee, you

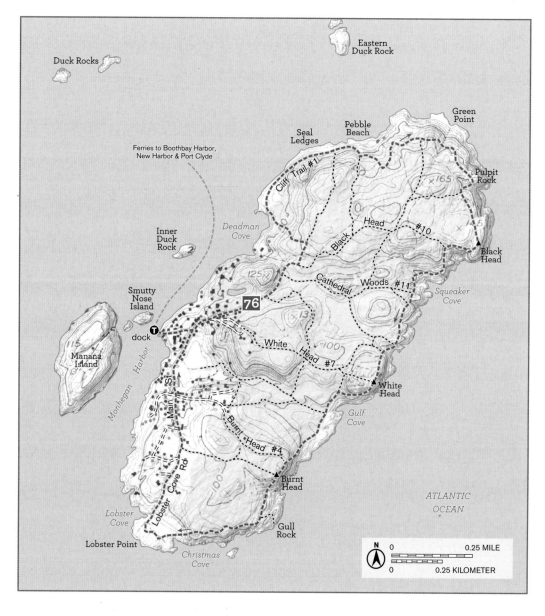

can purchase a detailed map on the boat and at various places on the island.

To reach the Cliff Trail's northern terminus, follow the dirt road east from the town dock. In 0.1 mile, turn left on Main Street and stay left again in another 0.1 mile. The gravel road levels off and slowly becomes more rustic. After passing two trails departing right, reach the start of the Cliff Trail on the left, 0.6 mile from the dock.

The hike begins in earnest now. Over the next 3.9 miles, your route will never stray far from the shoreline. Be alert for small wooden "1" Cliff Trail markers at the many intersections along the way. While the Cliff Trail, with few exceptions, is easy to navigate, the terrain is often rugged and challenging. Take your time and enjoy the incredible ocean scenery around every bend in the trail. In a few places along the eastern shore, there are alternative Cliff Trails labeled "1A." These options are less difficult, but also longer and less scenic.

The natural features encountered along the way include Seal Ledges and Pebble Beach in 0.5 mile, Pulpit Rock in 1.3 miles, Black Head in 1.6 miles, Squeaker Cove in 2 miles, White Head in 2.4 miles, Burnt Head in 3 miles, a spur trail left to Gull Rock in 3.2 miles, and the remains of various shipwrecks near Christmas Cove in 3.8 miles. In terms of rugged beauty, the stretch between Pulpit Rock and White Head is the most spectacular. It is also the most challenging, with frequent steep ups and downs. There are many places to take breaks and marvel at the stunning beauty, but be alert for poison ivy in places (mostly accompanied with signage).

The Cliff Trail ends at Lobster Cove, where a rock staircase leads to Lobster Cove Road. Follow this dirt route (becomes Main Street) 0.6 mile back to the village. Time permitting, check out the charming galleries and small stores, or grab a bite to eat at one of the restaurants. During spring and fall migration, Monhegan Village is a popular stopping point for songbirds. It is a great place to spot northern orioles, scarlet tanagers, indigo buntings, and other colorful avian life.

Shorter Options: Consider using the Black Head and White Head Trails in conjunction with the Cliff Trail. This will maximize your time exploring the coastline's most scenic section. For a quieter trek, check out the many paths that meander through the island's interior evergreen forests. A popular choice is the Cathedral Woods Trail. It features small fairy houses.

77 Ragged Mountain

Distance: 7.2-mile loop
Difficulty: moderate–challenging
Hiking time: 4 hours
Elevation gain: 1525 feet
High point: 1300 feet

Management: Coastal Mountains Land Trust (CMLT)
Season: year-round
Map: CMLT website
GPS coordinates: 44.21893°, −69.17156°

Getting there: From the junction of Routes 17 and 90 in West Rockport, follow Route 17 west. Drive 2.7 miles and turn right onto Hope Street. Continue 0.6 mile to the parking area for the Thorndike Brook Trailhead on the right.

Founded in 1986, the Coastal Mountains Land Trust has conserved more than 5000 acres around the Camden Hills and near the shores of Penobscot Bay. Their preserves feature nearly 50 miles of hiking trails that explore scenic mountain ridges, wildlife-rich wetlands, productive blueberry barrens, and maturing hardwood forests. This recommended circuit is one of a

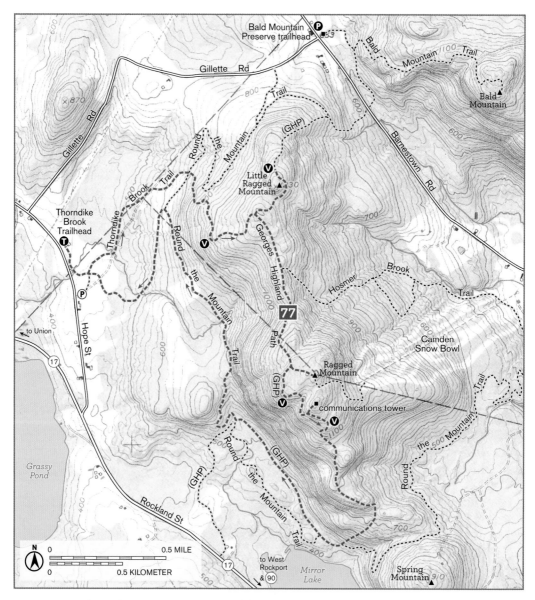

growing number of itineraries now possible through the development of the trust's Round the Mountain Trail, a multiuse corridor that, when complete, will circle Ragged Mountain and the Camden Snow Bowl.

Begin along the wide path that departs south from the kiosk. Hike around a dammed wetland, enter the forest, and reach a junction in 0.2 mile. Turn left onto the much-narrower Thorndike Brook Trail. The first third of this 1.4-mile path is easy as it meanders across a small brook, rises gradually, and heads straight at an intersection with the Round the Mountain Trail. Ascend more aggressively over the next 0.6 mile to the top of a large ledge offering multiple views across the bucolic countryside. At the final vista, swing left and climb 0.3 mile to a three-way junction with the Georges Highland Path, an inviting long-distance trail maintained by the Georges River Land Trust.

To the left, the trail leads 0.2 mile to an attractive rocky outcrop near the top of Little Ragged Mountain. This is a worthwhile diversion. Upon returning to the junction, turn left to continue on the Georges Highland Path. After weaving through pleasant forests, a brief scramble leads to a scenic promontory in 0.7 mile—on a clear day, Mount Washington can be seen on the western horizon. To the left, a red-blazed trail heads 0.1 mile through the boreal forest to Ragged Mountain's high point and views of Penobscot Bay. Return to the Georges Highland Path and turn left.

The next 0.3 mile is the hike's most spectacular stretch. Watch your footing and closely follow the cairns across the undulating terrain. Other than a brief descent into the forest, most of this section traverses open ledges with extensive views. A final steep pitch up the rocky slope leads to an unmarked spur that rises quickly to an open ledge at the base of the mountain's communications tower.

Continuing east, the Georges Highland Path descends steadily 0.7 mile, occasionally offering panoramas to Acadia's distant summits or more-intimate scenes of Mirror Lake far below. As the openings in the forest grow smaller and less frequent, the trees become more impressive. Swinging right, the trail descends steeply and reaches a junction with the Round the Mountain Trail in 0.4 mile.

Turn right as the two routes coincide briefly, and stay right on the Georges Highland Path as they diverge. Although there is little elevation change over the next 0.6 mile, the footing is uneven in places. Pass beneath an impressive scree slope before arriving at another intersection.

Hike north on the easy-to-follow Round the Mountain Trail. It is the perfect 2-mile conclusion to the day's loop. After a brief climb, the remaining stretch is downhill or flat. Near the halfway point, at a sharp bend, stay left toward the Thorndike Brook Trailhead. Along the way, scan the forested habitat for warblers, thrushes, woodpeckers, and other resident avian species.

Other Options: Rather than the longer loop, head 5.2 miles roundtrip out and back along the Thorndike Brook and Georges Highland Path to Ragged Mountain's communications tower. Better yet, visit the Coastal Mountain Land Trust website for information on other access points to the mountain's growing network of trails, and discover their other properties: nearby Bald Mountain and Beech Hill are great choices.

Ragged Mountain's summit area offers countless viewpoints.

Maine Land Trust Network

A program of Maine Coast Heritage Trust, the Maine Land Trust Network brings together more than eighty conservation organizations protecting land throughout the state. Together, these membership-based nonprofits have conserved more than 2.7 million acres in Maine and provide over 1200 miles of hiking trails at locations in all sixteen counties.

78 *Camden Hills*

Distance: 7.3-mile loop
Difficulty: moderate–challenging
Hiking time: 5 hours
Elevation gain: 1775 feet
High point: 1380 feet

Management: Maine BPL
Season: year-round
Map: BPL website
GPS coordinates: 44.22662°, −69.07847°

Getting there: From Route 1 near downtown Camden, follow Route 52 northwest 1.2 miles to the trailhead on the right. Parking is available along the east side of the road.

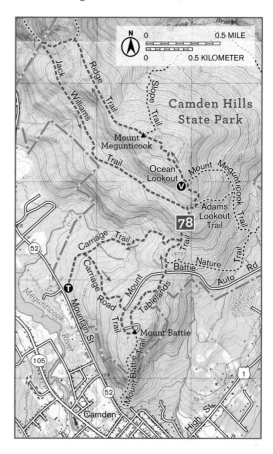

Heading to Mount Battie for panoramic views of Penobscot Bay or venturing to the edge of Mount Megunticook's dramatic Ocean Lookout are memorable hikes on their own. This recommended itinerary visits both natural features by forming two distinct loops across rocky landscapes, beneath towering treetops, and through diverse habitats, where wildflowers and songbirds abound.

Head northeast up the Carriage Road Trail. At a junction in 0.3 mile, swing right and begin a modest ascent. The path meanders 0.8 mile up Mount Battie's west side, ending at the auto road. Follow the pavement right and hike 0.1 mile to the summit of the 800-foot peak. Mount Battie provides splendid views of Camden Harbor and Penobscot Bay. The scenery from the top of a stone tower is even more extensive and includes the Camden Snow Bowl and Bald Mountain.

The journey continues along the 1.5-mile Tablelands Trail, which departs near the center of the mountain's parking area. Across thinly forested ledges, watch your step as you drop steadily to the north. Soon, a steep pitch leads to the edge of the auto road. Safely cross and proceed over a couple of small ridges and past a junction with the Nature Trail. At the next

Enjoying the scenery atop Mount Megunticook's Ocean Lookout

intersection, the Carriage Trail departs left. It drops 1.2 miles back to Route 52, providing a quicker end to the day's travels. Continue straight to complete the longer excursion.

After the first of two significant climbs, the rock-strewn Tablelands Trail soon plateaus at a junction with the Jack Williams Trail. Stay straight and scramble up the increasingly steep slope. Through stunted oaks, the route affords ever-expanding vistas at a safe distance from the edge of the sheer cliff face. The Ocean Lookout's impressive perch provides incredible 270-degree views that on clear days include Isle au Haut to the south and Mount Washington on the western horizon.

From the top of the lookout, pick up the Ridge Trail and climb 0.5 mile to the wooded summit of Mount Megunticook—the park's highest point. Now it is time to explore a quieter section of Camden Hills by staying on the Ridge Trail. A brief descent through the boreal forest leads to a relaxing walk through a brighter stand of hardwood trees. After passing a ledge with pastoral scenes across the rolling landscape, drop more aggressively back into the evergreens.

One mile beyond the summit, turn sharply left onto the Jack Williams Trail. This lightly used 1.6-mile route drops quickly at first, but soon climbs moderately. Ascend the rolling landscape under towering birch and maple, occasionally across small streams. The trail ends near the base of Ocean Lookout's massive rock face.

Bear right on the Tablelands Trail and hike 0.5 mile to the Carriage Trail. This path descends moderately, winds under an intriguing ledge, and parallels a small cascading stream before dropping steadily to the valley floor. Take your time. Numerous small brook crossings follow; generally the water is not too high. The final stretch is along flat terrain until the end.

Shorter Options: If you are looking for a shorter adventure, omit the Ridge and Jack Williams Trails to complete a 4.5-mile trek to Mount Battie and Ocean Lookout.

79 *Great Pond Mountain Wildlands*

Distance: 5.5 miles roundtrip	*Management:* Great Pond Mountain
Difficulty: moderate	Conservation Trust (GPMCT)
Hiking time: 3 hours	*Season:* year-round
Elevation gain: 1000 feet	*Map:* GPMCT website
High point: 1030 feet	*GPS coordinates:* 44.59310°, −68.68807°

Getting there: From the junction of Routes 1 and 15 in Orland, follow Route 1 east 1.6 miles. Turn left onto Hatchery Road and drive 1.5 miles to Craig Brook National Fish Hatchery. Just beyond the building, swing right onto the dirt road (gated in winter). Drive 0.5 mile up the narrow road to the parking area on left. *Note:* Portions of the route traverse multiuse trails used by mountain bikers.

Great Pond Mountain Conservation Trust—a membership-based organization dedicated to protecting biodiversity, clean water, scenic beauty, working landscapes, and outdoor recreation—acquired the bulk of its Wildlands preserve in 2007. Now spanning nearly 5000 acres, it has become a four-season destination featuring miles of hiking and multiuse trails to remote ponds and bald summits. This moderate loop to

the preserve's highest point is a great introduction to an area that begs further exploration to its more remote corners.

Most visitors to Great Pond Mountain opt for the shortest route that begins to the east. The slightly longer trek described here visits quieter settings with access to additional places to explore. Proceed through the gate on the Dead River Road, a wide multiuse trail corridor once

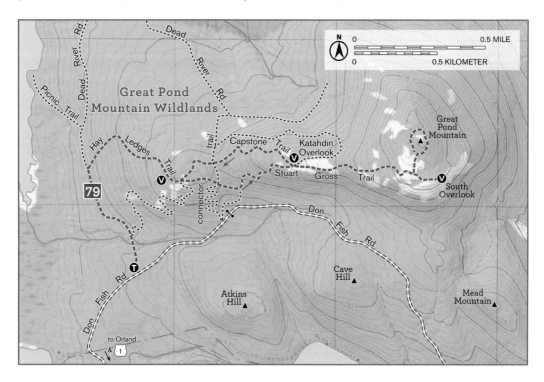

used to haul timber. Prior to its acquisition, the property was subject to significant harvesting in places. Now the trust manages the Wildlands with a goal of restoring older stands of trees and balancing the needs of diverse wildlife. In 2022, the trust was awarded the Hancock County Tree Farm of the Year.

Reach the start of the Hay Ledges Trail in 0.5 mile. Turn right and begin a modest ascent through the young forest. Marked with blue diamonds, the path meanders up the slope. In 0.6 mile, check out the short spur leading to a meadow with pleasant scenes across Alamoosook Lake to the Camden Hills. The Hay Ledges Trail levels off. Proceed straight through two four-way intersections, then descend into a saddle. The route swings right and ends.

An inviting spur leads to South Overlook.

Head left on the mountain's most popular route—the Stuart Gross Trail. After weaving around ledges and rising steadily, it emerges atop a semi-open landscape in 0.3 mile, near the upper terminus of the Capstone Trail. Over the next 0.7 mile, the forest grows thinner, affording pleasant views of Blue Hill and Acadia National Park. Watch your step, as much of the route traverses polished granite that can be slick when wet. A final steep pitch leads to a mostly barren expanse.

To the right, check out the spur that drops 0.2 mile to the South Overlook. The main trail continues to form a 0.3-mile circuit that showcases a northern panorama and visits Great Pond Mountain's 1030-foot wooded high point. There are numerous locations around the summit to enjoy a picnic and capture the sweeping views.

Begin the descent by retracing your steps to the Capstone Trail and turning right. This popular mountain bike route soon arrives at Katahdin Overlook, where Maine's highest peak is visible on very clear days. Stay left and be alert for bikers as you wind 0.6 mile down the switchbacks to an intersection with a connector trail. Continue straight another 0.2 mile before rejoining the Hay Ledges Trail to complete your journey.

Extend Your Trip: Consider extending the hike 0.8 mile by visiting the nearby Picnic Trail. This 0.3-mile spur off the Dead River Road visits a quiet spot on the edge of a great pond with views of the undeveloped far shore, a recent addition to the Wildlands. Take advantage of its convenient picnic table while scanning the waters for resident wildlife.

80 *Great Head, Beehive, Gorham Mountain, and Ocean Path*

Distance: 7.8-mile loop
Difficulty: challenging
Hiking time: 6 hours
Elevation gain: 1200 feet
High point: 538 feet

Management: Acadia NP
Season: May–Nov
Map: ANP website
GPS coordinates: 44.33023°, −68.18414°

Getting there: From Acadia National Park's Hulls Cove Visitor Center, follow Park Loop Road south 3 miles. Turn left and follow Park Loop Road 5.4 miles to the Sand Beach Entrance Station (a reservation may be required). Continue another 0.5 mile to the Sand Beach parking area on the left. Alternatively, from late June to mid-October, use the free and convenient Island Explorer bus service (routes beginning at the Hulls Cove Visitor Center or the Bar Harbor Village Green), which stops here throughout the day. *Notes:* Entrance fee required. Dogs prohibited on the Beehive Trail.

Sand Beach lies in the heart of Acadia's most-storied stretch of coastline and is surrounded by many popular destinations, including Thunder Hole, the Beehive, Otter Cliff, Gorham Mountain, and Great Head. This recommended loop, which can easily be divided into three or more separate hikes, is a comprehensive tour that maximizes outside exploration and minimizes sitting in the car.

At the parking lot's southern end, descend stairs to the beach and head left across the sandy 0.2-mile expanse. Depending on the tide and time of year, you may need to cross a small stream before joining the Great Head Trail, which ascends rock steps to a junction. Bear right and scramble up granite ledges to stunning beach views. Remain on the main route as it descends to shoreline vistas before rising to Great Head's

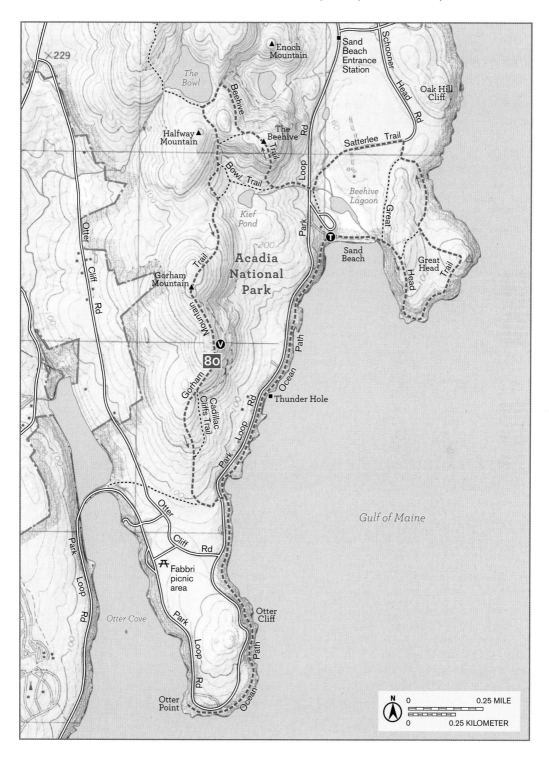

Looking north toward Great Head from Otter Cliff

145-foot high point, 0.8 mile from the beach. This stunning promontory is surrounded by alluring coastal scenery.

While rough at first, the Great Head Trail soon eases en route to a parking area 0.6 mile north. Walk through the parking lot and then follow the road left to a gate and the start of the Satterlee Trail. This wide corridor leads 0.3 mile, to where a spur exits right to Park Loop Road.

Use caution crossing to the Bowl Trail, a rocky path that rises at a moderate grade. In 0.2 mile,

head right onto the Beehive Trail and scale the increasingly steep slope. To navigate the terrain, the well-designed route uses bridges, ladders, and iron rungs, sometimes on the edge of sheer granite walls. Watch your step and enjoy the limitless beauty along the 0.3-mile scramble to Beehive's 538-foot south peak, where a breathtaking panorama awaits.

Proceed north along the ridge across a less rugged path. Through stunted pine forest, the trail traverses a mostly open landscape to the north peak. Beyond, the route drops to the Bowl, a secluded pond nestled atop the ridge. Parallel the pond's shore to a three-way intersection, then take the Bowl Trail south 0.2 mile through a picturesque birch forest.

Turn right onto a short connector that leads to the Gorham Mountain Trail. Stay right again to begin a modest 0.3-mile climb to the trail's namesake 525-foot summit and impressive views of Acadia's highest peaks. Continuing southeast, hike to numerous viewpoints high above the ocean. Soon a steady drop ensues but quickly eases near the first of two junctions with the Cadillac Cliffs Trail. Choose this slightly more difficult alternative to explore caves, ledges, and other geologic features. Beyond the second junction, the final 0.3-mile stretch ends at a parking lot.

Cross Park Loop Road to join the Ocean Path. This 2.2-mile well-groomed trail connects Sand Beach with Otter Point, passing some of Acadia's most-enduring natural features. Turn right and hike 1.2 miles over Otter Cliff's scenic ledges to additional oceanside perches that end at Otter Point before retracing your steps.

Heading north, enjoy the Ocean Path's easiest section, a 0.9-mile stroll that never strays far from the water. Occasionally, spurs diverge right, affording more-intimate shots of the granite shore. The most popular of these is Thunder Hole, where waves crash into a narrow chasm. Use caution when leaving the main path as the surface can be very slippery when wet. A final 0.1-mile descent ends at the Sand Beach parking lot and an end to the day's journey.

Shorter Options: For shorter excursions, consider exploring Sand Beach and Great Head, a 2-mile loop, the Beehive and the Bowl, a 1.9-mile loop, or Gorham Mountain and the Ocean Path, a 2.8-mile loop. To maximize easy terrain, follow the Ocean Path 4.4 miles roundtrip from Sand Beach to Otter Point. There are multiple Island Explorer bus stops along this stretch, allowing for a variety of beginning and ending points.

81 *Cadillac Mountain Traverse*

Distance: 6.5 miles one-way	*Management:* Acadia NP
Difficulty: moderate–challenging	*Season:* Jun–Oct
Hiking time: 4 hours	*Map:* ANP website
Elevation gain: 1600 feet	*GPS coordinates:* 44.31283°, −68.21478°
High point: 1530 feet	

Getting there: To complete this hike, take the free and convenient Island Explorer bus service from the Bar Harbor Village Green to the Blackwoods Campground. Pick up a bus at the Cadillac North Ridge Trail to return to the Village Green. If you are staying at Blackwoods Campground, there are trails from both campsite loops that lead to the main trailhead on Route 3. Use the Island Explorer bus service to return to the campground.
Notes: Non-bus service option (see Other Options). Entrance fee required.

The highest peak on the country's eastern seaboard, Cadillac Mountain is one of the first spots in the nation to welcome the day's sunrise. There are multiple trails available to scale this alluring summit covered in a vast expanse of ancient granite ledges. This route maximizes stunning scenery and takes advantage of the park's complimentary shuttle service to avoid the hassle of finding a parking space for this very popular mountain hike.

To reach the trailhead from the Island Explorer bus stop in the Blackwoods Campground, head 0.3 mile west through Loop B, the campground's northern loop. Near the northwest corner, pick up the trail that leads 0.2 mile to an intersection with the Cadillac South Ridge Trail. Turn right to reach Route 3. Carefully cross to the north side of the pavement and climb the rock steps to a kiosk and the start of the hike.

The South Ridge Trail is a long, gradual ascent of Cadillac that features three legs of similar lengths. The first segment begins in a dense evergreen forest, where boardwalks occasionally provide relief from the root-covered ground. Enjoy the shade as you wind methodically 1 mile with modest elevation gain to a junction.

Turn right on the Eagle Crag Trail and scramble 0.2 mile to an open ledge with resplendent views of Champlain Mountain and Cadillac's summit area. The Eagle Crag Trail ends in 0.1 mile. Bear right and begin the trek's second leg. While this 1.1-mile portion rises more aggressively, the trail's granite surface provides better footing, unless wet or icy. Weave through the thinning pines as more scenery comes into view, culminating with a 360-degree panorama atop 1073-foot Dike Peak. Drop 0.1 mile farther to reach a four-way junction. The Featherbed, a tiny pond, lies to the left. This forested saddle is a good place to grab a snack before tackling the final third of the ascent.

The South Ridge Trail leads through an intersection with the Canon Brook Trail. Plod 0.1 mile up the day's steepest climb. The route quickly moderates while traversing smooth open ledges with views in all directions. Much of Mount Desert Island and surrounding bays and peninsulas are in view as you pass a junction with the Cadillac West Face Trail in 0.6 mile and approach the summit road soon after.

The blue-blazed path swings right, heads over a forested knob, and then drops to a service road before arriving at the park's 1530-foot high point. Mostly forested, the summit is not as popular as the slightly lower barren area located 0.1 mile ahead, just beyond the trail's end. Before beginning your descent from the parking area, take a stroll on the paved loop trail that circles past signs describing the many natural features in view.

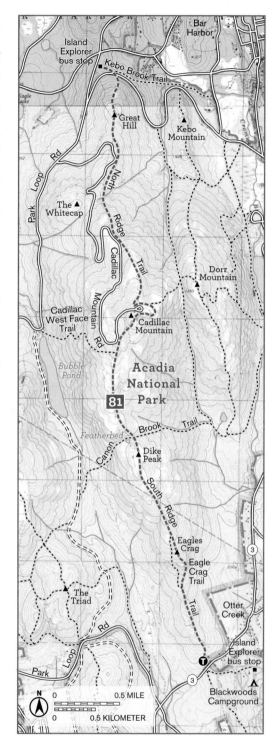

Locate the North Ridge Trail, which departs where the summit road exits. The upper portion of this 2.2-mile route remains almost entirely in the open. Although it is well blazed, early unmarked paths diverge in multiple directions. Take your time; the route quickly becomes easier to follow. On clear days, the seemingly endless horizon across Frenchman Bay to distant interior hills and mountains is breathtaking.

After descending the barren landscape, approach the summit road in 0.7 mile. The trail drops into the forest before emerging from the trees once again as it approaches the pavement a last time in 0.5 mile. Watch your footing over the final mile as you make your way to Great Hill and one last vista. Carefully proceed down a steep pitch to a parking area. To grab an Island Explorer bus, cross the road and take the

Descending the North Ridge Trail with Frenchman Bay in the distance

staircase left to a junction with the Kebo Brook Trail. Stay left and hike 0.1 mile to the bus stop.

Other Options: If the Island Explorer is not available, find parking along Route 3 near the start of the South Ridge Trail. Hiking 7.4 miles out and back on this route makes for a rewarding trip throughout the year, although it can be icy in winter.

82 *Jordan Pond and the Bubbles*

Distance: 4.2-mile loop
Difficulty: moderate
Hiking time: 3 hours
Elevation gain: 800 feet
High point: 866 feet

Management: Acadia NP
Season: Apr–Nov
Map: ANP website
GPS coordinates: 44.32222°, −68.25304°

Getting there: From Acadia National Park's Hulls Cove Visitor Center, follow Park Loop Road south 3 miles to a three-way intersection. Turn right onto Park Loop Road and drive south 4.4 miles to the Jordan Pond parking area on the right (a reservation may be required). Alternatively, from late June to mid-October, use the free and convenient Island Explorer bus; buses originating at the Hulls Cove Visitor Center stop at the Jordan Pond House throughout the day. *Note:* Entrance fee required.

This scenic hike visits two of Acadia National Park's signature features by combining a mostly level loop around Jordan Pond's picturesque shoreline with quick scrambles to a pair of rounded peaks—the Bubbles—that dominate its northern backdrop. Along the way, there are ample opportunities to spot resident wildlife, marvel at geologic remnants from the last ice age, and enjoy breathtaking scenery in all directions.

From the parking area's northernmost loop, follow the wide path that leads straight to the pond's boat launch. Alternatively, from the bus

Jordan Pond from just below the top of South Bubble

stop near the Jordan Pond House, take the shortest route north to the pond's shore and turn right
to quickly reach the boat-launch site.

From the boat launch, head east along the
Jordan Pond Path. It parallels the water's edge,
offering vistas of the expansive water body with
the Bubbles rising in the distance. In 0.2 mile,
the well-manicured path crosses a stone bridge
dividing the pond from a small marsh. Remain
on the Jordan Pond Path as it traverses level
terrain 0.9 mile, never far from the water.

After crossing a wooden bridge, arrive at a
four-way intersection. Continue straight on the
Bubbles Trail—leaving the level terrain for now.
Rising steeply 0.3 mile, the blue-blazed route

snakes up South Bubble's granite slopes. Enter
an open landscape with eagle-eye views of the
sparkling pond below. Level off before reaching
the high point. To the right, check out the short
spur that drops to Bubble Rock. Miraculously,
the large boulder has not fallen from this perch,
where a receding glacier deposited it.

Stay on the Bubbles Trail and drop gradually
0.3 mile north to a junction. Before heading left
to return to Jordan Pond, follow the Bubbles
Divide Trail right and immediately bear left
on the Bubbles Trail. Rising steadily across
a semi-open landscape, this well-used route
ascends North Bubble in 0.2 mile. Higher than its
southern neighbor, this rounded peak provides

gorgeous shots of Cadillac, Pemetic, and Sargent Mountains, as well as a different perspective of Jordan Pond.

Retrace your steps to the Bubbles Divide Trail and turn right. After crossing the saddle between the two peaks, begin a steep, rocky descent. Take your time and watch your footing. The 0.2-mile stretch eventually eases before ending at the Jordan Pond Path. Follow the more inviting corridor right, where two bridges lead across streams entering the sprawling water body.

Hike through an intersection with the Deer Brook Trail and begin paralleling the western shore. This mostly level section proceeds 1.4 miles, usually with the aid of bog bridging. Take advantage of the many scenic spots along the way, where there are gaps in the cedar-dominated forest. Upon arriving at a carriage road, turn left, cross the outlet stream, and turn left again. Take one last photo of the Bubbles before completing your adventure. If you have time, consider a stop at the Jordan Pond House for tea and popovers—reservations are strongly recommended.

Extend Your Trip: To explore another summit vista and add some challenging terrain, extend the described hike by heading up the Deer Brook Trail, a route that climbs aggressively 0.7 mile to the Penobscot Mountain Trail. Follow this path south over its namesake peak and across more than a mile of open granite ledges. Descend the Spring Trail 0.3 mile to reach the Jordan Pond House. This alternative ending to the hike results in a 4.8-mile loop.

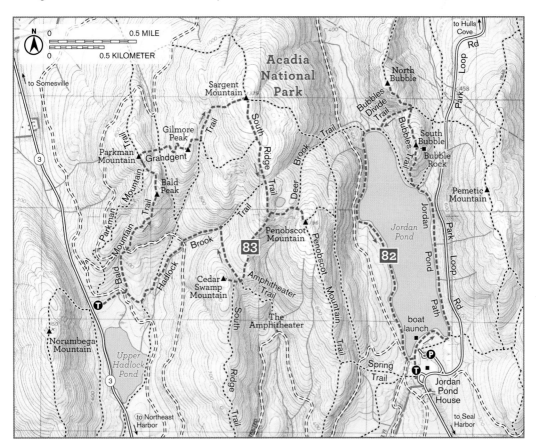

83 *Sargent Mountain Multi-Peak Loop*

Distance: 6.1-mile loop
Difficulty: challenging
Hiking time: 4 hours
Elevation gain: 1925 feet
High point: 1373 feet

Management: Acadia NP
Season: May–Nov
Map: ANP website
GPS coordinates: 44.32592°, –68.29134°

Getting there: From the junction of Routes 102 and 3/198 in Somesville, follow Route 3/198 toward Northeast Harbor. Drive 4.1 miles to the parking area on the right. **Note:** Entrance fee required.

Acadia's highest roadless peak and its five surrounding summit pinnacles are the perfect collection of destinations for hikers looking to maximize scenic beauty in the crown jewel of the Atlantic. Throw in a hidden high-elevation pond and cascading streams to complete this epic trek in the heart of Mount Desert Island.

Carefully cross the pavement to the cedar post. Enter the evergreen forest and continue straight on the Hadlock Brook Trail. The path descends 0.2 mile to a small stream and trail junction. Turn left on the Bald Mountain Trail, which soon crosses a carriage road. Follow the route as it parallels the bubbling stream 0.2 mile to a second carriage road crossing.

Rise more aggressively up the rocky slope. In 0.1 mile, the trail descends into a small saddle before scrambling up an exposed ledge that affords breathtaking views across Upper Hadlock Pond. If the rocks are slick, watch your footing as you make your way to Bald Peak's 974-foot high point. Enjoy views in all directions, including Sargent Mountain towering to the east.

The trail continues down ledges into a deep col before rising to a junction with the Parkman Mountain Trail in 0.2 mile. Turn right to quickly

Gilmore Peak along the Grandgent Trail

scale its namesake peak. Parkman's 941-foot treeless summit offers exceptional scenery, especially of Somes Sound's upper reaches lying to the northwest.

Join the 1.3-mile Grandgent Trail. It descends east into an evergreen forest draped in boulders before heading straight through a four-way junction. Rise aggressively to the day's third destination—the 1036-foot mostly treeless summit of Gilmore Peak. Follow the trail down to a four-way junction and stay left. After skirting past a small wetland, a more daunting incline travels over increasingly open ledges and ends at the large cairn atop the excursion's highest locale. At 1373 feet, Sargent Mountain's windswept high point rises above all but one of its neighbors and offers exquisite views of islands, inlets, mountains, and bays in all directions.

The adventure's next chapter is along the mountain's South Ridge Trail, one of the park's most inviting routes. At first the elevation changes very little across an open expanse. Hike straight, passing junctions with the Maple Spring and Hadlock Brook Trails. In 0.8 mile, turn left for a 0.6-mile roundtrip diversion to Penobscot Mountain's wide-open summit. The route to get there heads steeply down to Sargent Mountain Pond and meanders into a saddle before a short scramble leads to the 1194-foot high point.

Retrace your steps to the South Ridge Trail and bear left. Dropping rapidly over the next 0.5 mile, the rugged path makes its way around the upper reaches of the Amphitheater, a wide bowl in the mountain's slopes. At a four-way intersection with the Amphitheater Trail, continue straight on the South Ridge Trail. A short drop is followed by a 0.1-mile climb to the Cedar Swamp Mountain spur. This short, mostly level path leads to the sixth and final summit, a 942-foot peak that provides a great perspective on the day's previously visited destinations.

Return to the Amphitheater Trail and veer left. The forested path descends 0.4 mile and ends at a junction with the Hadlock Brook Trail. Turn left and follow this well-used corridor to Hadlock Falls, near the first of two carriage road crossings. The falls are especially impressive in the spring or after a rainstorm. After crossing the second carriage road, rise gently to Route 3/198 to complete the circuit.

Shorter Options: Combine the Bald Mountain and Parkman Mountain Trails to complete an excellent 2.5-mile loop from this trailhead. Similarly, cut the final two peaks out of the described route and follow the Hadlock Brook Trail from Sargent's South Ridge for an enjoyable 4-mile hike.

84 Black Mountain

Distance: 2.5-mile loop
Difficulty: moderate
Hiking time: 2 hours
Elevation gain: 915 feet
High point: 1049 feet

Management: Maine BPL
Season: Apr–Nov
Map: BPL website
GPS coordinates: 44.57750°, −68.10486°

Getting there: From the junction of Routes 1 and 183 in Sullivan, drive north on Route 183. In 4.3 miles, turn left and enter the Donnell Pond Public Reserve, near a sign welcoming you to the state-owned lands. Continue 0.3 mile and stay right at the fork pointing toward Black Mountain. Follow the dirt road 2.1 miles to the small parking area on the right.

Spanning nearly 15,000 acres across expansive lakes, remote forests, and mostly barren summits, the Donnell Pond Public Reserve's landscape is reminiscent of nearby Acadia National Park but with far fewer visitors and a bit longer distance to salt water. This short loop is a great introduction to the area and offers breathtaking scenery from atop Black Mountain's ledge-covered heights. More ambitious hikers can extend their travels by adding a rewarding circuit over nearby Caribou Mountain.

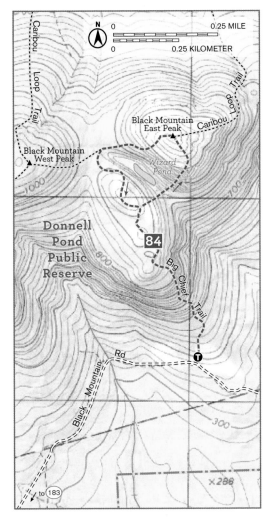

The Big Chief trailhead is located beyond the parking area to the left. Join this blue-blazed route as it rises moderately at first, winding through a boulder field to the base of an impressive ledge. Swing left of the ledge and then climb steadily to the right. Gaps in the forest appear and grow larger, offering views of Tunk Lake and the ocean in the distance. Follow the blue blazes and cairns to a junction 0.6 mile from the start.

Stay right and watch your step as you descend 0.2 mile to Wizard Pond's outlet stream. A final steep climb commences. In the forest to start, soon enter a sparsely vegetated landscape. The trail weaves across the granite ledges, finding the path of least resistance to Black Mountain's 1049-foot East Peak. Enjoy sweeping views in all directions. The most picturesque vistas are toward Mount Desert Island's highest peaks rising to the southwest and those of Tunk Lake's waters sprawling to the east. Check out Schoodic Mountain to the west and Tunk Mountain to the north—two destinations worthy of future hiking adventures in the area.

From a large cairn west of the summit sign, head down the ledges toward the mountain's West Peak. The trail swings left down the open terrain before heading back into the inviting evergreen forest. Arrive at a three-way junction 0.3 mile from the summit. Straight ahead, the trail rises steeply to the mountain's forested West Peak. Instead, turn left and follow the Big Chief Trail as it reemerges from the surrounding trees and ascends a small knoll in 0.2 mile. Enjoy views as the trail proceeds 0.3 mile across mostly open terrain to complete the loop around Wizard Pond. Retrace your steps 0.6 mile back to the start.

Extend Your Trip: Interested in a challenging, more remote trek? Add to your travels the 6.5-mile loop over Caribou Mountain. Begin this extension from Black Mountain's East Peak. After hiking across scenic ledges, the loop drops into a landscape of boulders and wildlife-rich wetlands. A steep climb leads to a traverse of the Caribou Mountain ridge, which features numerous viewpoints. An attractive descent of Caribou Mountain is followed by an aggressive climb to the top of Black Mountain's West Peak. Turn left to make your way back to the Big Chief Trail.

Black Mountain's East Peak affords splendid views of Acadia National Park.

85 *Cutler Coast*

Distance: 9.7-mile loop
Difficulty: challenging
Hiking time: 7 hours
Elevation gain: 1240 feet
High point: 210 feet

Management: Maine BPL
Season: year-round
Map: BPL website
GPS coordinates: 44.69851°, −67.15796°

Getting there: The Cutler Coast Trailhead is located on Route 191 north of Cutler. From Route 1 in East Machias, follow Route 191 east 16.9 miles to the parking area on the right. From Route 189, halfway between Whiting and Lubec, follow Route 191 south 10 miles and turn left into the parking area. *Note:* Backcountry campsites available.

The 12,334-acre Cutler Coast Public Reserve, located along Maine's spectacular Bold Coast, was protected by the state in the 1990s with the help of Maine Coast Heritage Trust and the Land for Maine's Future program. Hikers can choose either a 5.2-mile loop or a more rugged 9.7-mile circuit. Both feature rocky cliffs, invigorating ocean breezes, breathtaking oceanside vistas, and ample opportunities to spot resident wildlife in the surrounding vegetation and within the crashing surf below.

Follow the evergreen-lined path 0.4 mile to the Inland Trail junction. Continue straight for a relaxing 1-mile trek over a series of small ridges and around forested bogs. The Coastal Trail turns right as it nears the water, but first check out the scenic vantage point located on a short spur that descends straight to a large rock outcrop near a deep chasm in the shoreline. Watch your footing as you descend to the perch high above the pounding waves.

Leaving the vista, follow the Coastal Trail southwest high above the shore. Overall, the elevation changes little, but the route is far from flat. Pass steep walls and secluded rock beaches as the trail winds through windswept forest and open meadows, passing one dramatic viewpoint after another. At 1.5 miles, the Black Point Brook Cutoff exits right and leads 0.5 mile to the Inland Trail. Use this option to complete a 5.2-mile loop.

The Coastal Trail winds high above Maine's rugged Bold Coast.

While the Coastal Trail's southern section is less dramatic and more rustic, it is well worth the extra effort. Bear left to reach a stone beach at Black Point Cove. Hike up a steep incline and pass the first of five backcountry campsites scattered over the next 2 miles, each available on a first-come, first-served basis (there is limited fresh water available—best to pack in what you will need). Over rolling terrain, the trail meanders through an inviting forest lined with ledges and ferns before descending to an attractive campsite at the edge of Long Point Cove. Scale a rock staircase up the hillside and, before long, emerge onto the wide-open expanse near Long Point. Look for whales and other sea life offshore, and gaze out to the steep cliffs of Grand Manan

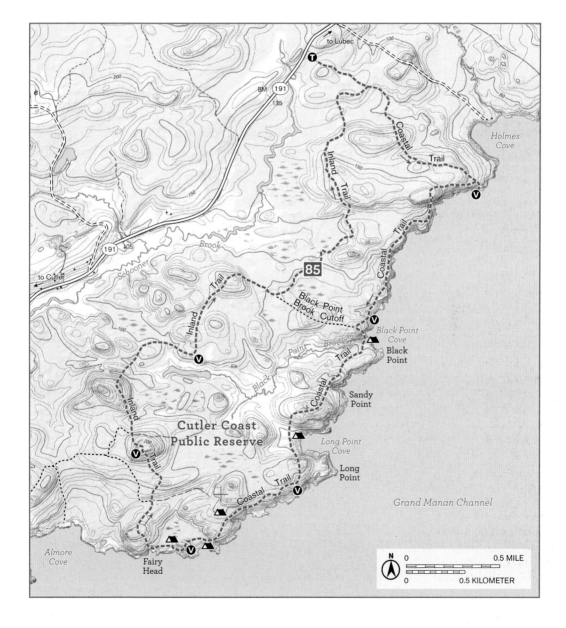

Island in New Brunswick, on the far side of the channel that bears its name.

Follow the blue blazes closely, as the Coastal Trail weaves into the forest occasionally but remains mostly along the immediate shoreline. Eventually the route crosses the outlet of a small bog and reenters the woods. This is the start of the 4.2-mile Inland Trail. During late spring and summer, be prepared for insects as the route passes numerous wetlands. The Inland Trail winds through pretty forests and gradually climbs a series of small hills, two with short spurs that lead to limited views. After passing a sizable beaver pond, climb a semi-open knob where a short outlook trail exits right to an expansive vista of the wetland.

The main route continues northeast to another rocky summit, swings sharply right, and descends 0.2 mile to a junction with the Black Point Brook Cutoff. Turn left, remaining on the Inland Trail. The recently reconstructed path weaves 1.7 miles through a pleasant evergreen forest before ending at the Coastal Trail. Turn left and hike 0.4 mile back to the parking area.

Nearby Options: Maine Coast Heritage Trust, a membership-based conservation organization, owns and manages a collection of nearby preserves that offer access to equally scenic corners of the Bold Coast. Check out their website for information on the Bog Brook Cove, Boot Head, and Hamilton Cove Preserves (see Resources).

86 *Quoddy Head*

Distance: 4-mile loop
Difficulty: moderate
Hiking time: 3 hours
Elevation gain: 400 feet
High point: 140 feet

Management: Maine BPL
Season: year-round
Map: BPL website
GPS coordinates: 44.81389°, −66.95247°

Green Point is a must-visit stop along the Coastal Trail.

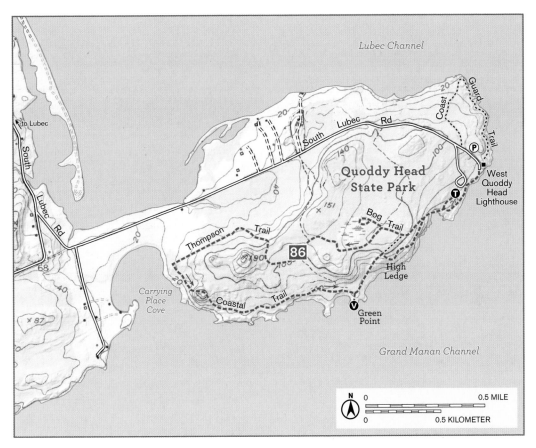

Getting there: Beginning at the junction of Routes 189 and 191 in West Lubec, follow Route 189 east 4.2 miles and then turn right onto South Lubec Road. Follow this road 4.7 miles to the parking area entrance on the right. **Note:** Entrance fee required.

Ironically, West Quoddy Head forms the easternmost spot in the United States—its eastern brother is located across the border on Campobello Island, in New Brunswick. Quoddy Head State Park, purchased by the state in 1962, is comprised of 532 acres of rugged headlands, more than 5.5 miles of hiking trails, and a picturesque lighthouse built in 1858. Open throughout the year, Quoddy Head is a wonderful spot to witness the raw power of the ocean, enjoy glimpses of its many wild creatures, and photograph an iconic Maine coastline.

From the parking lot and picnic area, follow the Inland Trail west along flat ground. After reaching a small cove at the base of an impressive ocean cliff, the path quickly rises to a trail junction. Stay right on the Inland Trail as it slowly levels off and arrives at the start of the Bog Trail. Turn northwest and wind through the evergreen trees. At an intersection with the Thompson Trail, stay right and follow the path onto a long boardwalk that weaves over the acidic bog. Look for pitcher plants, baked-apple berry, and other vegetation common to more-northern environs. After circling through the open expanse, return to and then join the Thompson Trail on the right.

The 1.2-mile Thompson Trail cuts through the heart of the peninsula. After crossing wetlands, it veers right and climbs over a small ridge. Before long, the wide path descends toward the water and ends at the Coastal Trail, near the shores of Carrying Place Cove. Named by boaters seeking to avoid the stronger currents east of Quoddy Head, the cove has a nice beach for exploring.

The 2-mile journey along the Coastal Trail is the highlight of the trek, with one spectacular vista after another. While the elevation change is minor, the path is far from level, a point quickly understood while ascending a low rocky knoll. Take your time and explore the many promontories, including the short spur to Green Point. Across the blue expanse lie the impressive cliffs of New Brunswick's Grand Manan Island. Nearby, the rugged shoreline is pounded by the surf; scan for seals, ducks, lobster boats, and an occasional whale in the channel.

Beyond Green Point, the trail rises steadily to a junction. The Inland Trail provides the most direct route back. Instead, continue the adventure on the Coastal Trail to the right. Stay left at an unmarked intersection and drop to High Ledge's scenic perch. Cautiously proceed east along the prominent headlands that follow. Enjoy dramatic scenes high above the steep ledges of Gullivers Hole before rejoining the Inland Trail. Hike around the cove, but this time stay right, remaining along the water's edge.

Follow the flat path past viewpoints and a beach-access spur. Head through the picnic area near the parking lot and continue another 0.1 mile to check out the West Quoddy Head Lighthouse, the nation's easternmost point. Retrace your steps back through the picnic area to complete the hike.

Other Options: Just north of the lighthouse, the Coast Guard Trail forms a 1-mile loop around a scenic peninsula featuring a series of precipitous oceanside clifftops—a wonderful optional extension to the day's hike. The Thompson Trail and the western portion of the Coastal Trail are the park's most rugged and least-manicured options. For a more straightforward adventure, limit your hike to stops at the bog, Green Point, High Ledge, and the lighthouse.

87 *Goose Eye and Carlo*

Distance: 7.7-mile loop
Difficulty: challenging–strenuous
Hiking time: 6 hours
Elevation gain: 2700 feet
High point: 3870 feet

Management: Maine PL
Season: May–Nov
Map: Maine Trail Finder website
GPS coordinates: 44.51062°, −71.04322°

Getting there: From Route 16, just south of downtown Berlin, New Hampshire, follow Unity Street across the James Cleveland Bridge. Drive 0.8 mile and swing right onto Coos Street. In 0.1 mile, stay left on Hutchins Street. Continue 0.9 mile and then turn right on Success Pond Road. Follow this dirt road 8 miles (logging trucks have right-of-way) to the parking area on the right. **Notes:** The route starts on private land. Backcountry campsite available.

One of the most rugged sections of the Appalachian Trail's journey from Georgia to Maine is the wild, rugged, and remote stretch across the Mahoosuc Range. This challenging loop visits two summits in the heart of the ridge.

Along the journey, enjoy breathtaking vistas from windswept ledges, relax aside the banks of bubbling mountain streams, and, with a little luck, spot moose, spruce grouse, or other resident wildlife.

Mahoosuc Trail visits high-elevation bogs beneath the Goose Eye Mountain summit.

Follow the Carlo Col Trail as it coincides with an old logging road. It leads gently 0.2 mile east to a junction with the Goose Eye Trail and the start of the loop. Continue straight and in 0.3 mile, veer left at the fork in the road. Hike 0.1 mile farther, where a sign directs hikers left into the forest. Now on a narrower and more inviting corridor, cross a small stream before paralleling and occasionally recrossing it for the better part of the next mile.

As the blue-blazed route leaves the shrinking stream behind, climb steadily up the slope. While the incline is more strenuous, the footing is not difficult, as the northern hardwood forest transitions to spruce and fir. In the surrounding boreal forest, 2.5 miles from the start, arrive at a spur that leads to an overnight campsite. Remain on the main path and in 0.2 mile enter the boulder-draped Carlo Col at an intersection with the Mahoosuc Trail (Appalachian Trail).

Turn left on the well-trodden trail. Take your time, as the next 2 miles are the most scenic of the hike. Ascend steadily 0.5 mile up rock steps and across root-covered soil. The incline moderates as the forest canopy opens. From atop Mount Carlo's summit, enjoy scenes of Goose Eye Mountain and more-distant peaks rising above and through the gaps of the stunted forest. The trail proceeds across a high-elevation bog before descending to larger openings affording more impressive views.

After dropping steeply into a saddle, ascend the other side just as aggressively. Moderating a bit, the route weaves in and out of the vegetation, up a landscape dominated by exposed granite and boggy wetlands. As you approach the final climb, traverse the mostly open surroundings while enjoying exceptional views on all sides. Take your time on the ladders and iron rungs leading up the very steep pitch to a junction with the Goose Eye Trail.

Bear left (the Appalachian Trail continues right) and scramble 0.1 mile to the mountain's west peak, the highest of its three summits. From

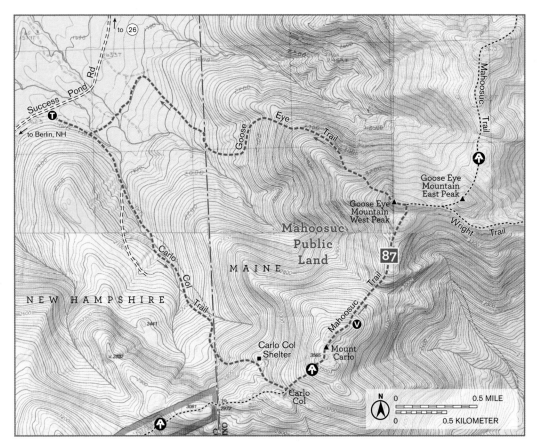

atop the barren pinnacle, the scenery is spectac-ular; the Presidential Range towers to the south and Old Speck looms in the north. Countless mountains, lakes, and valleys lie in all directions.

The Goose Eye Trail's initial descent west is tricky. Watch your step on the rocky, uneven terrain. It begins in the open but slowly enters the dense evergreen forest. The footing soon improves. Descend steadily down the mountain. After crossing back into New Hampshire, the incline eases significantly. Swinging to the left, the path briefly follows a logging road and then exits to the right. Cross a pair of streams before arriving at the Carlo Col Trail, 0.2 mile from the start.

88 Puzzle Mountain

Distance: 7.5 miles roundtrip
Difficulty: challenging
Hiking time: 5 hours
Elevation gain: 2650 feet
High point: 3120 feet

Management: Mahoosuc Land Trust
Season: year-round
Map: Maine Trail Finder website
GPS coordinates: 44.53897°, −70.82960°

Getting there: From the junction of Routes 26 and 2 in Newry, follow Route 26 north 4.7 miles to the parking area for the Grafton Loop on the right. ***Note:*** The route traverses private land.

This scenic day hike is the perfect introduction to the region's 38-mile Grafton Loop, which invites visitors to spend multiple days exploring hidden corners of the longer circuit. Despite its relatively low elevation compared to many of its neighbors, Puzzle Mountain features terrain as challenging and rugged as many of the higher summits in the region. Fortunately, these traits are accompanied with exceptional scenery and beautiful natural surroundings.

The journey starts easily in a stand of tall white pines. Cross a dirt road and rise more gradually as the forest transitions to northern hardwoods. In 0.5 mile, the route swings sharply right, and 0.4 mile farther bends left. Two additional turns lead to the base of a steep slope 1.5 miles from the start—no more opportunity to loosen up.

Take your time up the challenging terrain. While the soil is loose, the footing is generally easy to navigate. Higher up, rise into a boreal forest as the path makes its way around exposed granite to an occasional vista. Shortly after entering the Mahoosuc Land Trust's Stewart Family Preserve, the blue-blazed trail arrives atop Lunch Ledge. Featuring dramatic scenes north into Grafton Notch, the ledge is aptly named, with many spots to enjoy a snack.

To scale higher up the mountain and partake of more expansive views, continue 0.2 mile east

This ledge is aptly named Lunch.

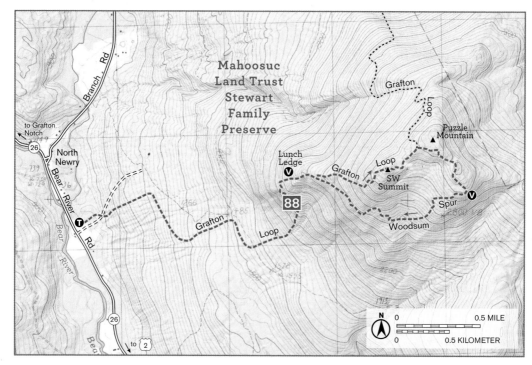

along the Grafton Loop to the lower junction with the Woodsum Spur. At this location, a 2.5-mile loop commences. Stay left and methodically scale the rugged landscape, often on exposed ledge. In and out of the trees, the path passes multiple viewpoints before arriving atop the mountain's open southwest summit in 0.6 mile. The views west toward Mount Washington and the Mahoosucs are especially impressive.

Carefully locate the cairns and blazes leading east from the high point. The Grafton Loop enters the forest and becomes easier to follow.

In 0.4 mile, bear right at the Woodsum Spur's upper junction. This more-lightly traveled corridor swings past Puzzle Mountain's wooded high point, drops into a saddle, and rises to another peak in 0.3 mile. Over the next 0.5 mile, watch your footing while descending a series of open ledges that feature expansive scenes south. Before long, the path swings right and meanders through quiet forested surroundings with an occasional brief climb. At the end of the 1.6-mile Woodsum Spur, turn left to retrace your steps 2.5 miles back to the start.

Shorter Options: Limit your travels to an out-and-back hike to Lunch Ledge, a 4.6-mile excursion.

Maine Appalachian Trail Club (MATC)

Since 1936, this organization of volunteers and trail enthusiasts has maintained the 267 miles of Appalachian Trail that wind through Maine. Many of the state's most remote and beautiful mountain locations are found along this corridor. Thanks to MATC-maintained trails, shelters, and campsites, hikers can enjoy this wild landscape.

89 *Baldpates and Table Rock*

Distance: 8.2 miles roundtrip
Difficulty: challenging–strenuous
Hiking time: 6 hours
Elevation gain: 3400 feet
High point: 3812 feet

Management: Maine BPL
Season: year-round
Map: BPL website
GPS coordinates: 44.58978°, −70.94695°

Getting there: From the junction of Routes 26 and 2 in Newry, follow Route 26 north 12.1 miles to the parking area on the left. **Notes:** Entrance fee required. Backcountry campsite available.

Located in the center of Maine's Grafton Notch State Park, this rewarding excursion features awe-inspiring panoramas from multiple vantage points. The terrain is occasionally rugged and challenging, but these traits are interspersed with more pleasant stretches beneath towering yellow birches and atop an open landscape of polished granite. If venturing to the summit of Baldpate Mountain's East Peak is too much, limit your journey to a much-shorter loop over Table Rock (see Shorter Options).

From the large Appalachian Trail (AT) parking lot, pick up the white-blazed route at an informative kiosk and follow it to the right. It quickly reaches Route 26. Cars travel fast here, so use caution when crossing. The path enters the woods near a large wooden "AT" sign, where a series of boardwalks wind to a junction with the Table Rock Trail.

The Table Rock Trail is not recommended for dogs or children, as it is very steep and rocky, especially as it approaches its namesake natural feature. There are two ways to reach the impressive clifftop and its stunning views of Grafton Notch. If you are looking for a less challenging adventure, bear left on the AT to the upper junction. Otherwise, turn right. The first half of the 0.8-mile climb on the Table Rock Trail rises modestly. Swing left to tackle the increasingly steep, rocky slope. Past an occasional viewpoint, arrive at the base of the ledge, where small caves and hidden crevices can be found. The path

bends right and then left before rising abruptly to the flat-topped cliff. Enjoy breathtaking scenes of Old Speck Mountain and other nearby peaks; watch your step near the edge!

Heading north, the Table Rock Trail drops steeply but soon levels off. Hike 0.5 mile to a junction with the AT and turn right. The white-blazed path climbs steadily and in 0.6 mile reaches a saddle on the ridge. While there is little overall elevation change, there are minor ups and downs over the next 0.8 mile that end at a spur to the Baldpate lean-to, an overnight shelter available on a first-come, first-served basis.

Enjoy the high-elevation landscape between Baldpate's east and west peaks

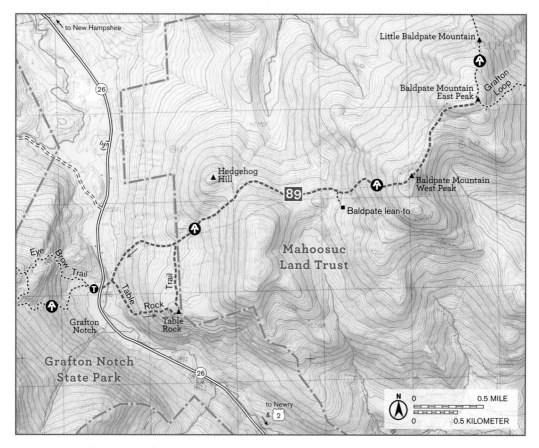

The terrain becomes difficult again. Weaving up rock staircases, across moss-lined ledges, and through the boreal forest, slowly plod 0.6 mile to the 3662-foot summit of Baldpate Mountain's West Peak. A few dozen steps beyond the forested high point, find an open landscape with exceptional views across the saddle to the East Peak, your next destination.

The 0.9-mile stretch that follows is the day's most spectacular. Most of the journey is exposed to the elements atop open ledges, with only the occasional patch of trees interrupting the views. Find wooden ladders to help navigate the most difficult sections and bog bridging to avoid the wetlands. Across the wide expanse between the two peaks, high-elevation bogs are prolific. The final ascent begins with a fun scramble, which is more difficult if wet or icy. This is followed by a mostly level stroll to the top, where mountains, lakes, and forests are visible in all directions. New Hampshire's Presidential Range rises to the southwest and Maine's High Peaks region dominates the northern horizon.

The hike is as rewarding as you return west to the trailhead. Skip the Table Rock Trail on the descent and stay on the AT throughout. It is 3.8 miles back to Route 26.

Shorter Options: For a shorter but invigorating adventure, stick to the 2.4-mile loop over Table Rock. Also, before leaving the area, check out nearby nature trails within Grafton Notch State Park that visit Screw Auger Falls, Moose Cave, and Mother Walker Falls.

90 *Tumbledown Mountain*

Distance: 6.4-mile loop
Difficulty: challenging
Hiking time: 4 hours
Elevation gain: 2200 feet
High point: 3060 feet

Management: Maine BPL
Season: May–Nov
Map: BPL website
GPS coordinates: 44.72920°, −70.53244°

Getting there: From Weld, follow Route 142 north 2.3 miles and turn left. Drive 0.5 mile, then stay right onto a dirt road (Byron Notch Road). In 2.3 miles, turn right at the intersection. The trailhead parking lot is located 1.5 miles ahead on the left. From Route 17 in Byron, follow Byron Notch Road 5.8 miles east to the Brook Trail parking area.
Notes: Camping prohibited at the pond. Byron Notch Road not maintained late fall through early spring.

Tumbledown Mountain is a rite of passage for innumerable Maine hikers. Surrounded by higher peaks to the north, the rugged mountain compensates for its relatively diminutive height with captivating natural features, including a high-elevation pond and sheer cliff faces. In recent decades, conservation groups have joined with the Land for Maine's Future and Forest Legacy programs to protect the mountain and its popular hiking-trail network. Choose this challenging 6.4-mile circuit midweek for greater solitude, or explore adjacent less-traveled paths that lead to equally stunning scenery from the summit of Little Jackson.

Begin the adventure by heading west on an uninspiring 1.3-mile walk along Byron Notch Road. The walk, slightly uphill, serves as a warm-up for the climb ahead. Upon reaching the Loop Trail sign, turn right and proceed up gentle grades. In 1 mile, the path reaches Tumbledown Boulder, an immense rock that marks a transition.

The Loop Trail reaches the day's first scenic perch.

Beyond the rock, the route is much more challenging. Paralleling an exposed ledge, a steep 0.3-mile climb ends on a small open peak with impressive views of Tumbledown Mountain's imposing southern wall. Descend briefly and then begin a relentless 0.6-mile ascent to the main ridge by methodically scaling the narrowing trail. As the final ledges envelop and

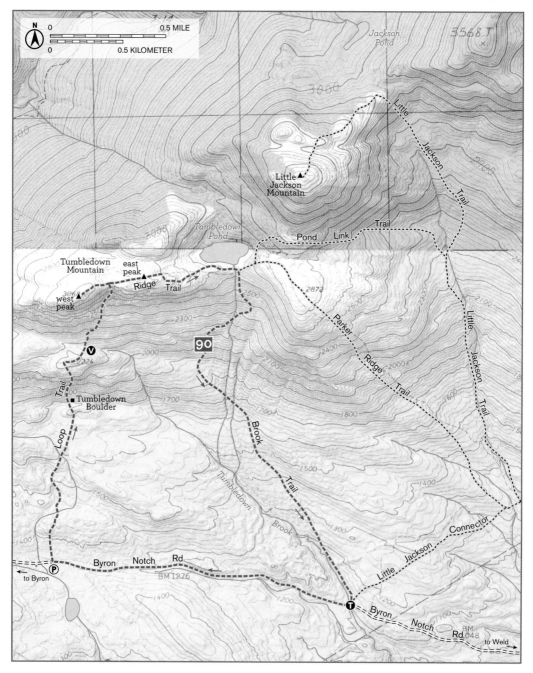

seemingly block the way, ascend a rock wall via iron rungs and carefully squeeze through a small cave affectionately referred to as "Fat Man's Misery." Not recommended for dogs or small children, the Loop Trail soon ends at a junction.

From the small saddle, turn left and rise steadily 0.2 mile to the west peak's rocky summit. Perched high above Tumbledown's precipitous slopes, this vantage point offers distant views of Mount Washington to the south and more-intimate shots of Maine's High Peaks region towering in the north.

Return east into the saddle and follow the Ridge Trail 0.2 mile as it scrambles up ledges to Tumbledown's wide-open east peak. Here, there are tremendous views across sprawling Webb Lake to Mount Blue and other peaks surrounding the large valley to the south. Continue along the Ridge Trail and carefully descend the polished granite surfaces. The path leads 0.5 mile to scenic Tumbledown Pond. This popular, over-loved water body is nonetheless a very picturesque location. It is a great place to relax on a warm summer day, but camping is no longer allowed near its shores.

Pick up the 2.2-mile Brook Trail beginning near the outlet stream. Along the first 0.5 mile, the footing is uneven and the incline challenging. Cross the brook and wind to a more gradual, wider corridor. The path recrosses the brook and continues another 1.2 miles, never straying too far from the running water. Other than the rocky, uneven surface, it is a relaxing end to the loop.

Shorter Options: For an alternative hike that avoids the Loop Trail's very challenging terrain, do an out-and-back along the Brook and Ridge Trails; it is 6 miles roundtrip to the west peak. A less-traveled option can be completed by following the Little Jackson Connector to the Parker Ridge Trail. Turn left and scale the scenic ridge before descending to Tumbledown Pond. Continue to the east peak and then return along the Brook Trail to complete a 5.8-mile circuit.

91 *Saddleback Mountain*

Distance: 10.2-mile loop
Difficulty: strenuous
Hiking time: 8 hours
Elevation gain: 3200 feet
High point: 4120 feet

Management: Maine Appalachian Trail Club
Season: May–Nov
Map: Maine Trail Finder website
GPS coordinates: 44.94609°, −70.52811°

Getting there: From the junction of Routes 4 and 16 in downtown Rangeley, follow Route 4 south 1 mile and turn left onto Dallas Hill Road. Drive 2.5 miles and then veer right onto Saddleback Mountain Road. Continue 4.5 miles to the base of the ski area. There is parking on the left just before the road reaches the lodge area. **Note:** The route begins on private land.

Saddleback Mountain features one of New England's most spectacular high-elevation ridgelines, with breathtaking views for more than 2.5 miles. This challenging loop adds a few stops at secluded ponds where, with a little luck, you might catch a glimpse of moose browsing, cedar waxwings feeding, or other resident wildlife quenching their thirst. End the scenic circuit by heading down the steep slopes of a popular ski resort that was resurrected in recent years.

From the lodge, follow the service road right, and turn left onto Rock Pond Road. This dirt roadway rises past condos to a dead end, 0.5 mile from the lodge. A large kiosk marks the

Alluring landscape between Saddleback Mountain and the Horn

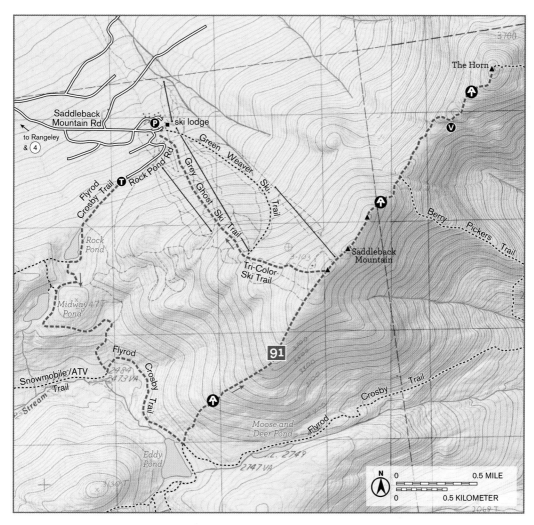

start of the Flyrod Crosby Trail. The day's hike will explore 2.9 miles of this long-distance route, named for a storied woman guide from this region that's famous for its angling traditions.

Much of the Flyrod Crosby Trail is multiuse, but this initial section is open to foot traffic only. Follow the wide path 0.5 mile to Rock Pond and then 0.4 mile farther to a spur that departs right to Midway Pond. Approach both quietly to increase your chances of spotting wildlife. Continue another 1.1 miles across mostly level terrain before descending to a wider corridor and turning left. While this next stretch is open for motorized recreation, it only lasts 0.9 mile.

At a junction with the Appalachian Trail (AT), consider a brief diversion south 0.1 mile along the AT to scenic Eddy Pond. Otherwise, continue your journey north on the more rustic hiking path. The initial 0.8-mile climb up the white-blazed trail is straightforward, albeit challenging. The real fun begins at tree line, which features a spectacular 1-mile stretch to Saddleback's summit area.

Traversing a mostly open landscape, enjoy incredible scenes of lakes and mountains in all directions. Brief scrambles soon give way to more modest terrain. Weave through groves of stunted trees to the first of three promontories.

Here, a trail leaves left to the ski area; this is the route down. For now, hike ahead to the second and highest bump, the 4120-foot top of Saddleback Mountain. Looking north, check out Sugarloaf, Crocker Mountain, Mount Abraham, and countless other peaks toward the Quebec border.

While many hikers choose to head back from here, if the weather is cooperating and you have the energy, the 1.6-mile stretch to the Horn is amazingly beautiful. Follow the AT north 0.1 mile to the third distinct peak, and then begin the very steep descent into the saddle. Take your time and watch your step, especially if it is wet or icy. Although the trail is difficult to navigate, the scenery is extraordinary. In 0.3 mile, the terrain eases significantly.

Hike past a junction with the Berry Pickers Trail, and then cross the mostly flat expanse. Ascend quickly to a pinnacle with impressive views south. Although not as steep as the recent descent, the remaining 0.5-mile climb to the Horn's 4041-foot summit is not easy. Once there, breathe in the 360-degree panorama, with mountains and lakes spreading out in all directions.

Take your time and savor the challenging journey back to Saddleback before grabbing the path exiting right to the ski area. It is 1.7 miles to the ski lodge using the most direct route. The first 0.1 mile is a hiking trail. Then follow the Tri-Color Ski Trail left and head down the steep and much-wider slope. The terrain levels off near the top of a ski lift and the start of the Grey Ghost Trail (there is a slightly longer, more gradual route to the right using the Green Weaver Ski Trail). Enjoy excellent views as you aggressively descend the Grey Ghost Trail and before long arrive at the base lodge, a great place to grab a bite to eat before heading out.

Other Options: To complete a shorter 7-mile loop, omit the trip across the ridge to the Horn. Or if hiking down a ski trail is not desirable, journey out and back using the Flyrod Crosby and Appalachian Trails: 9.4 miles roundtrip to Saddleback and 12.6 miles roundtrip to the Horn.

92 *Bigelow Range*

Distance: 12.8-mile loop
Difficulty: strenuous
Hiking time: 10 hours/2 days
Elevation gain: 4100 feet
High point: 4145 feet

Management: Maine BPL
Season: May–Nov
Map: BPL website
GPS coordinates: 45.10976°, −70.33713°

Getting there: From Kingfield, take Route 27 north. Continue 3.3 miles past Sugarloaf Ski Area and turn right onto Stratton Brook Pond Road (just west of where the Appalachian Trail crosses Route 27). Follow this narrow dirt road 1.6 miles to the parking area. **Note:** Backcountry campsites available.

Bigelow Mountain is the centerpiece of a 36,000-acre preserve permanently protected by Maine voters in 1976. The mountain's spectacular ridgeline is an assortment of endless vistas, idyllic ponds, and wildlife-rich forests. Once proposed as another big ski area in northern New England, Bigelow Mountain is now a popular destination for hikers and backpackers.

This full-day or two-day loop traverses the ridge's highest locations across challenging terrain, but with immeasurable rewards.

The Fire Wardens Trail follows the dirt road left. Hike 0.5 mile to a bridge across the Stratton Brook Pond outlet stream. The route follows the narrowing roadway along the sprawling wetland. Continue left as a mountain bike trail diverges

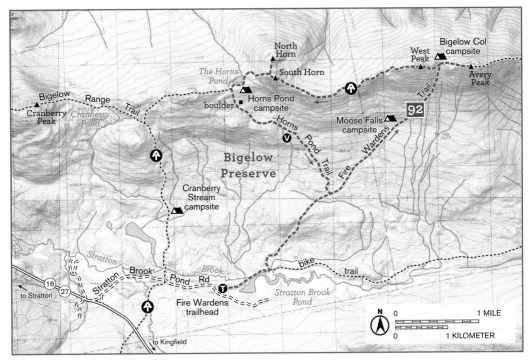

right. Ahead the corridor bends sharply right and soon after swings left onto a more rustic footway. Climb aggressively over the next mile, leveling off at an intersection with the Horns Pond Trail.

Continue straight on the Fire Wardens Trail. For the next 1.2 miles the path rises gradually through the maturing hardwood forest. After winding left, climb steeply to the Moose Falls campsite, which, along with two other overnight locations on the route, is maintained by the Maine Appalachian Trail Club (MATC). All three are available on a first-come, first-served basis.

Time to tackle the hike's most demanding section, a grueling mile-long ascent to the ridgeline. Rock steps lead up the mountainside and reach the day's second MATC campsite. Lying at a junction with the Appalachian Trail (AT), this overnight spot is nestled high atop the ridge in a narrow col.

Catch your breath before heading east on the AT. The white-blazed route scrambles 0.4 mile over a difficult maze of boulders to start. Continue to the barren alpine summit of 4088-foot Avery Peak. Named after Maine native Myron

Avery, arguably the visionary most responsible for the creation of the AT, the scenic peak appropriately enjoys expansive views that, on the clearest days, stretch from Mount Katahdin to Mount Washington.

Return to the saddle and hike west along the AT, scaling 0.3 mile up to the oft-windswept West Peak. The highest point on Bigelow Mountain, the 4145-foot summit provides an awe-inspiring 360-degree panorama, including stunning scenes of Flagstaff Lake and peaks north to the Quebec border. Use caution descending west down the exposed rock. Reenter the forest and continue the steady descent. The journey soon eases into a more relaxing jaunt along the high-elevation ridge, with an occasional glimpse of Sugarloaf Mountain through the trees.

Make your way to the base of South Horn, where an abrupt climb leads to the top of the scenic pinnacle, with vistas over its namesake pond below. The AT heads down the opposite side and quickly arrives at a 0.2-mile spur on the right that leads to the North Horn's impressive summit vista. Check out this worthwhile

Approaching the top of Bigelow's West Peak

diversion for its unique perspective of the Bigelow Range. When you return to the AT, watch your step down the steep, rugged slopes. The route eventually levels off and reaches another MATC campsite, where two paths lead right to the Horns Pond's placid waters nestled beneath imposing ledges.

The journey west resumes along the AT. Hike 0.1 mile to the Horns Pond Trail and turn left onto this blue-blazed route. In 0.4 mile, wrap around the base of a massive boulder that begs exploration. The trail proceeds through a windswept forest and reaches a wetland in 0.6 mile. Parallel the small stream to a spur right leading to an overgrown viewpoint. The final 1-mile stretch is a steady descent. Turn right on the Fire Wardens Trail and retrace your steps 2 miles back to the start.

93 *Borestone Mountain Sanctuary*

Distance: 5.6 miles roundtrip
Difficulty: moderate–challenging
Hiking time: 4 hours
Elevation gain: 1500 feet
High point: 1981 feet

Management: Maine Audubon
Season: May–Nov
Map: Maine Audubon website
GPS coordinates: 44.37808°, −69.43018°

Getting there: From Monson, follow Route 15 north. In 0.5 mile, turn right onto Elliotsville Road. Drive 7.7 miles and then turn left onto Mountain Road (after crossing Big Wilson Stream). Continue 0.7 mile to the parking area on the left. *Notes:* Entrance fee required for non-members. Dogs prohibited.

The relatively low elevation atop Borestone Mountain—the centerpiece of Maine Audubon's northernmost sanctuary—belies its terrain, which mirrors Maine's highest peaks. The route to the summit will get your blood flowing and requires some rock scrambling that is likely to thrill young aspiring hikers. Everyone that reaches the mountain's collection of three high-elevation viewpoints will revel in panoramic scenes that rival any others in New England.

Enter the sanctuary on the opposite side of the road near a large gate. Immediately turn left onto the 1.1-mile Base Trail. Blazed with green triangles, this route wastes little time ascending the steep slope. Numerous rock steps wind through a dense evergreen forest that suggests a much-higher elevation. After leveling off, a spur leads right to the Greenwood Overlook. Visit this scenic spot on the descent. For now, proceed straight 0.4 mile to the Access Road. Stay left on this wider corridor and pass a privy. Ahead, reach the visitor center on the picturesque shores of Sunrise Pond. Pay your entrance fee and check out the handful of displays.

Before heading to the summit, explore the 0.5-mile Peregrine Trail. This lightly used path is occasionally closed to accommodate guests staying at the sanctuary's lodges. It enters the forest across from the visitor center and stays close to Sunrise Pond's western shore. At a sign, the red-blazed route swings left and moderately rises to the top of a steep cliff. Watch your step near the edge; the views east over Midday Pond are breathtaking.

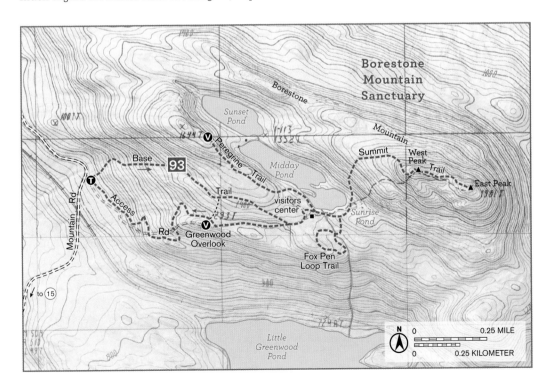

Onawa Lake and Barren Mountain from Borestone's West Peak

Back at the visitor center, turn left onto the 1-mile Summit Trail. It swings south of Sunrise Pond, heads over the pond's outlet, and climbs slowly at first. The incline grows steeper as numerous rock steps lead up the ledge-covered, root-filled trail. Take your time and watch your footing. The final pitch to the West Peak's open summit is tricky in spots, but iron rungs ease the way. Once atop the rocky pinnacle, marvel at the incredible scenery north across Onawa Lake to Barren Mountain.

To reach the higher East Peak, follow the green-blazed Summit Trail 0.3 mile farther. A short drop is followed by a gradual climb. The East Peak is less pointy and more open,

providing a broader area to hang out and admire the stunning landscapes in all directions.

As you retrace your steps down the Summit Trail, use caution descending the West Peak, especially if wet or icy. Before reaching the visitor center, take a slight detour onto the 0.4-mile Fox Pen Loop Trail. This short diversion crosses a small wetland before looping past a viewpoint and an imposing ledge.

From the visitor center, rejoin the Access Road. Follow this wide and easy-to-follow route 1.2 miles back to the parking area. Just before the halfway point, turn left onto the spur leading to the Greenwood Overlook and one last view of the surrounding landscape.

Extend Your Trip: Maine Audubon invites exploration of its other seven sanctuaries in the state. Most of them are located closer to the coast and offer wonderful opportunities to spot resident birds and other wildlife.

94 *Eagle Rock*

Distance: 6.8 miles roundtrip
Difficulty: moderate–challenging
Hiking time: 4 hours
Elevation gain: 1900 feet
High point: 2525 feet

Management: Maine BPL
Season: May–Oct
Map: BPL website
GPS coordinates: 45.48676°, –69.74143°

Getting there: From the center of Greenville, follow Route 15 north for 5 miles. Turn left onto North Road, near a sign for Little Moose Public Land. Head up the dirt road. Stay straight in 1.6 miles, and 2.1 miles farther, stay straight again. The road descends before leveling off and arriving at the parking area in 1.4 miles. *Note:* The route crosses private property.

Maine's Little Moose Public Land, just a short drive from Greenville and the shores of Moosehead Lake, includes more than 15,000 acres of hidden ponds and secluded mountaintop vistas. Of the many miles of trails to explore, choose one of the region's newer options—this trek to the top of Eagle Rock—for incredible 360-degree views. The journey there affords ample opportunity to spot resident songbirds, carpets of wildflowers, and, with a little luck, a moose.

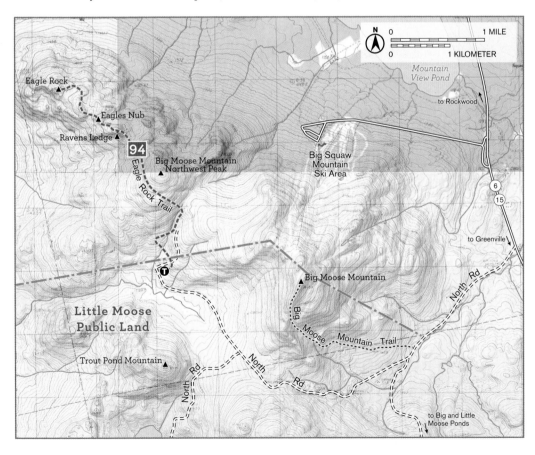

The blue-blazed trail begins easily, rising to a forest road in 0.2 mile. Enter private lands that are actively managed for forest products. The remaining path, protected with a conservation easement, crosses the dirt road, then descends to a small brook. Over the next 0.6 mile, climb steadily along the stream, occasionally moving from one side to the other. Rising away from the water, the trail enters a stand of northern hardwoods as the ascent continues.

Level off near the hike's highest point and wrap around the top of Big Moose Mountain's Northwest Peak. The trail descends gradually, reaching a saddle on the ridge in 0.6 mile. Enjoy this brief reprieve, then scale 0.3 mile up a steep ledge-covered knob, where limited views appear through the thinning canopy. At a well-marked junction, a spur departs left and rises 0.1 mile to the top of Ravens Ledge. Watch your footing on the edge of this precipitous cliff and enjoy the spectacular scenes north and west.

The main trail continues another 1.2 miles to Eagle Rock. Meander down the narrow ridgeline and proceed through the moss-carpeted boreal forest. The inviting path leads across an increasingly ledge-covered landscape, while heading over Eagles Nub. After a final descent, watch your footing and scramble up Eagle Rock's exposed granite pinnacle.

There are few spots in northern Maine with more exceptional views. To the east, beyond the

Eagle Rock's open summit provides a great perspective of Moosehead Lake.

sprawling waters of Moosehead Lake, Mount Katahdin towers on the horizon. In all directions near and far lie lakes, forests, and rolling ridges. After enjoying a refreshing picnic, retrace your steps 3.4 miles back to the start.

Nearby Options: Scale the highest peak in the public land by exploring the 4.2-mile roundtrip trek to the top of Big Moose Mountain. There are views from the summit and from a couple of spots along the way. To the south, a similar-length loop visits Big and Little Moose Ponds before climbing to prominent ledges with sweeping panoramas.

95 *Mount Kineo*

Distance: 3.4-mile loop	*Management:* Maine BPL
Difficulty: moderate–challenging	*Season:* May–Oct
Hiking time: 3 hours	*Map:* BPL website
Elevation gain: 875 feet	*GPS coordinates:* 45.67702°, −69.73884°
High point: 1806 feet	

Getting there: Drive north on Route 15 from Greenville. Continue 1.5 miles past Moosehead Lake's West Outlet (the second of two Kennebec River crossings) and turn right onto Village Road. Drive 0.3 mile to the Rockwood boat launch. The trailhead is located across the lake. The Kineo Shuttle, a private boat, runs daily from Memorial Day through early October. Crossing the water by canoe or kayak is possible but can be dangerous. The shortest distance is 0.7 mile. *Notes:* Entrance fee required. Backcountry campsites available.

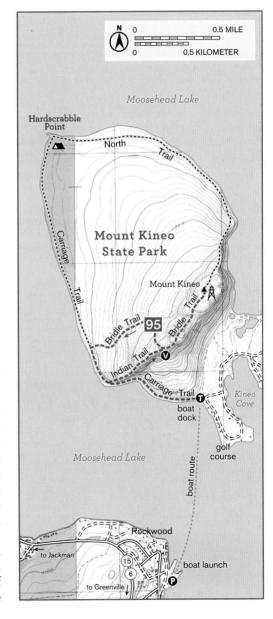

Mount Kineo's summit tower presents an extraordinary panorama of endless waters, forested hillsides, and distant peaks in all directions. In 1990, the mountain and more than 800 acres surrounding it were permanently protected by the state, with assistance from the Maine chapter of the Nature Conservancy and funding from the Land for Maine's Future program. Thanks to these efforts, hikers can scale Kineo's rugged slopes and enjoy one of New England's most iconic viewpoints.

The 10-minute boat ride across Moosehead Lake offers the first views of the day. Check out the dramatic 700-foot cliffs on Kineo's eastern flank. They emerge from the deepest depths of New England's largest lake. American Indians, who searched for stone tools at the base of the cliffs, believed Kineo comprised the remains of a large cow moose slain by a god.

From the dock, turn left onto the Carriage Trail and enter Mount Kineo State Park. The route features minor elevation changes while hugging the lake's picturesque shoreline. Continue beneath the base of a talus slope, pass the mountain's lower cliffs, and reach the start of the Indian Trail, 0.6 mile from the dock.

Turn right and begin an aggressive 0.4-mile climb up the steep slopes. Remaining close to the edge of the adjoining cliff, the challenging path offers one spectacular vista after another. (Take extra care and watch children closely; the trail often approaches precipitous drops.) Beyond a grassy ledge offering stunning views of the lake below, arrive at a junction with the Bridle Trail and swing right.

Proceed up and over a small knoll, and soon rise to the wooded summit and the base of a tall observation tower. Scale the five sets of stairs that lead above the canopy to behold the

Mount Kineo's Indian Trail features a series of breathtaking vistas.

breadth of Moosehead Lake and its boundless surroundings. On a clear day, enjoy scenes of Baxter State Park rising in the east, beyond the imposing Spencer Mountains. Looking south, spot the ridges that form Maine's famous 100-Mile Wilderness. The views appear endless in all directions.

The 1.8-mile return to the dock could take an hour or more (allow plenty of time, to avoid missing the last boat). On the descent, skip the Indian Trail and remain exclusively on the more gradual and more forested Bridle Trail. In 1 mile, arrive at the shoreline. Turn left on the Carriage Trail to reach the dock. Be sure to look for common loons riding the waves offshore. Along with the many boats in the area, the birds are searching the cold waters for the bounty of fish for which Moosehead Lake is famous.

Extend Your Trip: If time permits, consider a longer exploration of the entire peninsula. Combine the Carriage, Indian, and less-traveled North Trail to complete a 5.8-mile circuit. At Hardscrabble Point, there are picnic tables and grassy tent sites available for overnight use.

96 Gulf Hagas

Distance: 9.7-mile loop	**Management:** North Maine Woods,
Difficulty: challenging	Appalachian Mountain Club
Hiking time: 7 hours	**Season:** May–Oct
Elevation gain: 1225 feet	**Map:** Maine Trail Finder website
High point: 1160 feet	**GPS coordinates:** 45.49854°, −69.35709°

Getting there: From Brownville Junction, follow Route 11 north 4.8 miles and then turn left onto the road to Katahdin Ironworks (KI). Follow this logging road 6.3 miles to KI Checkpoint, where you pay the entry fee. Drive 2.4 miles ahead and stay left at a fork. Cross the Pleasant River in 1.4 miles. In 2.9 miles, pass a large parking lot on the right (alternative access). Continue straight 4.3 miles to an intersection. Alternatively, to reach this same intersection from downtown Greenville, follow Pleasant Street past the municipal airport and in 3.6 miles, cross Big Wilson Stream. Continue up the logging road 8.6 miles to Hedgehog Checkpoint. Stop and pay the entry fee. In 1.9 miles, arrive at the intersection. From the intersection, turn left and follow the KI Road 1 mile to the parking area. Remember that logging trucks have the right-of-way on these private roads. **Note:** Entrance fee required.

Often described as the Grand Canyon of Maine, Gulf Hagas offers stunning rewards for those seeking intimate views of its steep walls, rushing river, and tumbling cascades. This scenic loop meanders past hidden wetlands and through pleasant forests to the edge of the deep chasm, a slate gorge unlike any other New England site. Save for the time when dynamite was employed to aid the logging drives that occurred here, it is a location that has changed very slowly as the water has polished its sides.

Traditionally, hikers have accessed the gulf from the east, a slightly shorter but more adventurous route than the one described here. The eastern access follows the Appalachian Trail and includes fording the river, which can be challenging. In 2003, the Appalachian Mountain Club (AMC) acquired 37,000 acres that abut Gulf Hagas, as well as sporting camps they now manage for overnight visits. Since acquiring this land, AMC has more than doubled their conservation property and developed more than 50 miles of trails, including a Gulf Hagas access point from the west. The day's journey begins here.

Head northeast on the wide path that quickly intersects the Camp-to-Camp Trail. Stay left and proceed 0.6 mile over level terrain. After passing a small wetland, the route reaches a dirt road. Turn right and follow the road over a bridge that spans the West Branch of the Pleasant River. This is the start of the 1.3-mile Head of the Gulf Trail. Once across the rushing water, continue up the narrowing road. The trail immediately swings right onto a more welcoming course. With little elevation change, hike south past Lloyd Pond, a short spur right to the river, and eventually to a trail junction.

Turn right onto the Gulf Hagas Rim Trail and descend 0.1 mile to the Head of the Gulf—now the real fun begins. For nearly 3 miles, the Rim Trail sinks deeper aside the rugged gorge. As you wind over the undulating terrain, use extra care on the slate bedrock that abounds; it can be very slippery when wet. Explore the many side trails (all 0.2 mile roundtrip or less) that

Billings Falls

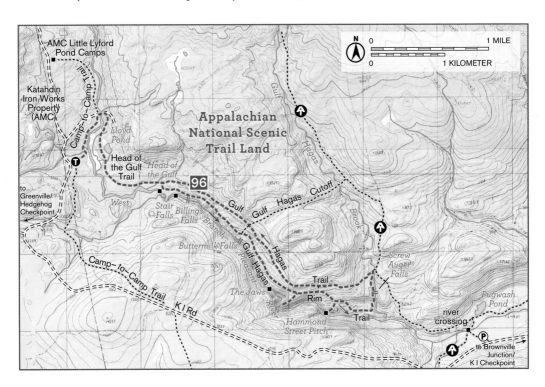

showcase Stair Falls, Billings Falls, Buttermilk Falls, The Jaws, Hammond Street Pitch, and countless other unnamed natural features. Eventually the path veers away from the river and begins to climb along Gulf Hagas Brook. After passing two spurs that lead right to impressive shots of Screw Auger Falls, the Rim Trail ends at a large boulder with a commemorative plaque.

To the right, the Appalachian Trail leads 1.5 miles to the eastern access point. Turn left and follow the Gulf Hagas Trail (sometimes called Pleasant River Road). With modest elevation gain, this 2.2-mile route provides a straightforward return to the Head of the Gulf Trail. Continue another 1.9 miles to conclude the day's trek.

Shorter Options: For those seeking a shorter excursion into the gulf, consider using the 0.1-mile connector trail that leads northeast from Buttermilk Falls. This less-strenuous 6-mile alternative still includes the most scenic portions of the Gulf Hagas Rim Trail.

97 *Debsconeag Lakes Wilderness*

Distance: 8.6-mile loop	***Management:*** The Nature Conservancy in Maine (TNC)
Difficulty: moderate–challenging	
Hiking time: 6 hours	***Season:*** Jun–Oct
Elevation gain: 1675 feet	***Map:*** TNC website
High point: 1650 feet	***GPS coordinates:*** 45.84800°, −69.06993°

Getting there: From Abol Bridge on the Golden Road north of Millinocket, head west 5.2 miles and then turn left onto the well-signed dirt road. Drive 0.2 mile to the trailhead parking lot. ***Notes:*** Dogs prohibited. Backcountry campsites available.

Located south of Maine's famed Baxter State Park, the Nature Conservancy's 46,271-acre Debsconeag Lakes Wilderness Area contains the highest concentration of remote, pristine ponds in New England. This 8.6-mile excursion visits a handful of these secluded water bodies, as well as a scenic ridgeline offering sweeping views of nearby summits. The Debsconeag Lakes Wilderness is an ideal destination for hikers seeking solitude, wildlife-viewing opportunities, and hidden geologic formations.

Head across a bridge spanning Horserace Brook and join an old woods road. The yellow-blazed route continues gently 0.5 mile to a junction and the start of the loop. Stay left, following the blue markers toward Rainbow Lake. The trees that surround the inviting path grow taller and more impressive as you meander up the hillside. Hike beneath the base of a large ledge before leveling

Unique perspective of Katahdin from the Orange Trail

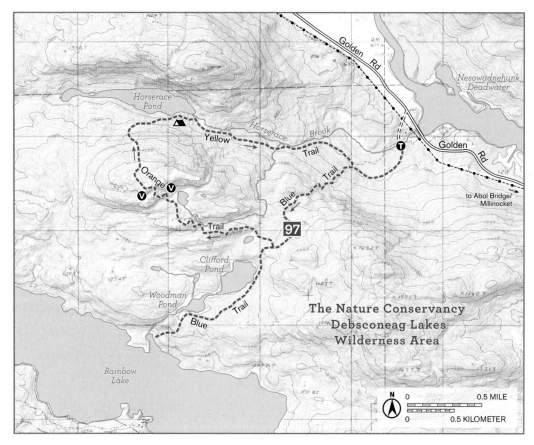

off across an evergreen-shaded plateau. Arrive at a junction 1.4 miles from the start.

While the main loop continues right, for now stay straight on the blue-blazed path. This 1.3-mile spur to Rainbow Lake drops nearly 350 feet over a rolling landscape. En route, approach the shores of Clifford and Woodman Ponds. Both water bodies offer ample opportunities to spot wildlife in the surrounding wetland habitat. The trail ends at a tiny cove on the shores of Rainbow Lake, a perfect locale to scan the waters for common loons and spotted sandpipers.

Upon returning to the main loop, turn left and follow the orange blazes. Over the next 1.4 miles, the well-designed trail weaves through moss-covered terrain. Pass scatterings of large boulders, scramble up ledge-covered slopes, skirt the edges of tiny ponds, and visit a series of scenic bluffs. Most of the vistas afford dramatic

scenes of Katahdin and aerial shots of Rainbow Lake, with few signs of civilization in sight.

From the final view near the loop's high point, the trail proceeds north another 0.6 mile to Horserace Pond. The orange blazes direct you across level terrain at first, but not for long. Drop steadily through the mature spruce forest. Weaving between rocks and ledge, the footing is uneven in places, especially as you approach the sprawling wetland. The picturesque water body, nestled between the sides of steep abutting slopes, is the perfect place to enjoy a warm summer's day. There are also overnight campsites available nearby on a first-come, first-served basis.

Leave the shores behind and pick up the yellow-blazed route that parallels Horserace Brook for the better part of its 1.3-mile course. The grade is mostly gentle, but watch your step on the roots and rocks along the way. Scan the lush forest for wildflowers blooming in the early summer and for prolific bright-colored mushrooms sprouting later in the season. Complete the loop and stay left at the junction to hike 0.5 mile back to the start. If you have not been fortunate enough to spot a moose on your journey, be alert for one as you return south along the Golden Road.

Extend Your Trip: Another popular hike in the Debsconeag Lakes Wilderness is the 2-mile roundtrip trek to the Ice Cave, a crevice between large rocks that typically retains ice into August. Also check out TNC's Trout Mountain Preserve just south of Baxter's Togue Pond Gate. At the end of its 2.7-mile trail, an impressive tower leads above the trees, affording exceptional views of Mount Katahdin.

98 *Mount O-J-I*

Distance: 8.7 miles roundtrip	*Management:* Baxter SP
Difficulty: challenging–strenuous	*Season:* Jun–Oct
Hiking time: 6 hours	*Map:* BSP website
Elevation gain: 2550 feet	*GPS coordinates:* 45.90337°, −69.03727°
High point: 3410 feet	

Getting there: After registering at Baxter State Park's Togue Pond Gatehouse, follow the Park Tote Road west 10.4 miles and then turn right into the day-use parking lot. *Notes:* Day-use fee for non-residents. Dogs prohibited.

Scenes of Doubletop Mountain from just above Old Jay Eye Rock

Mount O-J-I's steep slopes feature extensive slides that still exhibit evidence of the three letter shapes for which it was named. In recent decades, Baxter State Park has redesigned the route to its summit. No longer scaling the highest portions of the peak's slides, the current trail takes a longer, more methodical course. While still challenging, there are plenty of rewards for the hard work, including exceptional views from various rocky promontories.

The hike rises very little to start, but the trail's rough footing demands attention. Wrap around a wetland expanded by resident beavers, and proceed 1.2 miles to the base of a slide. The terrain becomes more inviting as you approach the first climb. Rise 0.3 mile before swinging sharply left. Moderating again, the path meanders 0.4 mile to the base of another slide. Cross this small chasm and then climb a series of switchbacks that plod 0.8 mile to the base of a large ledge and a junction just beyond.

To the left, a spur ascends modestly 0.2 mile to the West Peak. Here, enjoy exceptional shots of Mount O-J-I's slides and Mount Katahdin in the distance. For better lighting, check out this worthwhile diversion on the descent.

The main path swings right and grows more difficult with elevation. Reach a sharp right turn in 0.7 mile. The next 0.2-mile pitch features tight scrambles through narrow gaps in the ledge and will require the use of all four limbs at times. Use caution and, with patience, you will arrive at the scenic pinnacle of Old Jay Eye Rock, a pointy perch showcasing dramatic scenery, including Doubletop Mountain rising high above Nesowadnehunk Stream.

Rejoin the trek to the summit, now only 0.5 mile away. Though it requires extra care at first, the blue-blazed route quickly becomes easier to follow. Across an open expanse, the views of

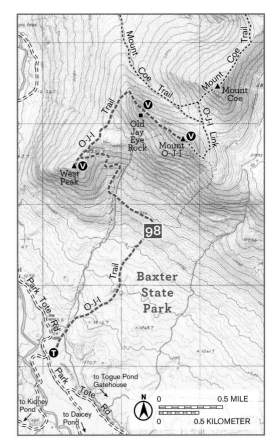

Mount Coe and South Brother provide an awesome backdrop. Reenter the dense boreal forest and continue climbing to the wooded high point. Upon reaching the summit sign, proceed a few dozen steps farther to an exposed ledge. Here, bask in exquisite views of Mount Katahdin and the Klondike, a vast forested wetland far removed from civilization.

To complete the day's journey, retrace your steps back to the start. Take your time, especially around Old Jay Eye Rock.

Nearby Options: If, upon returning to the trailhead, you are still itching for some outdoor adventure, consider checking out nearby Daicey Pond. Here, you can follow the Appalachian Trail 1.5 miles to Niagara Falls, explore the 1.4-mile Daicey Pond Nature Trail, or rent a kayak to paddle among the loons.

99 *Doubletop Mountain*

Distance: 7.2 miles roundtrip
Difficulty: challenging
Hiking time: 6 hours
Elevation gain: 2500 feet
High point: 3489 feet

Management: Baxter SP
Season: Jun–Oct
Map: BSP website
GPS coordinates: 45.97670°, −69.07743°

Getting there: After registering at Baxter State Park's Togue Pond Gatehouse, follow the Park Tote Road west 16.6 miles and turn left into Nesowadnehunk Field Campground— the day-use parking is located 0.2 mile on the right. **Notes:** Day-use fee required for non-residents. Dogs prohibited.

Looking north from Doubletop Mountain's South Peak

Doubletop rises like a giant prism on Baxter State Park's western boundary. The mountain's ledge-scarred slopes and rocky summit outcrops are a formidable setting for this exhilarating northern New England hike. The summit is accessible by two trails; this recommended trek from the north is a bit shorter and a slightly less challenging route. Both paths lead to the awe-inspiring ridgeline that connects the mountain's two rocky pinnacles, with comprehensive views of Baxter State Park.

From the parking area, follow the dirt road southwest and cross over a bridge that spans Nesowadnehunk Stream. Just beyond the slow-moving water, turn left and hike past campsites to reach the Doubletop Mountain Trailhead, 0.3 mile from the parking area.

During the journey's initial 1.4 miles, the quaint path rises gradually away from the stream and meanders through an inviting northern hardwood forest. This is a great opportunity to loosen leg muscles and scan the surrounding habitat for warbling songbirds and colorful wildflowers. As the forest transitions to conifers, the trail abruptly descends 0.1 mile to a large stream. Carefully cross, fuel up, and prepare for the difficult ascent that follows.

While the route is extremely steep, the footing over the next 0.6 mile is largely forgiving, especially early on. Take your time, and with a little luck you might spot an eastern toad or more-reclusive wildlife species exploring the surrounding habitat. The footing grows rockier, but soon the incline levels off. Make your way 0.7 mile across the high-elevation plateau that follows. Weaving through an evergreen tunnel, the increasingly relaxing path meanders between dense carpets of verdant moss. Late in the summer, plentiful mushrooms add a splash of bright colors to the lush surroundings.

The final 0.4-mile climb is steady, but not nearly as challenging as the last one. Slowly wind through the thinning canopy of spruce and fir. As the surface transitions to ledge, emerge atop the 3489-foot North Peak and magnificent views east across Baxter State Park's highest mountains.

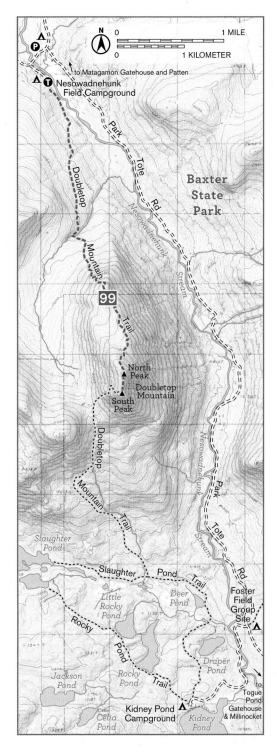

Doubletop's precipitous slopes drop thousands of feet to the valley below.

Although a bit lower, the 3455-foot South Peak is well worth a visit. Journey 0.2 mile across the narrow summit spine to its more open and stunning landscape. From your perch on the edge of dramatic cliffs, revel in aerial scenes in all directions, including west to the summits circling Moosehead Lake and north across Chesuncook Lake toward the headwaters of the Allagash River. From here, retrace your steps 3.6 miles back to the start.

Extend Your Trip: If you can spot a car or get picked up at a different trailhead, consider tackling Doubletop beginning at Kidney Pond and ending at Nesowadnehunk Field Campground. This 8.6-mile trek begins gradually near the shores of secluded ponds before ascending increasingly steep slopes. The final push to the south peak is especially challenging and can be extremely difficult to descend.

100 *Katahdin*

Distance: 11.4-mile loop
Difficulty: strenuous
Hiking time: 10 hours
Elevation gain: 4500 feet
High point: 5267 feet

Management: Baxter SP
Season: Jun–Oct
Map: BSP website
GPS coordinates: 45.91913°, −68.85744°

Getting there: From Baxter State Park's Togue Pond Gatehouse, follow the road right and drive 7.8 miles to Roaring Brook Campground. There are two ways to ensure access to the trailhead: stay in the campground, or reserve a day-use parking spot in advance for a small fee. Reserved day-use spots go quickly, and remaining spaces are filled on a first-come, first-served basis. **Notes:** Day-use fee required for non-residents. Dogs prohibited.

Towering majestically—high above a landscape of sprawling lakes, vast forests, and lower peaks—Katahdin showcases steep headwalls, sweeping ridgelines, and deep ravines like no other. Its rugged beauty has lured outdoor adventurers, experienced and novice alike, for more than two hundred years. While many visitors underestimate the physical and natural challenges the iconic mountain presents, those who are prepared and successfully complete the journey will have memories to last a lifetime.

After registering at the ranger station, where a weather update is available, follow the well-used Chimney Pond Trail 0.1 mile to the start of the Helon Taylor Trail on the left. Leading 3.5 miles to the 4902-foot summit of Pamola Peak, this rugged path wastes little time ascending Keep Ridge. As it rises through the mixed forest, the initial incline is moderate. After leveling off, descend to a small brook crossing and brace yourself for the challenge ahead. The route meanders through the thinning evergreen forest and emerges above tree line for the final 1.2-mile stretch. While the terrain is steep, the footing is straightforward, and the views are spectacular.

Atop Pamola Peak, enjoy the day's first views into South Basin and across the deep abyss to Katahdin's Baxter Peak. If the weather is not cooperating, turn back; otherwise, it is time to carefully tackle the mountain's infamous Knife Edge Trail. Descend abruptly into a small gap, only to immediately scramble up Chimney Peak. Follow the blue blazes along a narrow spine with many precipitous drop offs. While there are several spots that demand extra caution, the surrounding landscape is breathtakingly beautiful. The route becomes less precarious as you aggressively rise up the South Peak. From here,

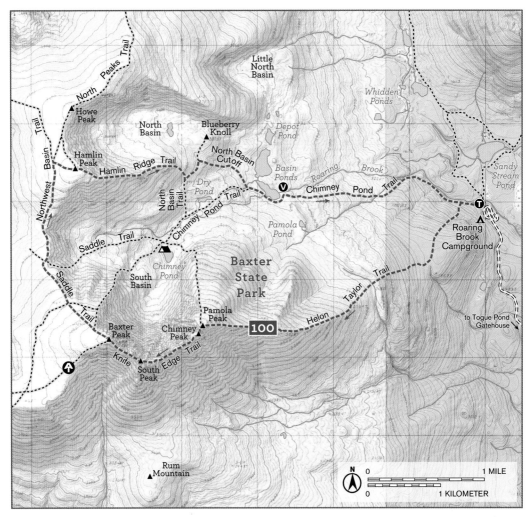

navigate 0.3 mile of boulder-hopping to the top of Maine.

Not surprisingly, Katahdin's 5267-foot Baxter Peak is a popular destination. It attracts many day hikers and those venturing along the Appalachian Trail. On clear days, the view from the summit is seemingly endless, encompassing much of northern Maine. When it is time to find solitude, head northwest down the Saddle Trail. It descends steadily 1.1 miles. When the weather is nice, the biggest fear is slipping on the loose rocks because it is hard to take your eyes off the scenery.

Near the col, the Saddle Trail swings right. It drops to Chimney Pond, offering an easier (though not easy) end to the day if the weather is less than ideal or the legs are too tired. Otherwise, proceed straight on the Northwest Basin Trail. Immediately notice the narrower path and thicker alpine vegetation. Rising steadily 0.9 mile, this less-traveled trail winds to a four-way intersection, where two routes lead deep into the heart of the park's wilderness area. Turn sharply right and hike 0.2 mile to Maine's second-highest summit. As you stand atop Katahdin's Hamlin Peak and gaze at the stunning perspective of Baxter Peak, the distant crowds are now a faded memory.

Remain on the Hamlin Ridge Trail. It descends 1.5 miles steeply down the narrow rock ridge that divides Katahdin's North and South Basins. While difficult in places, the scenic trail can be safely navigated with appropriate caution. Take advantage of the less rugged sections to enjoy the panorama east to Katahdin Lake. Eventually, the route drops rapidly into the shady evergreen forest.

At a junction with the North Basin Trail, turn left. The level terrain is a welcome sight. In 0.2 mile, swing right onto the 0.7-mile North Basin Cutoff. If you have not had enough, follow the North Basin Trail straight 0.2 mile to Blueberry Knoll's unique vista. Although rocky in places, the cutoff is not difficult. Upon reaching the Chimney Pond Trail, turn left. The remaining 2.1 miles back to Roaring Brook crosses uneven terrain, but it is otherwise a relaxing end to the circuit. Check out the short spur to Basin Ponds and exceptional views looking back to the peak.

Shorter Options: Katahdin's weather is unpredictable and unforgiving. Its terrain is also extremely challenging. If the forecast is not ideal or you are looking for a less rigorous itinerary, there are many options to consider. Hike 6 miles roundtrip along the Chimney Pond Trail into the impressive amphitheater-shaped basin. Or head 1 mile north to Sandy Stream Pond for exceptional views of the mountain and excellent opportunities to spot moose.

Admiring Katahdin's Knife Edge between stretches of its challenging terrain

Katahdin rises between the gap formed by Mount Coe and Mount O-J-I

Acknowledgments

I would be remiss if I failed to acknowledge the many people who played a part in the evolution of this book. So I thank those who joined me on the trail, posed for photographs, and reviewed draft material. And I especially want to thank my wife, Maria; son, Anthony; and daughter, Sabrina, for your support throughout this process. You each played a vital role in making this book a reality. Thanks so much for your patience and help along the way. I hope you remember most the many adventures we shared together. My fondest memories include enjoying a glorious fall day on Monhegan Island's rugged cliffs, discovering the pine marten in the heart of the Debsconeag Lakes Wilderness, learning that Alander Mountain is really home to timber rattlesnakes (the signs don't lie!), watching the plovers forage as the waves lapped the shore of Napatree Point, celebrating Father's Day in the heart of the Mahoosuc Range, rising through the early-morning mist to the top of Watatic, and wondering when my hiking partner would realize the Long Trail continued well beyond the summit of Mount Grant.

Resources

Acadia National Park
P.O. Box 177
Bar Harbor, ME 04609
Phone: (207) 288-3338
www.nps.gov/acad/index.htm

Appalachian Mountain Club
10 City Square
Boston, MA 02129
Phone: (617) 523-0655
www.outdoors.org

Appalachian National Scenic Trail
P.O. Box 50
Harpers Ferry, WV 25425
Phone: (304) 535-6278
www.nps.gov/appa

Appalachian Trail Conservancy
P.O. Box 807
Harpers Ferry, WV 25425-0807
Phone: (304) 535-6331
www.appalachiantrail.org

Ashburnham Conservation Trust
P.O. Box 354
Ashburnham, MA 01430-0354
Phone: (978) 827-6427
www.AshburnhamConservationTrust.org

Audubon Society of Rhode Island
12 Sanderson Road
Smithfield, RI 02917
Phone: (401) 949-5454
www.asri.org

Baxter State Park
64 Balsam Drive
Millinocket, ME 04462
Phone: (207) 723-5140
https://baxterstatepark.org

Bay Circuit Trail & Greenway
www.baycircuit.org

Belknap Range Conservation Coalition
PO Box 151
Gilmanton IW, NH 03837
www.belknaprange.org

Berkshire Natural Resources Council
309 Pittsfield Rd., Suite B
Lenox, MA 01240
Phone: (413) 499-0596
www.bnrc.org

Block Island Conservancy
P.O. Box 84
Block Island, RI 02807
Phone: (401) 466-3111
www.biconservancy.org

Cape Cod National Seashore
99 Marconi Site Road
Wellfleet, MA 02667
Phone: (508) 255-3421
www.nps.gov/caco

Coastal Mountains Land Trust
101 Mount Battie Street
Camden, Maine 04843
Phone: (207) 236-7091
www.coastalmountains.org

Bunchberries are encountered frequently in early summer.

Connecticut Department of Energy and Environmental Protection
79 Elm Street
Hartford, CT 06106-5127
Phone: (860) 424-3000
https://portal.ct.gov/DEEP

Connecticut Forest and Park Association
16 Meriden Road
Rockfall, CT 06481
Phone: (860) 346-8733
www.ctwoodlands.org

Friends of Acadia
P.O. Box 45
Bar Harbor, ME 04609
Phone: (800) 625-0321
www.friendsofacadia.org

Friends of the Wapack
P.O. Box 115
West Peterborough, NH 03468
www.wapack.org

Great Pond Mountain Conservation Trust
PO Box 266
Orland, ME 04472
Phone: (207) 469-6929
www.greatpondtrust.org

Green Mountain Club
4711 Waterbury-Stowe Road
Waterbury Center, VT 05677
Phone: (802) 244-7037
www.greenmountainclub.org

Green Mountain National Forest
P.O. Box 220
Rutland, VT 05702
Phone: (802) 747-6700
www.fs.usda.gov/gmfl

Harris Center for Conservation Education
83 King's Highway
Hancock, NH 03449
Phone: (603) 525-3394
www.harriscenter.org

Island Explorer
www.exploreacadia.com

Kineo Shuttle
https://destinationmooseheadlake.com/kineo-shuttle-schedule

Lakes Region Conservation Trust
PO Box 766
156 Dane Road
Center Harbor, NH 03226
Phone: (603) 253-3301
https://lrct.org

Mahoosuc Land Trust
P.O. Box 981
Bethel, ME 04217
Phone: (207) 824-3806
www.mahoosuc.org

Maine Appalachian Trail Club
P.O. Box 7564
Portland, ME 04112
www.matc.org

Maine Audubon
20 Gilsland Farm Road
Falmouth, Maine 04105
Phone: (207) 781-2330
https://maineaudubon.org

Maine Bureau of Parks and Lands
22 State House Station
Augusta, ME 04333
Phone: (207) 287-3200
www.maine.gov/dacf/parks

Maine Coast Heritage Trust
1 Bowdoin Mill Island, Suite 201
Topsham, ME 04086
Phone: (207) 729-7366
www.mcht.org

Maine Trail Finder
www.mainetrailfinder.com

Massachusetts Department of Conservation and Recreation
251 Causeway Street, 9th Floor
Boston, MA 02114
Phone: (617) 626-1250
www.mass.gov/orgs/department-of-conservation-recreation

Midstate Trail
www.midstatetrail.org

Minute Man National Historic Park
174 Liberty St.
Concord, MA 01742
Phone: (978) 369-6993
www.nps.gov/mima

Monhegan Associates
Box 97
Monhegan, ME 04852
https://monheganassociates.org

Mount Agamenticus Conservation Program
186 York Street
York, ME 03909
Phone: (207) 361-1102
http://agamenticus.org

New Hampshire Audubon
84 Silk Farm Road
Concord, NH 03301
Phone: (603) 224-9909
www.nhaudubon.org

New Hampshire Division of Forests and Lands
172 Pembroke Road
Concord, New Hampshire 03301
Phone: (603) 271-2214
www.nh.gov/nhdfl

New Hampshire State Parks
172 Pembroke Road
Concord, NH 03301
Phone: (603) 271-3556
www.nhstateparks.org
www.nhtrails.org

North Maine Woods
92 Main Street
Ashland, ME 04732
Phone: (207) 435-6213
www.northmainewoods.org

Rhode Island Division of Parks and Recreation
1100 Tower Hill Road
North Kingstown, RI 02852
Phone: 401-667-6200
www.riparks.com

Sachuest Point National Wildlife Refuge
www.fws.gov/refuge/sachuest-point

Silvio O. Conte National Fish and Wildlife Refuge
Pondicherry Division
289 Airport Road
Whitefield, NH 03598
Phone: (802) 962-5240
www.fws.gov/refuge/silvio-o-conte

Society for the Protection of New Hampshire Forests
54 Portsmouth Street
Concord, NH 03301
Phone: (603) 224-9945
https://forestsociety.org

Steep Rock Association
P.O. Box 279
Washington Depot, CT 06794
Phone: (860) 868-9131
https://steeprockassoc.org

Stowe Land Trust
P.O. Box 284
Stowe, VT 05672-0284
Phone: (802) 253-7221
www.stowelandtrust.org

The Nature Conservancy
www.nature.org

Maine Chapter
14 Maine Street, Suite 401
Brunswick, ME 04011
Phone: (207) 729-5181

Rhode Island Chapter
159 Waterman Street
Providence, RI 02906
Phone: (401) 331-7110

Palm warblers arrive in April while heading to nesting sites in northern New England and beyond.

The Trustees of Reservations
200 High Street
Boston, MA 02110
Phone: (617) 542-7696
https://thetrustees.org

Trail Finder
www.trailfinder.info

Vermont Department of Forests, Parks, and Recreation
1 National Life Drive, Davis 2
Montpelier, VT 05620-3801
Phone: (802) 272-4156
https://fpr.vermont.gov

Vermont Land Trust
8 Bailey Avenue
Montpelier, VT 05602-2161
Phone: (802) 223-5234
www.vlt.org

Wapack National Wildlife Refuge
25 Plowshare Lane
Greenfield, NH 03047
Phone: (978) 465-5753
www.fws.gov/refuge/wapack

Watch Hill Conservancy
One Bay Street
Watch Hill, RI 02891
Phone: (401) 315-5399
https://thewatchhillconservancy.org

White Mountain National Forest
71 White Mountain Drive
Campton, NH 03223
Phone: (603) 536-6100
www.fs.usda.gov/whitemountain

Index

About the Author

Jeffrey Romano has been hiking throughout New England for nearly fifty years. Born in Connecticut, Jeff grew up in southern New Hampshire. He earned a BA in politics from Saint Anselm College and a JD from Vermont Law School and has worked for various nonprofit organizations over the past three decades. Jeff currently manages public policy activities for Maine Coast Heritage Trust.

When not advocating for land conservation in the Maine State House, he is often exploring the outdoors of New England with his family and dreaming about future adventures in Italia—*Forza Azzurri!* An avid bird-watcher, Jeff lives in Hallowell, Maine, with his wife, Maria, and their children, Sabrina and Anthony. He is also the author of *Best Loop Hikes: New Hampshire's White Mountains to the Maine Coast*; *Day Hiking New England*; and *Hike the Parks: Acadia National Park*, all three published by Mountaineers Books.

Author Jeff Romano (left) with his son, Anthony (right), on Katahdin's Pamola Peak.

recreation · lifestyle · conservation

MOUNTAINEERS BOOKS is a leading publisher of mountaineering literature and guides—including our flagship title, *Mountaineering: The Freedom of the Hills*—as well as adventure narratives, natural history, and general outdoor recreation. Through our two imprints, Skipstone and Braided River, we also publish titles on sustainability and conservation. We are committed to supporting the environmental and educational goals of our organization by providing expert information on human-powered adventure, sustainable practices at home and on the trail, and preservation of wilderness.

The Mountaineers, founded in 1906, is a 501(c)(3) nonprofit outdoor recreation and conservation organization whose mission is to enrich lives and communities by helping people "explore, conserve, learn about, and enjoy the lands and waters of the Pacific Northwest and beyond." One of the largest such organizations in the United States, it sponsors classes and year-round outdoor activities throughout the Pacific Northwest, including climbing, hiking, backcountry skiing, snowshoeing, camping, kayaking, sailing, and more. The Mountaineers also supports its mission through its publishing division, Mountaineers Books, and promotes environmental education and citizen engagement. For more information, visit The Mountaineers Program Center, 7700 Sand Point Way NE, Seattle, WA 98115-3996; phone 206-521-6001; www.mountaineers.org; or email info@mountaineers.org.

Our publications are made possible through the generosity of donors and through sales of 700 titles on outdoor recreation, sustainable lifestyle, and conservation. To donate, purchase books, or learn more, visit us online:

MOUNTAINEERS BOOKS
1001 SW Klickitat Way, Suite 201 • Seattle, WA 98134
800-553-4453 • mbooks@mountaineersbooks.org • www.mountaineersbooks.org

An independent nonprofit publisher since 1960

 Mountaineers Books is proud to support the Leave No Trace Center for Outdoor Ethics, whose mission is to promote and inspire responsible outdoor recreation through education, research, and partnerships. The Leave No Trace program is focused specifically on human-powered (nonmotorized) recreation. For more information, visit www.lnt.org.

OTHER TITLES YOU MIGHT ENJOY FROM MOUNTAINEERS BOOKS

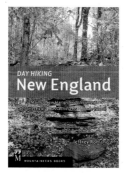

Day Hiking New England
Jeffrey Romano
115 relaxing strolls and challenging
hikes in Maine, New Hampshire,
Vermont, Connecticut, Massachusetts,
and Rhode Island

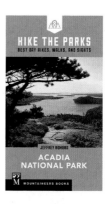

Hike the Parks:
Acadia National Park
Jeffrey Romano
Compact, full-color guide to the
best hikes for all skill levels

Best Hikes with Kids: Connecticut,
Massachusetts & Rhode Island
Cynthia Copeland, Thomas Lewis,
and Emily Kerr
80 fun-filled explorations
for little feet

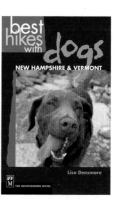

Best Hikes with Dogs:
New Hampshire & Vermont
Lisa Densmore
More than 50 dog-friendly trails

Paddling Southern Maine:
Day Trips for Recreational
Kayakers, Canoers, and SUPers
Sandy Moore and Kimberlee Bennett
More than 50 trips—most within an
hour's drive of Portland

www.mountaineersbooks.org